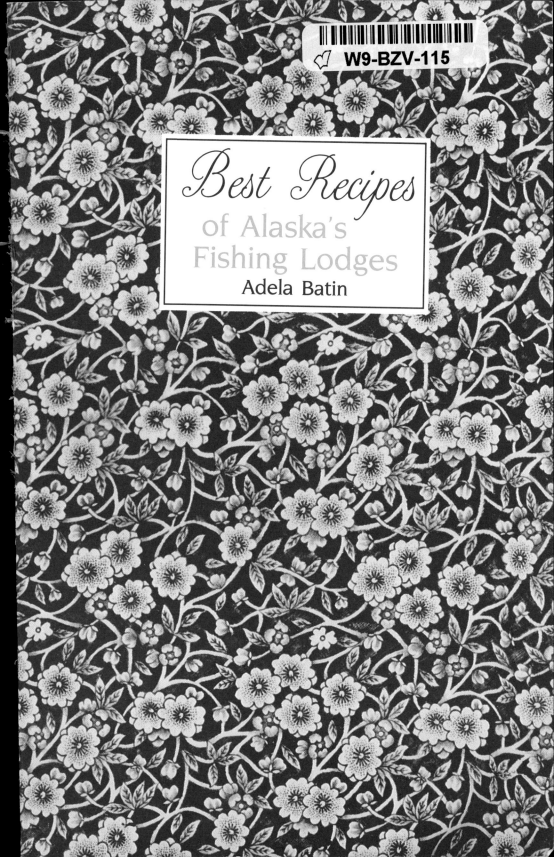

Best Recipes
of Alaska's
Fishing Lodges
Adela Batin

God give me stillness, give me time to stand
Unpressed by creeds and credits, undefiled
By dust of industry, and be a child
Reminded of my oneness with the land.
Let me stop running and be reconciled
To feel my feet send roots into the sand;
Let me put forth fresh blossoms from my hand.
Let me not lose my kinship with the wild.

And if I call this mine, remind me, God,
That it is only as my blood and bone
Are mine; not mine to waste, not mine to own,
But mine to be. I am the goldenrod,
The grain, the granite; I am stream and glen.
Remind me to preserve myself. Amen.

—Margaret Menamin

Reprinted with permission from the author and the Outdoor Writers Association of America

Best Recipes
of Alaska's
Fishing Lodges

Adela Batin

Photographs by Adela and Christopher Batin

Happy cooking!
Adela Batin

Published by Alaska Angler Publications
Fairbanks, Alaska

Best Recipes of Alaska's Fishing Lodges is part of the Alaska Angling and Hunting Library™, which is dedicated to providing only the very finest in Alaska fishing and hunting literature.

Published by Alaska Angler Publications, P. O. Box 83550, Fairbanks, Alaska 99708-3550 (907) 455-8000 Fax (907) 455-6691. Website: http://www.alaskaangler.com

First Edition, January 1994
Second Edition, May 1997

Cover photography and book design: Adela Ward Batin
Typography and production: Award Design, Fairbanks, Alaska
Photography: Adela and Christopher Batin
Coauthor and Sportfishing Consultant: Christopher Batin
Editor: Sharon Durgan Wilson

Author's Cataloging in Publication Data
Batin, Adela.
    Best recipes of Alaska's fishing lodges / Adela
Batin ; photographs by Adela and Christopher Batin.

    Includes Index.
    1. Cookery, Alaska.   2. Fishing—Alaska.
    3. Fishing lodges—Alaska.   I. Batin, Christopher.   II. Title.

TX715.B38   1997

Library of Congress Card Catalog Number: 93-071062
ISBN 0-916771-10-5 (Trade Edition)
ISBN 0-916771-16-4 (Hardcover)

Produced in the State of Alaska
Printed in the United States of America

Dedication

This book is dedicated to my mother,
Edna Schuster Johnson,
Who guided me with her spirit of adventure.

To Dotsie Boyer,
Who made me laugh when I felt only tears.

To Betty Moore,
Who fed me peach cobbler when I needed it most.

To Grandma Schuster,
Whose strength and wisdom
has been my source of inspiration.

To God,
Through your gift of sight
I see your beauty everywhere.

Acknowledgements

Many thanks to the following cooks who tested and reviewed the recipes in this book: Yvonne Bergstedt, Esther Green, Kathy Mayo, Karen Milne, Naomi Walsworth, Sheary Suiter, Marlis Panchyshyn, Lise McCann, Kathleen McLeod, Cathey Peterson, and Sharon and Bobby Wilson.

Special thanks to Karen Milne for her professional guidance; Sharon Wilson for her critical review and editorial suggestions; and my husband, Christopher, with whom I've shared these adventures.

Elaine's Pecan Salmon, Brooks Bread Pudding, Levelock Lemon Sauce and Brooks Cream were adapted from recipes in Paul Prudhomme's *Louisiana Kitchen*.

Table of Contents

Photo at left: Stephan Lake Lodge's needlepoint recipe box contains the recipes that have pleased thousands of guests for over 30 years. Cranberry bread, made with newly ripened cranberries picked within 100 feet from the kitchen door, is a favorite among lodge guides and guests.

Introduction

*B*est Recipes of Alaska's Fishing Lodges is more than just a cookbook. It's a celebration of a wilderness lifestyle that many of us dream about, but few live. Each chapter is seasoned with detailed descriptions of dining elegance amid spectacular wilderness scenery, garnished with cook profiles and frosted with anecdotes that entertain as well as inform.

This book gives you a variety of lodge experiences. Each lodge is unique in its location, the type of fishing it offers, the way meals are prepared, the type of food served, and the ambiance created by owners and personnel. Each year, thousands of anglers pay up to $4,000 a week to enjoy the services and partake in the sensational meals served at these world-famous lodges.

*T*his book is your link to the Alaska lodge experience. If you've stayed at one of these featured lodges, these recipes may help you savor those memories. If you've never been to Alaska, allow this book to be your guide.

These recipes represent the best meals sampled by my husband, Christopher, and I in our journeys to the state's fishing lodges. In 1984, I began compiling the information and recipes in this book because I wanted to record this segment of Alaska history. Some of these lodges no longer exist, and this will be your only chance to get a taste of what it was like to be there.

The recipes range from simple to complex, homestyle to gourmet. They are as varied as the cooks who prepared them. Each cook brings to the lodge a different culinary background, a wide range of cooking techniques, and a zest for living the Alaska adventure.

Cooks and chefs at Alaska's fishing lodges are unsung heroes. They are food preparation innovators working under the most basic conditions...experts at doing the impossible. Their menus must sometimes be planned months in advance, with food ordered and shipped by barge or flown in by bush plane. A 79-cent can of olives might end up costing the lodge owner $3.

The life of a lodge cook revolves around the kitchen. Kitchen staff often work 16 hours a day, with few days off. This puts a great deal of stress on the cook, who fixes three to four meals a day, plus appetizers and packout lunches. Yet somehow, the cook finds time to listen to everyone's fish stories. Hard work doesn't dampen the lodge cook's spirits. When an angler's day is spoiled by inclement weather or temperamental fish, the cook knows that she is the pinch hitter, the one-person cavalry who can set things right with a good meal. He or she knows that dinner is more than just sustenance: it is a time when anglers gather to share the day's events, to laugh, fill their bellies and feel good. Dinner is a time to make new friends, form new family bonds and mix with people from all walks of life who have come to unwind and "get back to nature."

These cooks have a strategic advantage... they prepare meals from Nature's bounty: freshly baked blueberry pie made with plump, ripe berries picked from a nearby tundra marsh; royal-tasting silver salmon caught hours before from a crystal-clear stream. Fresh salads of greens, herbs and vegetables grown in a garden surrounded by wilderness, where the only vermin are 1,100-pound moose and pesky black bear. Chowder from freshly dug clams, or an appetizer of elegant Dungeness crab caught in the traps you helped pull from the ocean.

$\mathcal{T}$he dining experiences at an Alaska fishing lodge are better than what you'll find in the world's finest restaurants. Where else could you relax and dine with wild rainbow trout jumping in the river only a stone's throw from your table? Where else could you gaze across a brilliant green tidal area to see deer peacefully grazing?

The aroma of meals prepared in the Alaska wilderness setting and the friendships formed with lodge guests are some of the best memories of my life. I invite you to experience this unique taste of Alaska for yourself.

Adela Batin

Fairbanks, Alaska

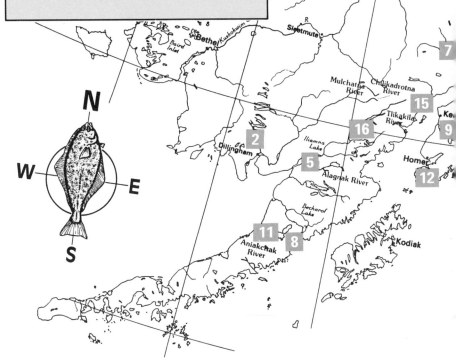

Map of Alaska

Location of featured lodges

1. Boardwalk Wilderness Lodge
2. Wood River Lodge
3. Stephan Lake Lodge
4. Camp Denali
5. Alaska Rainbow Lodge
6. Denali West Lodge
7. Riversong Lodge
8. Alaska Wilderness Safaris
9. Freebird Charters & Fish Camp
10. Princeton Hall
11. Painter Creek Lodge
12. Kachemak Bay Wilderness Lodge
13. Growler Island Wilderness Camp
14. Gates of the Arctic Lodge
15. Silver Salmon Creek Lodge
16. Iliamna Lake Resort

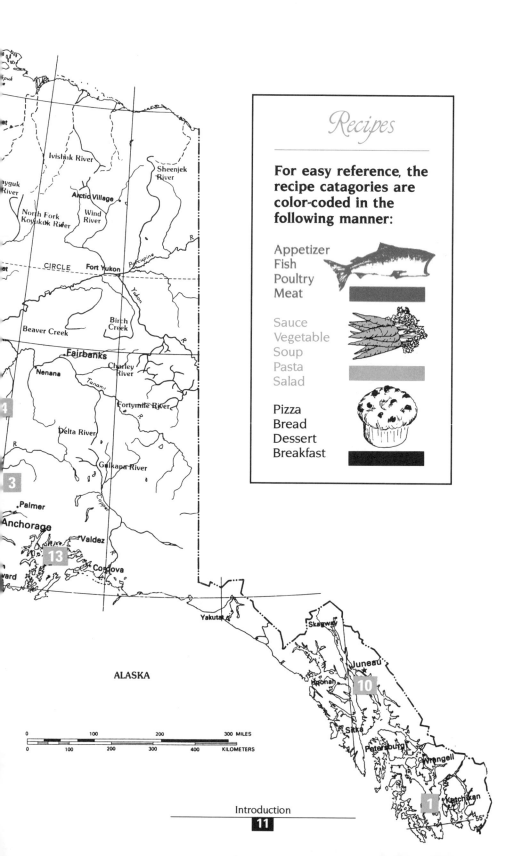

Recipes

For easy reference, the recipe catagories are color-coded in the following manner:

Appetizer
Fish
Poultry
Meat

Sauce
Vegetable
Soup
Pasta
Salad

Pizza
Bread
Dessert
Breakfast

Ivishak River
Sheenjek River
ayguk River
Arctic Village
North Fork Koyukuk River
Wind River
CIRCLE
Fort Yukon
Porcupine
Yukon
Beaver Creek
Birch Creek
Fairbanks
Charley River
Nenana
Tanana
Fortymile River
Delta River
Gulkana River
Palmer
Anchorage
Valdez
Cordova
Yakutat
Skagway
Juneau
Hoonah
Sitka
Petersburg
Wrangell
Ketchikan

ALASKA

| 0 | 100 | 200 | 300 MILES |
| 0 | 100 | 200 | 300 | 400 | KILOMETERS |

How to Fillet Salmon

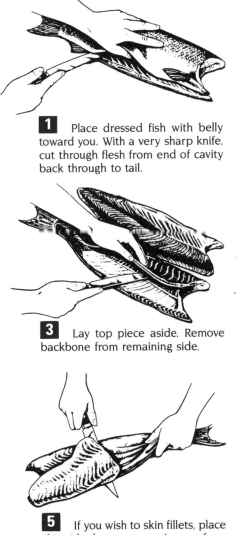

1 Place dressed fish with belly toward you. With a very sharp knife, cut through flesh from end of cavity back through to tail.

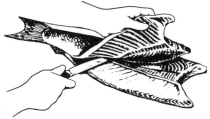

2 Place knife blade against backbone and cut along backbone from head end to tail on one side of fish, severing ribs and top piece from backbone.

3 Lay top piece aside. Remove backbone from remaining side.

4 With a smaller knife, trim away rib and fin bones from both pieces. Pull out pin bones, if desired.

5 If you wish to skin fillets, place skin-side-down on cutting surface. Hold tail end tightly. With sharp knife, cut down through the flesh to skin. Flatten knife against skin and cut flesh away by sliding it toward head end while holding tail end of skin firmly.

6 Prepared salmon fillets can be baked, poached or grilled, or cut into serving-sized portions.

Illustrations courtesy of the Alaska Seafood Marketing Institute

Weights & Measures

1 cc=**1 ml**
dash=**less than 1/8 teaspoon**
3 teaspoons=**1 tablespoon** (15 ml)
2 tablespoons=**1 liquid ounce** (30 ml)
4 tablespoons=**¼ cup** (2 liquid ounces or 60 ml)
5⅓ tablespoons=**⅓ cup**
8 tablespoons=**½ cup** (120 ml)
10⅔ tablespoons=**⅔ cup**
12 tablespoons=**¾ cup**
16 tablespoons=**1 cup** (8 liquid ounces or 240 ml)
1 cup=**½ pint**
2 cups=**1 pint** (16 liquid oz. or 500 ml)
2 pints (4 cups)=**1 quart** (or 950 ml)
4 quarts (liquid)=**1 gallon**
8 quarts (solid)=**1 peck**
4 pecks=**1 bushel**
16 ounces=**1 pound**

King salmon—average weight 11 to 30 pounds
Chum salmon—average weight 9 pounds
Sockeye salmon—average weight 6 pounds
Silver salmon—average weight 4 to 12 pounds
Pink salmon—average weight 2 to 5 pounds

Cuts of Salmon

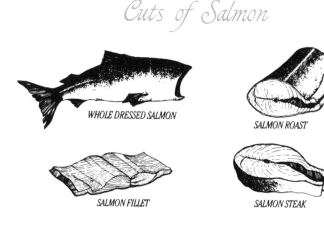

WHOLE DRESSED SALMON

SALMON ROAST

SALMON FILLET

SALMON STEAK

Boardwalk Wilderness Lodge

*B*oardwalk Wilderness Lodge on Prince of Wales Island offers a paramount Alaska lodge experience. You will enjoy some of the finest cuisine and hospitality found in southeast Alaska, with the added bonus of excellent action from king and silver salmon, rockfish, halibut and rainbow trout. The lodge features world-class steelhead and cutthroat fishing, possibly the best in North America.

Managers Sid and Kathy Cook started their lodge on a dream. "We won a choice 3½-acre parcel outside Thorne Bay in the state land lottery in 1981 that was perfect for a home and lodge," Sid Cook said. "The sheltered cove offered waterfront access and tall, dense stands of spruce and cedar—all the elements necessary for a prime sportfishing lodge." Already a competent carpenter, Sid took a six-week course in log-home building. Building a lodge in a remote location required logistical skills as well.

"There was neither electricity nor roads," he said. "Everything had to be hauled in by boat, and took five times longer than what we had planned. Building materials could only be moved in on high tide, and many trips were made in darkness. There were disappointing moments when barges sank and earth-moving equipment failed to work."

Persistence paid off. They felled their own timber, and with the help of friends and family, built a lodge from 12-inch-diameter Alaska Sitka spruce logs. Seven years later, they completed their lodge.

*T*he design of the lodge takes advantage of the scenic wilderness and a window seat and balcony overlooks a meadow where bears and deer feed regularly. The lodge is trimmed in pine and features Victorian decor with triangular windows, cathedral ceilings and comfortable beds with plush quilts. Ceiling fans, antiques and collectibles vie for your attention, and a log staircase exudes country elegance.

A typical day at Boardwalk starts with setting out the crab and shrimp pots, which fill in a matter of hours. Then it is a matter of choosing between a freshwater or saltwater fishing adventure.

Sid has spent 10 years learning the complex fisheries of Prince of Wales Island, which is the third largest island in the United States, surpassed only by Kodiak Island, the largest, and the big island of Hawaii. The island is 135 miles long and 45 miles across, covering 2,231 square miles with 990 miles of coastline.

"Most of these streams support coho, pink, sockeye and chum salmon during the summer months," said Sid. "Dollies start their run the second week in July, with catches of 30 or more fish per day commonplace. Soon after, the Dolly fishing tapers off with the influx of tens of thousands of pink salmon into the watershed. You can also catch chums and silvers until your arms tire."

For anglers who want to take fish home, Boardwalk vacuum-packs and freezes fish. They fillet-steak the salmon for ease of preparation. The fillets look elegant, fit easily into a pan, and best of all, have no bones.

An hour after arriving at Boardwalk, I was aboard a boat and our guide, Ron, rigged us up for silver salmon. Within 15 minutes, I was battling a dime-bright 18-pounder. Later that afternoon, I was fishing for cut-throat and Dolly Varden on a secluded stream.

The next fun-filled day of cave exploration and wildlife watching left me pleasantly exhausted. The Cooks prescribed the right cure. After Don Wharton, Board-walk's cook, served a gourmet meal of crab, halibut and deer tenderloin medallions, I was led to an outdoor hot tub overlooking a secluded inlet. I eased into the 105-degree water and found paradise. While sipping ice-cold sodas, we watched blacktail deer feed in an inter-tidal meadow 30 feet away from the tub. Before long, the bubbling water relaxed my sore muscles. I rested my head against the cedar backboard. Darkness settled in over the lodge and soon the northern lights began dancing over the horizon. Not in my most vivid imagina-tion could I think of a finer way to end the day.

On a much-welcomed day off, Kathy Cook (left) relaxes in the lodge hot tub with her daughter, Jamie, and lodge employees, Don and Brandy. During the hectic summer season, days off are few, but working at such a peaceful retreat offers many aesthetic benefits.

Don Wharton, *Cook, Boardwalk Wilderness Lodge*

This Fallbrook, California, native and his family transplanted to Alaska when Don was 13 years old. Don's mother, a single parent, took the kids camping and fishing since they didn't have a lot of money to spend on entertainment. They lived with friends on a float house in Ravina. The children were responsible for kitchen duties, housework and keeping up the exterior of the float house while their mom worked as a waitress at a restaurant in nearby Ketchikan.

Fascinated with restaurant work, Don started doing food prep at the restaurant where his mother was employed. His next job was at Charlie's, a fine-dining restaurant in Ketchikan, where he worked his way up from food prep to breakfast cook.

Wanting to increase his experience, Don spent five months in Arizona learning new ideas in food preparation. Missing Alaska, he returned to Ketchikan and to Charlie's as a dinner cook. After Don's sixth year at Charlie's, the restaurant closed. The owners introduced Don to Boardwalk Wilderness Lodge owners, Sid and Kathy Cook, who were looking for kitchen help.

Don's favorite aspect of working at Boardwalk is the opportunity to intermingle with guests. Typically, cooks don't get to meet the people they're cooking for in restaurants. Don will go out of his way to ensure each guest's food requests are met. After guests return from an exciting day of fishing, Don listens intently to everyone's fish stories while preparing hot hors d'oeuvres for the evening.

Don has a few stories of his own to tell. Every day he boats to the lodge, leaving his apartment in Thorne Bay at daybreak. One morning at 4:45 a.m., just as Don was pulling up to the dock at Boardwalk, his engine stopped. His adrenalin rushed as the tidal current pulled him out to sea. He tried to lasso the other boat at the dock. Not only was his rope waterlogged, but he couldn't find an object on the other boat to lasso. As he drifted away from shore, he contemplated his options: hit the rocks, jump overboard, or resort to creative crisis management. Remembering a cutting board over the stove in the boat's cabin, he grabbed it, leaned over the side of the boat, and paddled to the dock. It took him half an hour to paddle only 15 feet, but he made it to work on time!

Instead of serving meals family style, Don prefers to serve each guest individually. In this way, he can cater to individual requests, while making an elegant presentation of each food item on the plate.

Don caught his first big king salmon his first year as lodge cook. Not only is he hooked on working for Sid and Kathy, but he is also hooked on the fishing!

Smoked Halibut

1 **cup soy sauce**
½ **cup brown sugar**
3 **cloves garlic, crushed**
½ **cup salt**
2 **teaspoons black pepper**
2 **cups water**
3 **pounds halibut**

In a large glass or plastic bowl, *mix* soy sauce, brown sugar, garlic, salt, pepper and water until well-dissolved.

Cut halibut into slabs not to exceed one-inch thick. *Place* halibut in sauce. *Refrigerate* 1½ to 2 hours, *stirring* occasionally.

Remove halibut from refrigerator and *pat dry*. Let stand uncovered at room temperature for 45 minutes, or until a tacky glaze forms on fish. Meanwhile, *heat* smoker and have chips burning. *Smoke* halibut for 6 to 8 hours, or until done.

Serves 6—8

Prince of Wales Island offers some of Alaska's best saltwater sportfishing for halibut and king salmon as shown by Jeff Schuler (left) and Sid Cook (right). Guests delight in returning home with a 70-pound box filled with salmon, halibut and cod fillets.

Smoked Halibut Spread

*I*n Alaska, the female of the species wins in big ways: in sled dog racing, women win the Iditarod, while in the piscatorial realm, female halibut reach weights of up to 500 pounds and always outfight the 80-pound and smaller males.

While the chinook salmon may be the king of Alaska sportfish, this tasty spread proves halibut is the undisputed queen. Try it as a sandwich spread or use with crackers for hors d'oeuvres.

After breakfast each morning at Boardwalk Wilderness Lodge, Don Wharton sets out a selection of lunch makings and guests are invited to make their own lunches. This smoked halibut spread is my favorite for sandwiches.

½	**pound smoked or poached halibut or salmon**
1	**dill pickle, chopped**
2	**tablespoons finely chopped yellow onion**
½	**tomato, chopped**
¼	**teaspoon garlic powder**
¼	**teaspoon black pepper**
	dash of lemon juice
½	**cup mayonnaise**
¾	**teaspoon liquid smoke flavor**

In a bowl, *break* fish into small pieces. **Add** pickle, onion, tomato, garlic powder, pepper, lemon juice and mayonnaise. **Mix** until spread is desired consistency.

If poached fish is used, *add* liquid smoke until desired flavor is reached.

Serves 4

Savory Dill Salmon

6   **pounds of king or silver salmon fillets**
½   **cup butter**
¼   **cup lemon juice**
4   **tablespoons chopped fresh parsley**
3   **cloves garlic, chopped**
½   **teaspoon paprika**
¼   **teaspoon white pepper**

Preheat oven to 400 degrees. *Lay* salmon fillets, skin side down, in a lightly greased baking dish. *Set* aside.

Melt butter in saucepan. *Stir* in lemon juice, parsley and garlic, *sauteing* until garlic is slightly toasted. *Pour* over salmon fillets. *Sprinkle* paprika and pepper over salmon. *Bake* at 400 degrees for 15 to 20 minutes (until fish flakes easily, but is not quite done).

Remove from oven and *spread* dill sauce over fish. *Return* salmon to oven and *broil* for 2 to 3 minutes.

Serve immediately.

Dill Sauce

Dill Sauce is also delicious served on poached or cold salmon.

½   **cup mayonnaise**
½   **cup sour cream (or substitute plain yogurt for**
     a lighter sauce)
1   **tablespoon dried dillweed**
1   **tablespoon lemon juice**
½   **teaspoon salt**

In a small bowl, *blend* mayonnaise, sour cream, dillweed, lemon juice and salt. *Spread* on fish.

Serves 8–10

Butterfly Salmon Steaks

The guides at Boardwalk Wilderness Lodge prepare salmon steaks and vacuum seal serving-size portions to ensure easy preparation when clients return home.

This is how to make picture-perfect, boneless butterfly steaks:

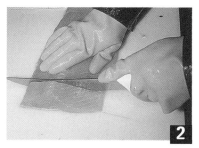

From your whole, cleaned salmon, cut fillets from side of salmon (see How to Fillet Salmon, page 12).

1. Trim off belly fat from fillet.

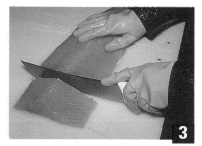

2. Make the first cut one inch wide, from end of fillet, cutting through the flesh, but not through the skin on the underneath side.

3. Make the second cut one inch away from the first, cutting all the way through the flesh and skin so the piece is free from the rest of the fillet.

4. Place knife under cut piece of fish and lift up. The piece will fall open at the first cut line, making a butterfly steak. The skin of the salmon will be holding the two sides together.

Cook's Cove Halibut

Nestled at the head of Cook's Cove is Boardwalk Wilderness Lodge. Residents of the Thorne Bay area commute between coves in boats, much like city-dwellers commute in their cars. The local school bus is actually a boat, which picks up the Cook's children and delivers them to the dock at the village of Thorne Bay.

Boardwalk Wilderness Lodge is open for steelhead fishing during the spring and fall. Sid and Kathy Cook guide and cook for steelhead anglers. This recipe is one of Kathy Cook's specialties.

2   **pounds halibut (1 pound pieces)**
6   **slices bacon, chopped**
1   **small onion, diced**
1   **cup evaporated milk**
3   **tablespoons lemon juice**
1   **small dill pickle, diced**
1   **teaspoon prepared mustard**
1½ **teaspoons parsley**
1½ **tablespoons cornstarch**
2   **tablespoons melted butter**
1½ **cups shredded Cheddar cheese**
2   **tablespoons dry bread crumbs**

Lightly *grease* baking dish. *Lay* one piece of fish in baking dish.

Saute bacon in fry pan until brown. *Add* onions and *cook* until they are slightly brown. *Remove* from heat and *cool* slightly. *Stir* in evaporated milk, lemon juice, pickle, mustard, parsley and cornstarch until well-blended. *Pour* half of mixture over fish.

Lay second piece of fish on top. *Brush* with melted butter. *Pour* remaining mixture on fish. *Sprinkle* with cheese and bread crumbs.

Bake uncovered at 375 degrees for 30 minutes.

Serves 8

Ital-aska Snapper

*A*laska red snapper, also known as yelloweye rockfish, is a delightful-tasting, white-fleshed fish found throughout Prince of Wales coastal waters. Your family and guests will enjoy this savory combination of two regional cuisines, Alaska and Italy. Use fresh Italian herbs to complement the delicate flavor of this fish.

6	snapper fillets
2	cups canned Italian-seasoned tomatoes
3	tablespoons finely chopped green onion
¾	teaspoon oregano
¾	teaspoon basil
1	tablespoon butter
1	cup grated Monterey Jack or mozarella cheese

Preheat oven to 450 degrees.

Lay fillets in shallow baking dish. In small bowl, *mix* tomatoes, green onion, oregano, basil. *Pour* mixture over fillets and *dot* butter on top. *Place* in oven and *bake* at 450 degrees for 15 minutes. *Remove* from oven, *sprinkle* with cheese. *Return* to oven and *bake* until cheese has melted.

Serves 6—8

The cuisine and accommodations of Boardwalk Wilderness Lodge have been featured in such prestigious magazines as Country Living and Western Outdoors. Here, Sid and Kathy Cook (middle and far right) are enjoying dinner with a lodge guest.

Ginger Turkey Breast

Anglers on a steelhead fishing trip to Staney Creek in May find the spring scents of cedar, hemlock and wild cucumber especially delightful. The scents complement the flavors of this marinated turkey breast which Don Wharton slices and serves in sandwiches for shore lunches.

As a main dish, serve with brown or wild rice, cooked julienned zucchini and baby carrots. Garnish with cilantro and mandarin orange slices. Also good cold, in a mixed green salad, with Sweetwater Lake Dressing.

2	inches ginger root, freshly grated
5	cloves garlic, crushed
1	cup brown sugar
2	cups soy sauce
¼	cup red wine vinegar
½	cup olive oil
2	cups water
1	whole boneless turkey breast

Mix ginger root, garlic, brown sugar, soy sauce, vinegar, olive oil and water. Set aside.

De-skin turkey breast and puncture breast meat with a fork or knife about 10 times. Place breast in marinade and refrigerate for 2 to 3 hours.

Place turkey breast under broiler in oven or on barbeque and broil for 45 minutes. Turn the breast every 10 minutes, basting the meat with the marinade. When the meat is done, place it back in the marinade sauce until ready to serve. Remove from sauce and slice against the grain to make thin slices.

Serves 4

Ketchikan Chicken

Ketchikan is the way Alaskans pronounce Szechuan.

1	**cup soy sauce**
¾	**cup olive oil**
¾	**cup brown sugar**
¼	**cup red wine vinegar**
2	**inches ginger, freshly grated**
5	**cloves garlic, crushed or chopped**
2	**tablespoons Dynasty Szechuan chili sauce**
1	**teaspoon Sun Luck or La Yu chili oil**
2	**cups water**
3	**tablespoons cornstarch**
4	**carrots, French-cut on diagonal**
1	**yellow onion, thinly sliced (stem to stern)**
1	**red bell pepper, thinly sliced**
1	**green bell pepper, thinly sliced**
¾	**pound snow peas, cleaned and de-stemmed**
3	**medium zucchini, French-cut**
1	**pound mushrooms, halved or quartered**
2	**pounds boneless chicken breast, jullienned**
2	**bunches green onions, French-cut**

In a small bowl, *mix* soy sauce, oil, brown sugar, wine vinegar, ginger, garlic, chili sauce, chili oil and water. *Taste* for spiciness. *Add* cornstarch, *stir* until dissolved; *set aside*.

Have a large serving bowl standing by. *Heat* wok until very hot. *Add* a little oil. *Saute* carrots in wok until done, but still crisp. *Place* carrots in bowl. *Reheat* wok and *repeat* procedure in this order: onion, bell peppers, snow peas, zucchini, mushrooms and chicken.

Reheat wok and *pour in* sauce, *stirring* constantly until thickened. *Add* green onions to sauce. *Pour* sauce over vegetables and chicken, *stir* and *serve* over rice.

Serves 8

Pepper Point Butter

*T*his recipe is named after a point off Baker Island near the western coast of Prince of Wales Island. The name is a translation of ''Punta de la Pimienta'' given in 1779 by Don Juan de la Bodega y Quadra and Francisco Antonio Maurelle. This delightful dipping sauce captures the peppery flavor of its Spanish origins and is excellent for crab, shrimp or ''Poor Man's Lobster,'' also known among Alaska commercial fishermen as ''poached halibut.''

1	**large red bell pepper (or ¾ cup prepared red peppers)**
3	**cloves garlic**
1	**stick butter**
¼	**cup vinegar**

Roast red pepper on grill or in oven until pepper blisters and turns black. *Place* in plastic bag until moisture gathers under the skin. This helps skin slide off for easier peeling. *Peel* pepper.

Put pepper and garlic in blender and *blend* until they become a smooth, almost liquid form. *Melt* butter in saucepan, *add* pepper mixture and *stir* to blend. *Remove* saucepan from heat and *cool* to room temperature. Add vinegar and *whisk*.

Makes 1 cup

Photo at right: Boardwalk Wilderness Lodge is aptly named for its ¼-mile long boardwalk extending from Thorne Bay to the main lodge located at the head of Cook's Cove.

Sweetwater Lake Dressing

*T*his zesty dressing tastes as fresh as springtime on Sweetwater Lake, a beautiful trout and char fishery on Prince of Wales Island. The ginger, honey and cilantro capture the essence of the area's sweet-smelling wildflowers, refreshing afternoon rainstorms and subsequent sunbursts breaking through the towering spruce.

This salad dressing also works as a marinade for chicken or fish.

Wash and prepare salad greens. Set aside.

½   **cup honey**
½   **cup soy sauce**
½   **cup red wine or rice vinegar**
4 - 5 **cloves garlic, chopped**
1½   **tablespoons chopped fresh ginger**
¼   **cup oil (sesame, olive or vegetable)**
1   **tablespoon toasted sesame seeds**
2 - 3 **tablespoons chopped cilantro**
       freshly grated carrot, grated cabbage, or
       sliced cucumber for garnish

Melt honey on low heat in a medium-size sauce pan. *Remove* from heat, *add* soy sauce, wine or vinegar, garlic and ginger. **Whisk. Add** oil, sesame seeds and fresh cilantro and *whisk again.*

Pour over mixed greens. *Top* with grated carrot or cabbage, or sliced cucumbers for garnish.

If cilantro is unavailable, parsley is a good substitute.

Makes 2 cups

Chocolate Leaves

$\mathcal{C}$hocolate leaves make an easy, elegant garnish for even the most simple dessert.

**1   cup chocolate chips
    non-poisonous leaves, cleaned and dried**

Melt chocolate in double boiler on top of stove, or in ovenproof container at 350 degrees for 5 minutes with oven door open. **Stir** chocolate until smooth. If the chocolate is too thick, **thin** with a tiny bit of butter.

Holding stem of leaf, **pull** the vein side of leaf through chocolate, being careful not to get chocolate on the top side of the leaf. **Place** leaf on cookie sheet with chocolate side up. **Chill** until chocolate loses its glossiness. **Peel** off leaf and **refrigerate** chocolate leaves until ready to use.

Citrus leaves work especially well for chocolate leaves, because they have a natural oil in them that helps keep the chocolate glossy when you pull off the leaf.

Chocolate Mousse is a popular dessert among lodge guests. Chocolate leaves, made with either brown or white chocolate, add a decorative touch.

Queen of Tarts

Crust:

1	**cup graham cracker crumbs**
⅓	**cup granulated sugar**
⅓	**cup chopped nuts**
1	**teaspoon cinnamon**
1	**teaspoon vanilla**
⅓	**cup butter, melted**

Preheat oven to 350 degrees.

Mix together graham cracker crumbs, sugar, nuts, cinnamon, vanilla and melted butter. Press firmly into a 10-inch pie plate or springform pan.

Bake at 350 degrees for 15 minutes.

Filling:

4	**8-ounce packages cream cheese, softened**
1	**cup sour cream**
½	**cup granulated sugar**
1	**teaspoon vanilla**
	rind of one orange
1	**pint fresh strawberries (or orange slices)**
1	**pint fresh raspberries or blueberries**
2	**tablespoons red currant jelly (or orange marmalade)**
1	**shot brandy (or 1 ounce orange liqueur)**

Beat cream cheese until light and fluffy. Add sour cream, sugar, vanilla and orange rind. Beat together. Pour mixture into cooled pastry crust and chill in refrigerator until firm.

Brush fruit to remove any particles or stems. Do not rinse, otherwise the fruit will leak. Remove pastry from refrigerator. Arrange fruit in a circular pattern on top of filling.

Melt current jelly and brandy. With a pastry brush, paint mixture on top of each berry. This will give it a pretty glaze. Refrigerate.

Serves 8

Photo at right: Dinner at Boardwalk can include several entrees such as fresh-caught Dungeness crab, salmon, shrimp and halibut. The Queen of Tarts dessert is shown in the foreground.

Wood River Lodge

*B*ristol Bay is the standard by which the world's best sportfishing is judged. To offer the ultimate Alaska fishing adventure, lodges must provide more than just world-class fishing. They must cater to your every whim. At some of the finest you can dine on king crab and New York steak, sample the best California wines, or sip Bailey's and coffee while relaxing fish-tired muscles in a bubbling hot tub. Of the hundreds of anglers who search for that special Alaska fishing experience each year, many choose Wood River Lodge in the Wood River-Tikchik Lake area of Bristol Bay.

The lodge is an oasis of luxury in a sea of wilderness fishing indulgence. Forget roughing it in a tent or trapper's cabin. Relax in a private cedar cabin with indoor bath. In the evening, the bed covers will be turned back, the heat turned up a bit to take off the chill, and Godiva chocolates placed on your pillow.

Why this pampering? Because you'll need all your energy to tackle the sportfish of Bristol Bay.

Deciding what to fish for in the Bristol Bay area is as

difficult a decision as where to fish. The decisions are made at breakfast, an elaborate affair consisting of Eggs Benedict, hash browns, oatmeal, pancakes, bacon, sausage, an assortment of fruit and lots of hot coffee and fruit juice.

*W*ithin the 54,700-square-mile area of Bristol Bay and the Kuskokwim, the lodge conducts most of its fishing in the massive Wood River-Tikchik Lakes area and the Togiak National Wildlife Refuge. Because there are no roads in these wilderness areas, the lodge flies guests to most of the fishing spots in either Cessna or DeHavilland Beaver floatplanes. Each plane can hold three to four anglers, pilot and gear. Although there is excellent fishing in front of the lodge, chief pilot and manager John Ortman tries to preserve that for after-dinner fishing.

"After a nine-hour day of fishing, some anglers still can't get enough," he said as he taxied us onto Lake Nerka and readied the floatplane for take-off. "The Agulowak River, which runs in front of the lodge, offers plenty of salmon, trout, grayling and char. Sometimes anglers who fish until 2 a.m. will rise again at 6 a.m. to fish before breakfast."

You'll anticipate lunch as much as the day's fishing. A shore lunch consists of fresh-caught salmon gently coated with lemon-pepper and butter. Your guide will slow-steam it in a cast-iron skillet over a driftwood fire, and fry up an accompaniment of seasoned potatoes and onions. A selection of fresh vegetables and a bottle of white zinfandel top off this meal. This is dining in the finest, most scenic "restaurant" in the world.

After a day of fish-catching action, relax and enjoy hors d'oeuvres served while you relax on a deck that overlooks the scenic Agulowak River.

After the day's fishing, take a quick shower and meet at the lodge for hors d'oeuvres of shrimp cocktail, shishkabob and Nerka char bits. Ice from the self-serve bar tinkles in glasses amid the flow of stories. Dinner is always an elaborate affair with spectacular halibut, chicken and beef entrees. Through the lodge's picture window, watch trout rise on the Agulowak River.

The lodge also offers a luxury cruise on the Wood River lakes via the lodge's customized houseboat. The hostess will serve 15 different types of antipasto and cheeses while enroute to the first fishing spot on Lake Nerka. Crystal champagne glasses are kept full, with plenty of fishing to enjoy throughout the day.

For lunch, we tasted gourmet coffees and teas, smoked pheasant, chilled shrimp and crab, fresh strawberries, the famous Wood River Salmon Log, and a variety of dips, breads and crackers. Everyone in our group agreed it was one of the finest gourmet lunches ever served on the lake.

At Wood River, as well as a few other lodges, the guides videotape your entire day, and each guest receives a copy of the week's fishing highlights.

"A video is much better than photos," said guest Carl Tabet. "You can see and hear the jokes and wisecracks, and relive the excitement of your trip time and time again. After watching today's action, I'm ready to book again for next year."

The next time you find yourself in the office, swamped by work and mired in deadlines, stop and remember those lucky few who indulge in the ultimate fishing experience known as Bristol Bay. If the siren song gets to you, make a reservation on the next flight north.

The Agulowak River flows right outside the door of your private cedar cabin.

Mary McCarley, *Cook, Wood River Lodge*

Mary decided to pursue a career in nursing while her husband, Don, was stationed in Colorado with the United States Air Force. After several years of study, Mary received her vocational nurse's license and worked in the nursing profession for the next 12 years.

When Don retired from the Air Force, the couple decided to return to Texas. Six years later they felt a desire to visit Alaska. During their sojourn, Don and Mary fell in love with Alaska. Mary particularly liked the Anchorage area. They returned to Texas, but realized they had left their hearts in Alaska.

Ten years later, mutual friends introduced Don and Mary to Wood River Lodge owners Ken and Helen Stockholm, who showed the couple slides of the lodge. Mary said she would never cook for a lodge, but might be interested in being a caretaker. In August 1984, Ken invited Don and Mary to try a winter as caretakers of Wood River Lodge. They agreed, and worked as caretakers for the next few years. Don accepted the lodge manager's position in 1986. Mary, however, had land-  ed a summer job as a maid at Aleknagik Mission Lodge.

Don spent all summer asking Mary to cook for Wood River Lodge. Mary, however, didn't feel totally confident in her abilities. While at Aleknagik, Mary helped in the kitchen on numerous occasions. She obtained first-hand kitchen experience by working with cook Patty Grant. Patty was a patient teacher and Mary soon achieved the cooking confidence she needed. Patty ran a well-organized kitchen and established a good example for Mary, who learned how to organize and structure her time.

In the fall of 1986, Mary finally gave Don a tentative "OK" about cooking at Wood River, but still felt unsure about her new-found skills. After spending a third winter at Wood River, Mary became comfortable with the lodge kitchen, and agreed to hire on as head cook for Wood River Lodge.

Mary says her position as cook has worked out well, but staying organized is her biggest challenge. She insists that meals run smoothly and be served on time.

All meals served at Wood River Lodge are from Mary's own southern, family-style recipes. Mary is surprised that she enjoys cooking at the lodge as much as she does, and her efforts have been extremely successful. She believes that cooking at a fishing lodge is the hardest job she has ever had, but it has also been the most fun. After sampling her meals, I'm glad Mary took the plunge to become head cook at Wood River. And so are the guests.

Steve O'Dell, *Assistant Cook, Wood River Lodge*

Mary McCarley's assistant cook, Steve O'Dell, is in charge of breakfasts, salads, cookies and maintaining the generator that provides electricity for the lodge. This unique combination of skills had its beginning when Steve served as a Marine Corps diesel mechanic. Little did he realize at the time that this skill would make him a valuable commodity in the fishing lodge business, where diesel generators flown in via bush plane provide the only source of electrical power.

After his discharge from the Marine Corps, Steve worked in several food industry jobs in New Orleans, Louisville and on the Mississippi Queen. To develop other talents, he took a sabbatical from the food industry, immersing himself in a three-year apprenticeship with a stained glass studio.

After the love of his life spurned his marriage proposal, Steve decided to seek his second love: Alaska. He boarded the Alaska ferry in Seattle. When he arrived in Haines, he met Virgil Scott. They traveled on to Fairbanks, where Steve helped Virgil open a home for the elderly and handicapped. Steve cooked for the residents of the home.

Steve eventually sojourned to Kodiak to work on a commercial fishing boat as a fisherman and cook. He also worked at a king crab cannery before returning to cook at Virgil's home and wait tables at a Fairbanks restaurant.

Because of his talents for cooking, his interest in people, and his love of fishing, Steve decided he wanted to work at a fishing lodge. He answered an ad in the Fairbanks Daily News-Miner, and was interviewed by Don McCarley, manager of Wood River Lodge. Because of his background in diesel mechanics and cooking, Steve was hired immediately.

Steve says that living and working in the wilderness has added to his spirituality; the solitude has enhanced his meditation. He also enjoys tying flies, which he tests at every opportunity.

"At Wood River Lodge, I work with some of the best people I've ever worked with in my life," says Steve. "And it gives me the opportunity to sample the incredible fishing that clients pay $4,000 a week to enjoy!"

Nerka Char Bits

Lake Nerka is a clear lake in the Wood River-Tikchik area. It has abundant populations of arctic char that enjoy a feeding frenzy on outmigrating salmon smolt in early spring. A similar frenzy happens at the lodge when this appetizer is served to hungry anglers!

1	**medium-sized char (2 to 3 pounds)**
2	**teaspoons seasoning salt**
2	**teaspoons seafood seasoning**
2	**teaspoons lemon pepper**
1	**12-ounce bottle of beer**
1	**cup flour**
	vegetable oil

*F*illet char and *cut* fillets into bite-sized pieces. Three hours prior to serving, *place* char bits, seasoning salt, seafood seasoning and lemon pepper in a ziploc bag; *shake* to coat fish pieces evenly. *Refrigerate* until ready to fry.

*H*eat oil in a deep-fryer or pan. *Stir* beer into flour until the batter is the consistency of syrup. *Dip* char bits into batter and *fry* in hot oil.

Serves 4—6

Arctic char rank near the top as a prime food fish and are easily caught on a variety of flies. Most anglers, however, practice catch and release, keeping only an occasional fish for the table.

Quek Quiche

Q uek is the Eskimo name meaning "small boat anchorage" and you'll see the similarities among the floating bits of broccoli in a delightful sea of eggs and cream. This quiche is a great appetizer you can prepare in advance and freeze. It's quick to reheat and serve when hungry anglers return home early or guests show up unexpectedly.

2	3-ounce packages cream cheese
1	cup butter
2	cups flour

Grease 48 muffin cups. **Blend** cream cheese and butter well. **Stir** in flour. **Shape** into 1-inch balls and press against bottom and sides of greased 1¾-inch muffin cups to form a miniature pastry shell.

Quiche Filling

2	tablespoons butter, melted
5	slices bacon, chopped
1	medium onion, chopped
¾	of a 10-ounce package of frozen broccoli, chopped and thawed
¼	pound Swiss cheese, shredded
1	cup cream
3	eggs
1	teaspoon salt

Brush pastries lightly with butter; *refrigerate* 30 minutes. In a pan, *fry* bacon, *adding* onion and *sauteing* until onion is clear and bacon is crumbly. **Drain** broccoli on paper towel. Into each cup *spoon* one teaspoon bacon/onion mixture and one teaspoon broccoli. **Top** with shredded cheese. In small bowl, *mix* cream, eggs and salt. **Spoon** 1 teaspoon mixture into each cup. **Bake** at 375 degrees for 25 minutes.

Makes 48

Marsh Mountain Mushrooms

Marsh Mountain, a prominent landmark in the Wood River area, is also known in discreet circles for growing some of the tastiest mushrooms in this part of Alaska. Whether you travel to the mountain to pick your own or pick up a fresh supply from your corner supermarket, these stuffed mushrooms make a great appetizer or an elegant garnish for grilled moose or sirloin steak.

1	dozen large mushrooms
2	tablespoons butter
1	medium onion, chopped
2	ounces pepperoni, chopped
¼	cup green pepper, diced
1	small clove garlic, minced
½	cup finely crushed crackers
3	tablespoons Parmesan cheese
1	tablespoon chopped fresh parsley
½	teaspoon seasoning salt
¼	teaspoon oregano
⅓	cup chicken broth

Wash mushrooms; remove stems, chop fine and reserve. Melt butter, add onion, pepperoni, green pepper, garlic and chopped mushroom stems. Cook until tender. Add cracker crumbs, cheese, parsley, seasoning salt and oregano. Mix well. Stir in broth. Spoon mixture into mushroom caps. Place caps in shallow pan with ¼-inch water covering bottom. Bake at 325 degrees for 25 minutes. Triple recipe if you're feeding a crowd.

Makes 12

Selawik Stuffed Salmon

1	teaspoon white pepper
¾	teaspoon cayenne or red pepper
¾	teaspoon black pepper
1	teaspoon salt
½	teaspoon onion powder
¼	teaspoon dried thyme
	dash of dried oregano
1	stick margarine
1	cup finely chopped onions
½	cup finely chopped celery
½	cup finely chopped green bell pepper
½	cup finley chopped green onion
1 ½	teaspoons minced garlic
½	pound peeled shrimp, chopped (or use 2 cans small shrimp)
½	pound crabmeat (canned, good quality, lump crabmeat)
1	cup fine bread crumbs
4	tablespoons butter
1	egg, well-beaten
3	tablespoons grated Parmesan cheese
1	whole sockeye or silver salmon (10-15 pounds)
	lemon pepper

Thoroughly *combine* white, cayenne and black peppers, salt, onion powder, thyme and oregano in a small bowl.

Melt one stick margarine in skillet over medium-high heat; when half melted, *add* onions, celery, bell pepper, green onions and garlic. *Saute* about 5 minutes, *stirring* occasionally. *Add* shrimp and crabmeat, *mix* well. If using fresh shrimp and crab, *cook* 5 to 7 minutes, *stirring* occasionally. *Add* bread crumbs; *stir* well, then *add* butter and continue *cooking* until butter melts. *Remove* from heat and *cool* slightly. *Combine* egg with Parmesan cheese; *add* to mixture in skillet and *mix* well. *Transfer* to bowl, *cover* and *chill* in refrigerator.

Meanwhile, *season* inside of cleaned, whole fish with lemon pepper and seasoning mixture. When ready to bake, *stuff* inside of fish with stuffing mix and *bake* at 375 degrees for 45 to 60 minutes or until done. Time depends on size and thickness of fish.

Serves 6—8

Wood River Lodge offers comfortable dining in a group atmosphere. Through a large picture window near the dining table, anglers can eat dinner while watching trout and char rise on the Agulowak River.

Tikchik Chicken

This long-standing Eskimo name describes a 45-mile-long series of lakes known for spectacular mountain and river scenery and fishing opportunities. This savory fried chicken dish is a parallel to the Tikchik wilderness area: both delight the senses.

1   **frying chicken**
    seasoning salt
1   **teaspoon granulated sugar**
2   **tablespoons ketchup**
3   **tablespoons vegetable oil**
1   **cup chopped onion**
1   **cup chopped celery**
1   **cup water**

Skin and *cut up* fryer. *Place* in a large bowl. *Season* well with seasoning salt. *Sprinkle* with sugar and ketchup. *Mix* well to distribute seasonings. *Marinate* for two to three hours in refrigerator.

Heat oil in cast iron skillet until very hot. *Brown* chicken pieces well on all sides, *turning* frequently.

Add chopped onions and celery to chicken drippings and well-browned chicken, *stirring* for a few minutes. *Add* 1 cup water. *Turn* heat to low; *cover* and *simmer* chicken for 1 hour until very tender.

Serves 4

Egegik Enchiladas

1   **pound ground beef, caribou or moose**
1   **can cream of chicken soup**
½   **pint sour cream**
2   **cans green chilies, chopped**
½   **teaspoon salt**
1   **cup grated longhorn cheese**
1   **cup grated Monterrey Jack cheese**
1   **cup finely chopped onion**
1   **dozen corn tortillas**
    hot grease for dipping shells

Brown the ground meat and *set aside*.

In a bowl, *stir* together cream of chicken soup, sour cream, chopped chilies and salt. *Add* cheese and onions.

Dip shells in hot grease 5 seconds each side. *Drain* well. *Spoon* 1 tablespoon meat and 2 tablespoons filling on shell and roll up. *Place* in shallow 9x13x2-inch pan. When all enchiladas are in pan, *spread* remaining meat and filling on top. *Sprinkle* with a little extra cheese.

Bake at 350 degrees for 35 minutes.

Serves 6—8

Co-manager Bernie Ortman and Chris Batin with a husky Wood-Tikchik lake trout. Bernie has developed a reputation for providing clients with only the best food, accommodations and fishing adventure.

Good News Bierochen

¼ cup granulated sugar	1 egg, well-beaten
3 teaspoons salt	2 packages yeast
6 tablespoons shortening	¼ cup warm water
1 cup scalded milk	6 cups flour
¾ cup cold water	

Combine sugar, salt, shortening and milk. Add cold water, then add well-beaten egg. Dissolve yeast in warm water. Stir dissolved yeast into the sugar mixture. Gradually add flour to the mixture. Knead approximately 5 minutes. Refrigerate overnight. When ready to use dough, let rise in warm place 1½ hours.

Filling

2 pounds ground beef, moose or caribou
1 large onion, chopped
1 large cabbage, shredded
½ cup finely chopped green pepper
1 teaspoon paprika
1 teaspoon black pepper
1 teaspoon garlic salt
½ cup butter, melted

Combine meat, onion, cabbage, green pepper and spices in skillet, cover and cook until done. Do not brown!

Grease four cookie sheets. Roll dough very thin and cut into 4-inch squares. Cup dough in your hand and fill with 1 heaping tablespoon of meat mixture. Fold edges and seal. Place, with edges down, on cookie sheets. Let rise 30 minutes. Bake at 375 degrees for 30 minutes. Brush tops with butter. Serve hot.

Makes 48

Togiak Twice-Baked Potatoes

6	large baker potatoes
1	teaspoon salt
¼	teaspoon pepper
¼	cup butter
¼	cup milk
1	cup sour cream
¼	cup Parmesan cheese
4	slices cooked bacon, crumbled
½	cup grated Cheddar cheese

Bake potatoes in 400 degree oven for 1 hour or until done. Cut potatoes in half lengthwise and scoop out insides, leaving shell. Prepare as for mashed potatoes. Whip potatoes with salt, pepper, butter and milk. Stir in sour cream and beat until well-mixed and smooth.

Refill potato shells (can use pastry tube with large tip). When all the shells are filled, sprinkle tops with a little parmesan cheese, crumbled bacon pieces and cheddar cheese. Bake at 350 degrees until hot and cheese melts.

Serves 12

A fly-out fishing trip to the Togiak River is an hour or more from the lodge by floatplane. It is impractical to return to the lodge for lunch so Wood River guides and pilots prepare hot shore-cooked lunches. Our favorite was fresh-caught salmon, gently coated with lemon pepper and butter and cooked in a cast-iron skillet. Seasoned potatoes and onions were served on the side.

Taku Salad

$\mathcal{D}$uring the exploration of Alaska in the 1800s, explorers named numerous geographical features throughout southeast Alaska "Taku" after a division of the Tlingit Indians living in the area. Explorers Anglicized the pronunciation on maps to "Taco Harbor and Taco Inlet." This dish commemorates this early literary merger of Mexico and Alaska.

1	sweet onion
4	tomatoes
1	head iceberg lettuce
6	ounces cheese, grated
8	ounces french dressing
	hot sauce
1	large bag plain or taco flavored corn chips
1	large avocado
1 ½	pounds ground beef, caribou or moose
1	can drained red kidney beans
¼	teaspoon salt
1	avocado, sliced
1	tomato, sliced

Chop onion, tomatoes and lettuce. Place vegetables in a large salad bowl. Toss with cheese, french dressing and hot sauce to taste. Crunch ¾ bag of taco chips and add chips to salad, reserving remaining chips for garnish. Slice and add avocado. Refrigerate.

Brown ground meat, add drained kidney beans and salt. Simmer 10 minutes. Mix into cold salad.

Toss and decorate with reserved chips, sliced avocado and tomato slices. Serve at once.

Serves 4—6

Agulukpak Pea Salad

The Agulukpak River is one of the premier rainbow trout fishing streams in the Wood-River Tikchik Lakes chain. Along with its sister river, the Agulowak (Eskimo word meaning "many rapids"), you'll experience no finer adventure in stream angling. Expect to run whitewater rapids, dodge car-sized boulders and watch millions of salmon migrate in long ribbons along the shoreline. The Agulukpak offers many physical sensations. Agulukpak Pea Salad is sure to please the culinary adventurer with its combination of flavorful ingredients and myriad taste sensations.

1	head iceberg lettuce, torn in small pieces
½	cup finely chopped sweet onions
½	cup finely chopped green pepper
1	small can water chesnuts, drained and sliced
1	package frozen peas
2	cups mayonnaise
1	heaping tablespoon granulated sugar
4	ounces Cheddar cheese, grated
6-8	pieces crisp cooked bacon, crumbled

Layer the lettuce, onions, green pepper, water chesnuts and peas in the order listed in a 9x13-inch dish. **Do not mix!**

Mix mayonnaise with sugar in a small bowl. With rubber spatula, *smooth* mixture over frozen peas. Then *sprinkle* with Cheddar cheese and *top* with bacon.

Cover tightly and *refrigerate* overnight.

Serves 12

Aleknagik Bread

Aleknagik was the name of the Eskimo village on a lake of the same name, at the base of the Wood-Tikchik lakes. Discovered in the 1850s, the village served as a base camp for explorations into the Wood River area. Aleknagik Bread is named after this village because it serves as an ideal base for the heartiest of sandwiches and is an excellent substitute for biscuits or rolls at the evening meal. Guests at Wood River Lodge request this bread in shore lunches.

5 ½ to 5¾ cups all purpose flour
2   packages dry yeast
½   cup cornmeal
2   cups boiling water
½   cup dark molasses
⅓   cup shortening
1   tablespoon salt
2   eggs
2   tablespoons butter, melted

In a large mixer bowl, *combine* 3 cups of flour and yeast. Gradually *stir* cornmeal into boiling water; *add* molasses, shortening and salt. *Cool* to lukewarm. *Combine* cornmeal mixture and flour mixture; *add* eggs. *Beat* at low speed with electric mixer for ½ minute, *scraping* bowl constantly. *Beat* 3 minutes at high speed.

By hand, *stir in* enough remaining flour to make a soft dough. *Knead* until smooth and elastic (7 to 10 minutes).

Place in a lightly greased bowl, *turn* once to grease surface. *Cover* and *let rise* in warm place until double (about 1½ hours).

Grease two 4½x8½x2½-inch loaf pans. *Punch* down dough and *divide* in half. *Cover* and *let rest* 10 minutes. *Shape* into 2 loaves and *place* in greased loaf pans. *Cover* and *let rise* until double (45 to 60 minutes).

Bake at 375 degrees about 40 minutes. *Brush* warm bread tops with melted butter.

Makes 2 loaves

Kokwok Wine Cake

The Kokwok River meanders through the Wood River-Tikchik wilderness. In late August the leaves of the beautiful white paper birch trees along the river turn golden and shimmer in the sunlight. Take a bite of this cake and you'll know what it is like to walk through a birch forest and watch the yellow birch leaves wavering in the autumn wind.

1   yellow cake mix
¾   cup oil
¾   cup golden sherry
1   small package instant vanilla pudding
4   eggs
1   teaspoon nutmeg

Preheat oven to 350 degrees. Grease and flour bundt pan.
Combine cake mix, oil, sherry, instant pudding, eggs and nutmeg in a bowl and beat for 5 minutes. Pour into bundt pan. Bake at 350 degrees for 45 to 50 minutes.

Glaze

1   tablespoon butter
1   cup powdered sugar
¼   cup golden sherry

Melt butter, stir in sugar and sherry. Poke holes in cake with ice pick. Pour glaze over cake.

Serves 16

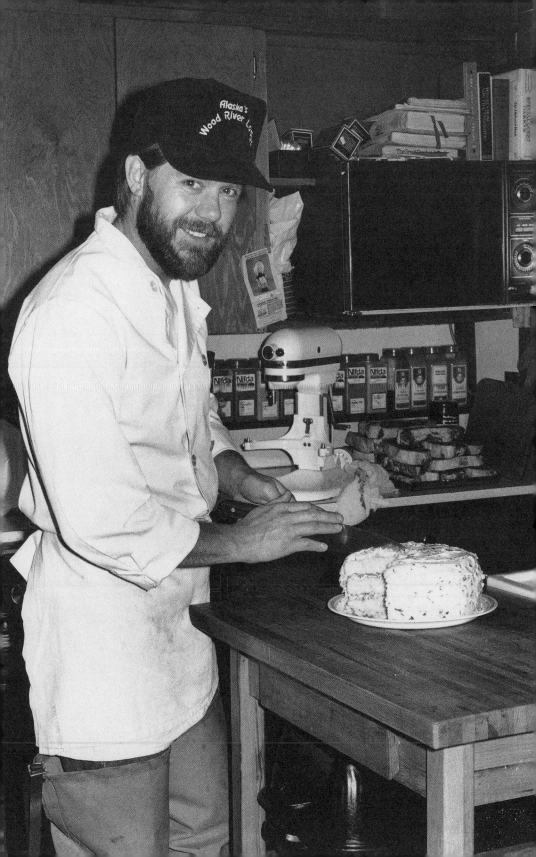

Kulik Cream Cake

2 cups granulated sugar
1 stick margarine, softened
⅓ cup shortening
5 eggs, yolks and whites separated
1 teaspoon baking soda
1 cup buttermilk
2 ¼ cups flour
1 small can flaked coconut
1 teaspoon vanilla

Preheat oven to 350 degrees. Grease and flour three 9-inch cake pans.

Cream together sugar, margarine and shortening. Add egg yolks, one at a time, beating well after each one (reserve egg whites). Add baking soda to buttermilk, then alternately add flour and buttermilk to creamed mixture. Stir in coconut. Beat egg whites until stiff and fold into mixture. Add vanilla. Pour into three cake pans. Bake at 350 degrees for 25 minutes.

Icing

1 8-ounce package cream cheese, softened
1 stick butter or margarine, softened
1 pound powdered sugar, sifted
1 teaspoon vanilla
1 cup chopped pecans

Cream together cream cheese and margarine, beating until smooth. Add powdered sugar and vanilla and beat until light and fluffy. Stir in pecans. Spread on cooled cake layers.

Serves 16

Photo at left: Steve O'Dell, assistant cook at Wood River Lodge, serving Kulik Cream Cake. Steve is as much at home fishing on the Agulowak River as he is in the kitchen. Says Steve, "One of the advantages of being a cook at a fishing lodge is that after the dishes are done, there's always time for fishing."

Bonanza Creek Surprise

The Bonanza Creek north of Wood River is one of 30 Bonanza Creeks throughout Alaska. Most were named by optimistic prospectors during the 1900s. I'm sure the prospectors must've exclaimed, "Bonanza!" when they struck gold in these creeks, which is what you'll do when you taste this dessert. The golden pineapple and bananas sit on a bed of graham crackers and hide under a froth of whipped cream, just like gold nuggets hide in the gravel bed, under the froth of the stream.

2	**cups graham cracker crumbs**
6	**tablespoons butter, melted**
2½	**cups powdered sugar**
2	**eggs**
1	**stick butter, softened**
1	**teaspoon vanilla**
4	**fresh bananas**
1	**20-ounce can crushed pineapple, well-drained**
2	**cups whipping cream**
½	**cup granulated sugar**
¼	**cup walnuts, chopped**
10	**maraschino cherries**

Mix graham cracker crumbs and melted butter and *press* into 9x12-inch pan; *chill*. *Beat* powdered sugar, eggs, butter and vanilla until fluffy; *spread* on top of crumbs.

Slice bananas and *place* on top of mixture. *Spread* crushed pineapple on top of bananas.

Pour chilled whipping cream into a chilled deep bowl. Gradually *add* granulated sugar while *whipping* cream; *continue* until fluffy and stiff. *Spread* whipped cream over the top. *Sprinkle* with nuts and *dot* with cherries. *Chill* for a few hours.

Serves 12—16

Pungokepuk Poppy Seed Cake

*W*hen anglers want the best rainbow fishing in the area, they visit the Pungokepuk River and carefully cast tiny dry flies to large 8- to 10-pound rainbow trout. There's not a better recipe to characterize this activity—the tiny poppy seeds pique the taste buds of your guests, like carefully presented dry flies entice Pungokepuk trout.

3	eggs
2¼	cups sugar
1¼	cups cooking oil
¼	cup milk
3	cups flour
2	teaspoons baking powder
1½	teaspoons salt
1¼	teaspoons vanilla
1¼	teaspoons butter flavoring
1¼	teaspoons almond flavor
1½	tablespoons poppy seed

Preheat oven to 350 degrees. *Grease* two 4½x8½x2½-inch loaf pans. In a bowl, *beat* eggs, *stir* in sugar, oil and milk until well-blended. *Sift* flour, baking powder and salt together and *add* to egg/sugar mixture. *Stir* in vanilla, butter flavoring, almond flavoring and poppy seed. *Beat* for 2 minutes. *Pour* into loaf pans.

Bake at 350 degrees for 1 hour. *Cool* slightly in pans.

Icing

¼	tsp. butter flavoring	¼	cup orange juice
¼	tsp. almond extract	⅔	cup sugar
¼	tsp. vanilla		

In a small saucepan, *combine* the above ingredients. *Heat* until sugar melts, then *pour* over warm loaves.

Makes 2 loaves

Arolik Raspberry Coffeecake

*I*n mid-August, anglers fly out to the Arolik and other rivers in the Togiak drainage to catch silver salmon and collect raspberries for this delicious dessert. Later at the lodge, when asked how their fishing was, they shamefacedly, but with an ear-to-ear grin, admit to spending more time picking and eating raspberries than fishing.

In Alaska there are eight types of raspberries: American Red Raspberry, Red Raspberry, Cloudberry, Baked Appleberry, Thimbleberry, Salmonberry, Trailing Raspberry and Five-Leaved Bramble.

1	**3-ounce package cream cheese**
¼	**cup butter, softened**
2½	**cups biscuit mix**
⅓	**cup milk**
½	**cup raspberry preserves**

Grease baking sheet.

In a small bowl, *blend* cream cheese and butter together. *Place* biscuit mix in a large bowl and *cut* cheese mixture into the biscuit mix until crumbly. *Stir* in milk. *Turn* out onto floured surface and *knead* 8 to 10 strokes.

On waxed paper, *roll* dough into an 8x12-inch rectangle. *Flip* onto greased baking sheet; *remove* waxed paper. *Spread* raspberry preserves down center of dough. *Make* 2½-inch cuts at 1-inch intervals on long sides. *Fold* strips over filling.

Bake at 425 degrees for 15 minutes. *Drizzle* icing over the warm cake.

Icing

½	**cup powdered sugar**
1	**teaspoon margarine, melted**
2	**tablespoons water**

Blend powdered sugar, margarine and water.

Serves 6—8

Park Ranger Cookies

At 1.4 million acres, the Wood-Tikchik State Park is Alaska's largest. When fishing or exploring this undeveloped wilderness, take time out to relax and absorb the magnificent scenery while eating lunch. Steve O'Dell, assistant cook at Wood River Lodge always makes sure there are plenty of these freshly-made ranger cookies packed in the guests' sack lunches. These big, bold cookies are certain to take the edge off a hungry angler, kayaker or hard-working man on the homefront. They'll make you feel like a kid again!

1	cup shortening or margarine
1	cup granulated sugar
1	cup packed brown sugar
2	tablespoons milk
2	eggs
1	teaspoon vanilla
2¼	cups flour
1	teaspoon baking soda
½	teaspoon baking powder
½	teaspoon salt
2	cups oatmeal
1	cup dried, shredded coconut
2	cups cornflakes
½	cup chopped nuts

Preheat oven to 350 degrees. Grease cookie sheet.

In a large bowl, cream shortening and sugars together. Continue to beat as you add milk, eggs and vanilla.

In a separate bowl, sift dry ingredients together. Add to creamed mixture, beating until well-blended. Stir in oatmeal, coconut, cornflakes and nuts. Drop by spoonfuls onto greased cookie sheet.

Bake at 350 degrees for 9 to 10 minutes.

Makes 5 dozen

Stephan Lake Lodge

S tephan Lake Lodge is in the heart of the
Talkeetna Mountains, a one-hour bush plane
flight from Anchorage. Built in the early 1960s, the spruce
log lodge sits on top of a gradually sloping, spruce-birch
hillside overlooking Stephan (pronounced Step-han) Lake.
The lodge is surrounded by a well-maintained lawn, with
fireweed and other wildflowers around the perimeter. Off
in the distance, the powerful Susitna River winds its way
through millennia-old bedrock canyons. Expect to see
moose, grizzly bear and caribou in the alpine meadows
across the lake.

When entering the lodge, prepare to indulge yourself in
complete Alaskana. The tangy-sweet smoke of birch burning in the circular fireplace provides an olfactory cue for
you to kick back, relax and enjoy. Neatly framed maps of
the area, marked with hiking trails, hang on the gnarled
log walls, which complement the tongue-and-groove
waxed floors. Superbly crafted wildlife and fish mounts
are displayed with painstaking care. Sit in the comfortable
chairs or couches hewn from local spruce logs and page

through the volumes of photo albums. You'll observe guests by the central fireplace, enthralled with brown bear stories told by the guides. Take a solitary stroll on the lodge grounds to see the walk-in root cellar, photograph the resident foxes looking for handouts, or listen to the shrill cry of an eagle gliding on the mountain wind.

Stephan Lake Lodge has earned a reputation for personal service and providing those "little extras" that make you feel good about being there. Owner and lodge manager Jim Bailey is quick with a handshake and a smile, and although he's lived in Alaska for over 20 years, he exudes a contagious enthusiasm for the adventures you are about to enjoy as if it were the first time for both of you.

Jim's personality is an integral part of each guest's experience at Stephan Lake Lodge. He entertains guests each night as he sits at the table and gives a humorous rendition of the day's events. This down-home approach is so endearing that many guests call the lodge home, and come back every year to claim their spot at the magnificent 10-foot dining table, hand-hewn from local birch and the epitome of

Red fox pup

rustic elegance. Here's a tip: sit on the left side of the table to enjoy a panoramic view of the lake and mountains.

Stephan Lake Lodge offers home-style cooking to satisfy a hearty appetite. Cook Renee' Olsen, prepares a variety of domestic and wild game dishes that include salmon, blacktail deer, moose and caribou. Desserts are a specialty, as are the plate-sized pancakes made with sweet alpine blueberries fresh-picked that morning.

After a scrumptious dinner, relax in a large spruce- and birch-heated sauna. The sauna is about 10 feet above the lake's edge. Once you've relaxed to the point of nodding off to sleep, take a running leap off the deck, into the clearwater lake for an invigorating thrill. Swim in the refreshing coolness of the lake and listen to the laughter of loons as the midnight sun burns brightly in the North.

$\mathcal{W}$atch grayling and rainbow trout dimple the surface of the lake, right in front of the lodge. Watching soon gives way to fishing, as the sight is too much for anglers to resist. The area offers excellent fishing for rainbow trout, arctic grayling and lake trout. I've caught as many as 30 rainbows a day from alpine streams. The silver and king salmon fishing is exciting in the clearwater streams, with 20 fish per day commonplace.

Brown bears are numerous throughout the area, as are Alaska-Yukon moose and black bear. Don't be surprised if Bailey slings a 375 H&H Magnum rifle over his shoulder as he heads for the fishing stream. He serves not only as fishing guide, but as the first line of defense against a brown bear who might have gotten up on the wrong side of bed. Luckily, he's never had an aggressive encounter with a bear while fishing, and humorously jokes that he has never had to feed a hard-to-please client to a bear. He says he doesn't want to give the bears indigestion. The best way to view bears is at the bear watch, a roomy photographer's blind overlooking a nearby salmon stream. Guests commonly observe from 10 to 20 bears a day.

Singer John Denver has visited Stephan Lake Lodge three times and foreign film crews have used the lodge as a base of operations for major films. Many European groups book the lodge for alpine hiking and mountaineering trips, as well as float trips down nearby rivers. Except for these occasional flurries of activity, the lodge is a quiet destination that allows total communion with Nature and unparalleled fishing opportunities. For more information on Stephan Lake Lodge, see page 303.

The hand-hewn log construction of Stephan Lake Lodge provides an atmosphere of rustic elegance.

Myrna Folkerts, *Cook, Stephan Lake Lodge*

Myrna and her husband, Bob, raised six children on their farm in Iowa. In 1981, after the children left home, Myrna and Bob came to Alaska. They wanted to live a simple life in the "bush." In August 1982, Jim Bailey invited them to Stephan Lake Lodge for the fall hunting season. They fell in love with Stephan Lake and the surrounding area.

Jim explained how rough it was to live in such a remote area. He said, "After six months, most people are ready to leave." But Myrna and Bob stayed on at Stephan Lake Lodge as caretakers, spending both summers and winters there for the next seven years.

In the summer Myrna cooks for lodge guests, while Bob maintains the lodge. In the winter, Myrna quilts and sews. She and Bob enjoy snowmaching, roaming around the hills, and watching wildlife. From mid-February through the end of March she rides her snowmachine along with Bob and Jim to bring in the year's supply of firewood.

Myrna says she loves the wilderness and the opportunity to meet new people at the lodge each year. "It's very difficult, though, making the transition each summer," Myrna says. "In the winter, it's just the snow, the animals and the two of us at the lodge. We experience culture shock when guests arrive and there's lots of activity going on."

Of all the meals Myrna serves at Stephan Lake Lodge, her "beer drop" is perhaps the most popular. Groups of hikers walk to the seven cabins scattered throughout the area, and float the rivers in between. On a real hot day, or when the hikers have reached the highest point in the mountains, Jim and Myrna fly over the hikers in Jim's Super Cub airplane and as a practical joke, Myrna drops a can of beer with 12 straws taped to it, one straw for each hiker.

Every fourth day, Myrna puts together an airdrop meal. Of course, this needs to be high energy, high "impact" food, such as banana bread, polish sausage and Alpine Apple Cake, because the food is dropped from a height of 500 feet. This is a special treat for the hikers, who are more than ready for the taste of fresh-baked goodies.

Myrna especially enjoys baking bread and desserts. The love she used to put into cooking for her large family she now puts into cooking for the "family" of Stephan Lake Lodge visitors.

Renee' Olsen, Cook, Stephan Lake Lodge

Renee' Olsen grew up fishing and hunting with her parents, and enjoyed each weekend they spent afield. She delighted in exploring new areas and the challenges of cooking over a campfire.

By the time she finished high school, Renee' decided to travel cross-country on a budget. In the process, she learned the basics of what she calls survival cooking. It became the foundation of her cooking career. "On the road, you don't carry many utensils," she said. "You use what is available." For instance, she says a beer can serves as excellent cookware.

"To boil rice, you fill a beer can with ¾ water and ¼ rice, close the flip top and cook. You can also stuff a baker potato into a can and put it in the coals, or use the can to make a one-serving stew."

Renee' refined her cooking style as she traveled. She abandoned her beer can cookery and applied her ingenuity to planning and preparing meals that landed her several jobs. She first cooked in Hawaii, and eventually arrived at the Double Musky in Girdwood, which she now calls home. She also cooked at a hunting camp on Kodiak Island, where she learned to cut wood, haul water and prepare king crab and venison.

Renee' said she didn't experience the "real Alaska" until she was hired as a cook at Stephan Lake Lodge. "I see lots of caribou and moose, a family of foxes who live near the lodge, and the waterfowl feeding in the shallows. Watching them helps me to unwind. The environment and the people allow me to put more tender, loving care into my meals. The area is so beautiful."

Renee' likes to work the element of surprise into her meals and desserts, such as the time she made a cake for a guest who was celebrating his 69th birthday. "I placed a Playboy centerfold on the platter under the cake," she said. "I was putting the final touches on the cake when the client walked in the front door, soaking wet. He was upset because he had fallen into the stream. He was also cold and hungry and somewhat depressed because his family wasn't around to help him celebrate his birthday. Before he had a chance to see the cake, I rushed him to his room so he could change clothes; then I brought him a glass of wine. After dinner, his eyes perked up when he saw the cake. He didn't know about the centerfold until half the cake was gone and the German clients began talking excitedly and pointing to the bottom of the cake plate. Taking a closer look, he was shocked, and then delighted. He said it was the best birthday cake he'd ever had."

Renee' classifies her style of cooking as "inventive," because she likes to try new things.

Chitina Chicken-Rice Bake

This entree is named after the Chitina River. Taken from an Indian word meaning "copper," this name also describes this hearty dish highly favored by guests and lodge staff.

The Chitina River country in the Wrangell-Saint Elias mountains is surrounded by rich veins of gold and copper ore. Early prospectors mining this area subsisted on a variety of chicken, grouse and ptarmigan dishes during the winter months, and probably would have given a poke of gold for this one. This dish is quick to fix, and makes a complete meal by adding rolls and a green salad.

1   10¾-ounce can cream of mushroom soup
1   cup milk
1   envelope dry onion soup mix
1   4-ounce can mushrooms, chopped
1   cup uncooked white or brown rice
1   10-ounce package frozen peas and carrots, thawed
1   2-pound chicken, cut up
1   teaspoon paprika

Preheat oven to 350 degrees.

Combine soup, milk, onion soup mix and mushrooms. *Reserve* ½ cup of mixture. *Stir* rice and vegetables into remaining soup mixture.

Pour soup/rice mixture into 9x13-inch pan, and *arrange* chicken pieces on top. *Pour* reserved soup mixture over top of chicken. *Sprinkle* with paprika. *Cover* tightly with foil. *Bake* for 1½ hours at 350 degrees, or until rice is tender.

Serves 4—6

Crispy Parmesan Chicken

6	tablespoons evaporated milk
6	tablespoons vegetable oil
16	chicken pieces
1½	cups crushed saltine crackers
⅔	cup Parmesan cheese, grated
1½	teaspoons salt
1	teaspoon celery salt
1	teaspoon garlic powder
1	teaspoon paprika
½	teaspoon onion powder
½	teaspoon pepper

Preheat oven to 375 degrees. In a bowl, *mix* evaporated milk and oil and *dip* chicken pieces. *Roll* chicken pieces in mixture of saltines, Parmesan cheese, salt, celery salt, garlic powder, paprika, onion powder and pepper. **Place** on a cookie sheet and *bake* at 375 degrees for 1 hour or until tender.

Serves 6—8

Lodge owner Jim Bailey pours wine for guests as they get ready to enjoy Myrna's Potlach Potatoes and Crispy Parmesan Chicken after a successful day of fishing.

Chili Alaska

A favorite among guests who fish the lake and return to the lodge for a hot lunch. Best served with freshly baked cornbread and topped with diced onion and grated Cheddar cheese.

Myrna ladles this chili, steaming hot, into a large-necked thermos for anglers who insist on spending a chilly Alaska day on the stream.

1	**pound ground beef, caribou or moose**
½	**pound ground pork**
1	**medium onion, sliced**
½	**medium green pepper, chopped**
1	**clove garlic, minced**
1	**28-ounce can whole tomatoes, cut up**
	or stewed tomatoes
2	**teaspoons chili powder**
1	**teaspoon ground cumin**
½	**teaspoon salt**
½	**teaspoon oregano**
¼	**teaspoon cayenne pepper**
¼	**teaspoon allspice**
1	**20-ounce can red kidney or pinto beans**
½	**cup diced onion**
½	**cup grated Cheddar cheese**

In a large pot, *brown* meat and onion; *add* green pepper and garlic, *cooking* until tender. Add tomatoes, chili powder, ground cumin, salt, oregano, cayenne pepper, allspice and beans. *Simmer* for at least 1 hour; more if possible.

Top individual bowls of chili with diced onion and grated cheese.

Serves 6

Moose Lake Goulash

*T*his popular dish is a favorite among anglers who spend a night at one of Stephan's outpost cabins. The flavorful dish, with its ripe tomatoes, reminds me of the red foliage that covers the mountains surrounding this cabin in mid-August. The hearty flavor satisfies the hungriest of anglers who have spent a day fishing for silver salmon and rainbow trout on a stream near the cabin.

1   **pound ground beef, caribou or moose**
½   **cup chopped onion**
1   **16-ounce can tomatoes, cut up**
½   **cup chopped celery**
½   **cup water**
1 ½ **teaspoons salt**
¼   **teaspoon pepper**
¼   **teaspoon dried basil leaves**
     dash dried marjoram leaves
3   **ounces uncooked egg noodles (about 1½ cups)**

Cook and *stir* meat and onion in large skillet until meat is browned. **Drain** off fat. **Stir** in undrained tomatoes, celery, water, salt, pepper, basil, marjoram and noodles.

Heat to boiling. **Reduce** heat; *cover* and *simmer, stirring* occasionally, until noodles are tender (about 20 minutes). **Add** small amount of water if necessary.

Serves 6

Alaska Meatloaf

1 ½ **pounds ground beef, caribou or moose**
1   **egg, beaten**
¾   **cup oatmeal**
¼   **cup chopped onion**
1   **teaspoon chili powder**
½   **teaspoon cornstarch**
½   **teaspoon dried red pepper flakes**
½   **teaspoon instant minced garlic**
½   **teaspoon ground cumin**
¼   **teaspoon dried oregano**
1   **8-ounce can tomato sauce**
½   **cup ketchup**

Preheat oven to 350 degrees.

In a large bowl, *combine* meat, egg, oatmeal, onion, chili powder, cornstarch, pepper flakes, garlic, cumin, oregano and tomato sauce. *Work* ingredients with hands or wooden spoon until well-mixed.

Place into loaf pan and gently *shape* into loaf. *Spread* ketchup on top of loaf. *Bake* at 350 degrees for 1 hour.

Serves 6

Located several miles from Stephan Lake Lodge, this cabin serves as a remote base camp for anglers searching for rainbow trout and salmon, and shutterbugs interested in photographing Alaska brown bears.

Stephan Swiss Steak

Ray Genet was the first European registered mountain guide to make a successful winter climb of Mount McKinley, North America's tallest mountain. Of Swiss origin, Ray also worked with Jim Bailey as a registered big game guide at Stephan Lake Lodge. When the hunt was over, Ray enjoyed dining on moose steak prepared in a zesty, flavorful manner. This recipe is a favorite among the lodge's Swiss and German clientele. Serve over rice.

1 ½ **pounds beef or moose steak, cut ¾-inch thick**
3 **tablespoons flour**
2 **teaspoons onion salt**
1 **tablespoon garlic powder**
1 **teaspoon pepper**
2 **tablespoons shortening**
1 **16-ounce can tomatoes, cut up or stewed**
1 **6-ounce can tomato paste**
3 **medium onions, sliced**
3 **bell peppers, red or green, chopped**
1 **tablespoon Worcestershire sauce**
1 **tablespoon beef base**
½ **cup water**
1 **tablespoon cornstarch**

Cut meat into six serving-size pieces; *pound* with meat tenderizer. *Combine* flour, onion salt, garlic powder and pepper. *Dredge* meat on both sides through mixture.

In a deep skillet, *heat* shortening and *brown* meat on both sides. *Add* tomatoes, tomato paste, onions, bell peppers and Worcestershire sauce over the top of the meat. *Cover* and let *simmer* 1 to 1½ hours until tender.

Mix beef base with water and cornstarch, *stirring* until dissolved. *Add* mixture to skillet, *let simmer, stirring* occasionally, until gravy thickens.

Serves 6

Potlatch Potatoes

A good dish to serve a hungry group of anglers. This dish is appropriately named after the Alaska Native potlatch, a ceremonial feast where a variety of traditional foods are prepared. The experience of a potlatch dinner creates a feeling of togetherness, as evidenced by lodge guest Roger Habisreutinger of South Carolina. He commented, "At Stephan Lake, we had the experience of a lifetime. We arrived as outsiders and leave as sourdoughs."

Double or triple the recipe for a larger crowd.

6	**medium potatoes**
1	**teaspoon salt**
¼	**teaspoon pepper**
3	**tablespoons snipped parsley**
¼	**cup chopped onion**
¾	**cup shredded sharp Cheddar cheese**
¾	**cup evaporated milk or half & half**
3	**tablespoons margarine**

Preheat oven to 350 degrees.

Cut potatoes into ¼-inch thick lengthwise strips. *Place* in the bottom of shallow 9x13-inch baking pan. *Sprinkle* salt and pepper over potatoes, then *layer* with parsley, onion and cheese. *Pour* in milk and *top* with margarine.

Cover and *cook* for one hour at 350 degrees.

Uncover and *cook* until tender, about 30 minutes longer.

Serves 6

Prospector Potato Salad

Potatoes are an important food item at Alaska fishing lodges. Because of their weight and bulk, potatoes are expensive to fly in on small bush planes. The early prospectors would have said these nuggets were worth their weight in gold!

2 **pounds white potatoes**
1 **teaspoon salt**
½ **cup diced bacon, uncooked**
½ **cup minced onion**
1½ **teaspoons flour**
4 **teaspoons granulated sugar**
1 **tablespoon salt**
¼ **teaspoon pepper**
¼ **cup vinegar**
½ **cup water**
2 **tablespoons snipped parsley**
½ **cup sliced radishes**

Place potatoes in large kettle, *add* one teaspoon salt and enough water to cover potatoes. *Boil* 20 to 30 minutes until done. *Cool* potatoes until cool enough to handle and *pull* off skins. *Cut* potatoes into quarter-inch slices.

Fry diced bacon until crisp. *Add* minced onion and *saute* until tender.

In a bowl, *combine* flour, sugar, salt and pepper. *Stir* in vinegar and water until smooth. *Add* to bacon. *Simmer, stirring* until slightly thickened.

Pour hot dressing over potatoes. *Add* snipped parsley and sliced radishes and *toss* lightly.

Variation

Omit radishes and *substitute* one tablespoon dried dill. *Reduce* parsley to 1 tablespoon.

Serves 6—8

Susitna Sunshine Carrots

This bright and colorful dish is named after the midnight sun seen from the mountaintops overlooking the Susitna River. In the northern Talkeetna Mountains, the sun shines for over 19 hours a day during early summer. Rather than rising in the east and setting in the west, the sun makes a lazy circle in the sky, dipping into the northwest at twilight and rising in the northeast a few hours later. At any time during the evening hours, there is enough light to read, tie flies or take a midnight stroll.

Myrna Folkerts takes advantage of nature's refrigerator to store the fresh vegetables she uses in meal preparation. Carrots, broccoli, cabbage, lettuce and potatoes keep well in the root cellar built into the hillside behind the lodge. The natural insulating qualities of the earth provide an average temperature of 38 to 42 degrees inside the root cellar while the 80-degree sun beats down outside. In the winter, with temperatures outside dipping down to 40 below zero, the perishables in the root cellar will not freeze.

2	**pounds carrots, sliced ½-inch thick**
2	**tablespoons brown sugar**
2	**teaspoons cornstarch**
½	**teaspoon ground ginger**
½	**cup orange juice**
4	**tablespoons butter**
	fresh parsley for garnish

Place carrots in ½-inch of water in a 2-quart saucepan. Cover and cook until tender, 15 to 20 minutes; drain. Place in serving bowl and keep hot.

In the same saucepan, combine brown sugar, cornstarch, ginger and orange juice; cook over medium heat until thickened. Add butter, stir until melted and pour over hot carrots. Garnish with parsley.

Serves 8

Kosina Corn Salad

Stephan Lake Lodge flies in all produce on a semi-weekly basis. Meals are often planned around cabbage, potatoes, carrots and other fresh produce that keeps its flavor and firmness while stored in the lodge's root cellar. Named after the very scenic and remote Kosina Creek, east of the lodge, this salad is ideal for those times when produce shipments are delayed, and the menu calls for a salad that has zest, yet is quick to prepare. Consider this recipe the next time you are out of lettuce and tomatoes.

4	**cups finely shredded cabbage**
½	**cup chopped green pepper**
½	**cup grated carrot**
¼	**cup chopped onion**
1	**16 ounce can whole kernel corn, drained**
½	**cup mayonnaise**
	dash of salt

In a salad bowl, *combine* cabbage, green pepper, carrot, onion and corn. *Stir* in mayonnaise and salt. *Toss. Chill* before serving.

Serves 8

Besides excellent fishing, Stephan Lake Lodge offers great family fun that includes hiking, canoeing, rafting and sightseeng.

Base Camp Bread

*M*yrna's first love is baking bread, and this is a favorite white-bread recipe among lodge guests. She serves it hot out of the oven to complement the evening meal. Early each morning, she careful-ly packs it in each angler's shore lunch. The guides serve it with freshly-caught salmon grilled over an open alder fire. Delicious!

2   **cups all-purpose flour**
3   **tablespoons granulated sugar**
2   **teaspoons salt**
2   **tablespoons active dry yeast**
2   **cups very warm water (120 to 130 degrees)**
¼   **cup vegetable oil**
2 - 3 **cups additional flour**

Combine 2 cups flour, sugar, salt and yeast. *Add* water and oil and *blend* well. *Stir* in additional flour until dough "cleans" the bowl. *Knead* on floured board, *working* in some flour, until dough is smooth and elastic, about 10 minutes.

Place dough in greased bowl, *cover* and *let rise* in a warm place (80 to 85 degrees) until double in size (1 to 1½ hours).

Grease two 8½x4½x2½-inch loaf pans. *Punch down* and *shape* dough into 2 loaves, *place* in loaf pans. *Cover* and *let rise* until doubled (1 hour).

Bake for 30 minutes at 375 degrees, until top is golden brown.

Makes 2 loaves

Monkey Muffins

$\mathcal{D}$uring Renee' Olsen's first year as a cook at Stephan Lake Lodge, she served a batch of banana bread muffins to a group of fishing clients from Germany. Having never tasted banana bread before, they jokingly dubbed them 'monkey muffins' and the name has stuck ever since.

1½   **cups all-purpose flour**
1½   **teaspoons baking soda**
½   **cup margarine, melted**
2   **eggs**
1   **tablespoon vanilla**
1   **cup granulated sugar**
3   **large ripe bananas, mashed**
½   **cup chopped macadamia nuts**

Preheat oven to 400 degrees. *Place* paper baking cups in muffin tins or *grease* muffin tins.

Sift flour and baking soda together.

In a separate bowl, *beat* together margarine, eggs, vanilla and sugar. *Add* mashed bananas and *stir*. *Blend* dry ingredients into mixture, being careful not to overmix. *Stir* in nuts.

Pour batter into muffin tins and *bake* at 400 degrees for 20 to 25 minutes or until golden brown.

Makes 14 muffins

Alaska Blueberry Muffins

*I*n mid-August, the alpine pastures near Stephan Lake Lodge provide an abundance of blueberries. While walking to the fishing streams, guests find it easy to become sidetracked by berries. It seems that for every handful of berries in the bucket, another handful gets eaten in the process of picking. Oftentimes, the sweet, succulent blueberries don't make it back to the kitchen, forcing Myrna to send out the guides to obtain this most important ingredient.

If cultivated blueberries are used, you can reduce the amount of sugar in this recipe to ¼ cup.

1	**egg**
½	**cup milk**
¼	**cup vegetable oil**
1 ½	**cups all-purpose flour**
½	**cup granulated sugar**
2	**teaspoons baking powder**
½	**teaspoon salt**
1	**cup Alaska blueberries**

Preheat oven to 400 degrees. *Grease* muffin tins or use paper baking cups.

Beat egg with fork, *stir* in milk and oil.

In a separate bowl, *blend* flour, sugar, baking powder and salt; *stir* into first mixture just until moistened. *Fold* in blueberries. *Do not overmix. Fill* muffin cups ⅔ full.

Bake 20 to 25 minutes or until golden brown. *Loosen* immediately with spatula.

Makes 12 muffins

Chickadee Cake

C hickadees are common in and around Stephan Lake, and are always searching for handouts at the lodge window. They rarely find, however, leftover Chickadee Cake, as all that remains of this delicious dessert are a few minute crumbs on an empty cake plate. For a treat, take the crumbs between thumb and forefinger, walk outside, and within minutes, chickadees will land on your finger and help themselves to the crumbs.

3   cups all-purpose flour
2   cups sugar
1   teaspoon salt
1   teaspoon baking soda
1   teaspoon cinnamon
3   eggs, beaten
1   cup vegetable oll
1   stick butter or margarine, melted
1½ teaspoons vanilla
1   8-ounce can crushed pineapple, undrained
2   cups chopped bananas
1½ cup chopped walnuts or pecans

Preheat oven to 350 degrees. *Grease* and *flour* 15½x10½x2-inch cake pan.

In a large bowl, *combine* flour, sugar, salt, baking soda and cinnamon. *Stir* in eggs, oil and melted butter or margarine and *blend* until dry ingredients are moistened, but *do not beat*. *Stir* in vanilla, pineapple, bananas and 1 cup of nuts. *Pour* batter into cake pan. *Bake* at 350 degrees for 30 to 35 minutes.

Cool cake in pan for 10 minutes, then remove from pan and cool completely. *Frost* with icing. *Sprinkle* top with remaining ½ cup of nuts.

Icing

Use icing on page 51, except *omit* nuts in icing.

Serves 16

Photo at right: Jim Bailey admires Gail Davis' arctic grayling, which she caught on ultralight tackle.

Alpine Apple Cake

*U*p in the Talkeetna alpine, Caribou Cabin is a hiking base camp with a spectacular view. The only thing better than the view is the Alpine Apple Cake which Myrna bakes for hikers to take with them to the cabin. Guests who return to Stephan year after year often request several containers of this tasty snack for their week-long journeys afield.

2	**eggs**
½	**cup vegetable oil**
2	**cups granulated sugar**
2	**teaspoons cinnamon**
½	**teaspoon nutmeg**
4	**cups peeled, diced apples**
2	**cups all purpose flour**
1	**teaspoon salt**
2	**teaspoons baking soda**
1	**cup chopped walnuts**

Preheat oven to 350 degrees. *Grease* a 9x13-inch baking pan.

In a large bowl, *beat* eggs, *add* oil, sugar, cinnamon, nutmeg and apples; *mix* well. In a separate bowl, *blend* flour, salt and baking soda; *stir* into the first mixture. *Blend* well. *Stir* in walnuts.

Pour into baking pan and *bake* for 40 to 45 minutes at 350 degrees.

Serve with a dollop of whipped cream on top if desired.

Serves 8

Denali Danish

$\mathcal{D}$enali means "The Great One" in the Athabascan Indian language, and aptly describes this rich dessert. Denali is also the local name for Mount McKinley, North America's highest mountain, which can be seen from the mountains near Stephan Lake. Myrna serves fresh-cut slices of this danish after dinner or as a morning pastry with scrambled eggs and caribou sausage.

1	cup butter
1¾	cups granulated sugar
4	eggs
1	teaspoon vanilla
2½	cups all-purpose flour
1½	teaspoons baking powder
½	teaspoon baking soda
1	30-ounce can of cherry, apple or lemon pie filling

Preheat oven to 350 degrees. Grease a 10x15-inch baking pan.

Cream butter and sugar together, add eggs and vanilla and beat well. Sift flour, baking powder and baking soda together. Add to first mixture and mix well. Spread in pan, reserving ¼ of batter. Spread pie filling on top of mixture. Dot with reserved batter and spread slightly.

Bake at 350 degrees for 45 minutes until golden brown. Drizzle with glaze while warm.

Glaze

½	cup sifted powdered sugar
¼	teaspoon vanilla
2	tablespoons water

Mix sugar, vanilla and water together until smooth.

Serves 12

Camp Denali

*D*enali National Park, the crown jewel of national parks, includes some of the most spectacular mountain and wilderness scenery in North America. Over 150 miles of snow-covered mountains arc through the center of the 5.7-million-acre park. Massive glaciers feed numerous rivers and streams. Most visitors view the sights from park buses that travel the 90-mile road from the park entrance to Wonder Lake and back. Private vehicles are generally not permitted within the main body of the park, so most visitors don't have time to kick back, relax and enjoy the best attractions.

This won't happen to you if you're a guest at Camp Denali or North Face Lodge. Located at the park road's terminus at Wonder Lake, Camp Denali is a nature center that offers an alternative to the standard lodge experience. Fishing takes a back seat to outdoor recreational opportunities and abundant wildlife viewing and photography.

Guests call Camp Denali "rustically elegant," with the emphasis on elegant. Nestled in an alpine meadow facing

Mount McKinley, the main lodge complex includes a central dining room, lounge and study cabin, and bathhouse. Spaced evenly along a wide ridge, each guest cabin has a view of the mountain. Country calico decorates the interior of each cabin and the comfortable beds are covered with quilts crafted at Camp Denali.

Guests claim repeatedly that the dining scenery is some of the finest in North America. Enjoy breakfast or lunch on your cabin porch and soak in the immensity of the Alaska Range.

If you require a television, telephones or swinging nightlife, look elsewhere for a vacation destination. At Camp Denali, your neighbors include 35 species of mammals and 156 species of birds. Spend your evenings developing film, researching plant and geological formations, or simply sitting by the fire with a good book.

The meals served at Camp Denali are as natural as the lodge surroundings. According to lodge co-owner Jerryne Cole, "It is essential that the food we serve be creative, appealing and nutritious."

Camp Denali cooks are masters at bringing out the natural flavor of foods by using complementary ingredients rather than fancy or overpowering sauces. Their sourdough breads, pancakes and rolls come from a starter kept in stoneware crocks. Favorite recipes of guests include the mile-high Vegetarian Lasagne and Muldrow Mud Cake.

Northface Lodge was acquired by Camp Denali owners, Wally and Jerryne Cole, in 1987. Designed with the charm of a comfortable north-country inn, Northface offers a hospitable, intimate atmosphere away from the crowds at Denali National Park.

$\mathcal{Y}$ou can fish for grayling in Moose Creek and lake trout in Wonder Lake, as well as take in natural history programs and burn energy by canoeing, rafting, biking, gold panning and hiking. When temperatures hit the upper 80s, guests are quick to sunbathe on the open tundra or take a dip in Moose Creek. I happened to experience the latter during a wild rafting trip down this exciting stretch of water.

Owners and managers Wallace and Jerryne Cole limit the number of guests at each lodge to maintain an atmosphere where nature, not man, dominates the scene.

It is a scene that would have made Sidney Lawrence, the famous Alaskan artist, envious. As I looked out my window of the "Forty-below Cabin," I could have sworn I was looking at a painting. But there is no grander painter than Nature itself. The magnificent Mount McKinley was framed by the window of our cabin.

This "painting" changed colors with the early-morning sunrise and the evening alpenglow on Mount McKinley. A warm glow enveloped me as I became mesmerized by this idyllic setting.

Photo at left: Camp Denali guests can view over 35 species of mammals, including caribou, ground squirrel, moose, grizzly bear, sheep, wolf and lynx. You may have the opportunity to view these animals during a morning stroll or while relaxing on the porch after the evening meal.

Photo below: North Face Lodge features 15 modern guest rooms, a dining room and living room accented by a native-stone fireplace. Guest rooms have private baths and central heating. Cozy down comforters adorn the rooms' twin beds. Outside, wide porches and a large patio invite relaxation and an opportunity to absorb nature's panorama.

Nancy Bale, *Baker, Camp Denali*

Nancy and her husband were in California dreaming of living someplace truly wild. Looking at a map of Alaska, they saw a road to Cantwell, just outside Mount McKinley National Park. During the summer of 1971, they drove the Alaska Highway to this area where they met Wally and Jerryne Cole and the people of Cantwell.

In the winter of 1972, Nancy and her husband acquired a homestead at the west end of Denali Park. For the past 13 years, they have spent the winters at their homestead, flying in after snowfall, and hiking out to Camp Denali in May. This 95-mile hike takes them 10 to 15 days, except when turned back by too much snow!

Nancy learned to cook and developed a knack for baking bread while a cook's helper at a lodge in Colorado. When Celia Hunter and Jenny Wood, the first owners of Camp Denali, offered her a job as lodge cook in 1974, she jumped at the chance. In those days, the lodge used mainly canned and dried food because of transportation difficulties into the lodge. But guests were there to see the great Mount McKinley, and didn't worry about meals.

The next year, Nancy worked as a baker at the Denali Park Hotel. The original hotel was destroyed by fire and replaced with the current structures.

In 1976, Wally and Jerryne Cole purchased Camp Denali from Celia and Jenny. Nancy came on again as lodge cook and has been there ever since. She cites the family atmosphere as one of the reasons.

"It's like Thanksgiving every day. We're one big family, and everyone learns to work together. The park setting is incredible. It would take many summers to see the park, so we spend much of our time off hiking."

What was originally a staff of eight has now grown to a staff of 30. Nancy used to make all the breads by hand but now has a separate bakery, complete with a convection oven that bakes 15 loaves of bread at one time. She sets the dough and bakes all the bread and cookies for both Camp Denali and Northface Lodge. Nancy bakes for as many as 100 people each day.

The staff makes committee decisions on menus and new recipes. Basic favorites are retained, but many new recipes have been introduced by creative kitchen workers over the years.

Camp Denali employs a gardener who grows parsley, lettuce, green onions, pea pods, radishes, spinach, rhubarb and flowers. Nancy grows chives and basil in a bay window of the bakery and uses this fresh basil in her Onion Herb Bread. She says, "Making bread is easy if you have a feel for it."

Kathleen Maslan, Cook, Camp Denali

Kathleen Maslan wears two hats. From September through May, she works as a second-grade teacher and sign language interpreter. Summer months she works as a cook at Camp Denali.

During her college days, Kathleen was a chef's assistant for several restaurants in Vermont and New Hampshire. Later she trained in food service management for the ski industry.

After graduating from college in 1989, Kathleen became involved in the local rescue squad. There she met Jerryne Cole, a registered nurse and co-owner of Camp Denali. Jerryne was searching for a lodge cook, and offered Kathleen the job.

"I remember telling her that while I had food preparation and management experience, I wasn't a formally trained chef," Kathleen said. "Jerryne told me that she would rather have a multi-talented individual who was willing to help wherever needed. I eventually agreed to try the position."

"Camp Denali is a very organized operation," she said. "Its people have a terrific ability to work together. I remember saying to myself, after a few days, 'Yes, this feels right. I fit in here.'"

Kathleen enjoys cooking one entree each evening instead of the dozens required in short-order cooking. Staff rotates every couple of weeks, so she works with a variety of people. She delights in getting to know each lodge guest, especially when they take the time to visit her in the kitchen. Whether they are from Europe, Australia or the United States, they all have a common goal: to learn more about the park and its wilderness treasures.

She has observed that many guests prefer low cholesterol foods. "Our most frequent request is for seafood," she said. "We receive guests from cruise ships who complain the food on board is too rich."

"Whenever possible, we serve food from the local area. Our sourdough is from a starter owned by Fanny Quigley, a gold miner in the Kantishna area. It dates back a number of years, and guests love its distinct flavor.

"We also serve huge Swedish pancakes at least once a week. We bring one out to each table, and a staff member cuts it into plate-size pieces. We serve it with lingonberry sauce, made from berries picked near the lodge."

Kathleen said the lodge has come a long way since its opening, when dried eggs and canned beans were regular items on the menu.

Its exceptional meals are now one of the major reasons why guests return to Camp Denali year after year. If you do visit the lodge, be sure to stop by the kitchen and say hi to Kathleen. She will enjoy chatting with you.

Sour Cream Halibut

*S*urpassed only by sourdough bread in popularity, Sour Cream Halibut is one of the many Alaskan dishes that have withstood the discriminating tastes of countless guests. It is one of Camp Denali's most frequently requested recipes.

⅓   **cup butter or margarine**
2   **tablespoons lemon juice**
4 - 5 **pounds filleted halibut or other white fish,**
      cut in ½-pound serving-size pieces
      lemon pepper
2   **cups sour cream**
½   **cup yogurt**
¾   **cup mayonnaise**
1   **cup soda crackers, crushed**

Preheat oven to 375 degrees.

Melt butter or margarine in the bottom of a 9x13-inch enamel baking dish. *Add* lemon juice. *Arrange* fish in pan and *sprinkle* with lemon pepper.

Mix together sour cream, yogurt and mayonnaise. *Spread* sour cream mixture on top of fillets and *bake* at 375 degrees for 20 minutes.

Top with crushed soda crackers and *bake* 15 to 20 minutes longer or until fish is done and crumbs are light golden brown.

Serves 8—10

Stifado

*T*his uniquely spiced stew has Mediterranean origins. Camp Denali cooks serve it in ramekins accompanied by sauteed vegetables, rice and cornbread.

⅓ **cup butter**
3 **pounds stew meat (beef, moose or caribou)**
  cut in 1½-inch cubes
2 **pounds tiny whole onions**
1 **6-ounce can tomato paste**
½ **cup water**
⅓ **cup dry red wine**
2 **tablespoons vinegar**
1 **tablespoon brown sugar**
1 **clove garlic, minced**
1-2 **bay leaves**
1-2 **cinnamon sticks**
¾ **teaspoon whole cloves**
½ **teaspoon cumin**
½ **cup raisins**
  toasted sesame seeds

Preheat oven to 325 degrees.

Melt butter in a dutch oven or other covered baking dish. *Add* stew meat and onions to the butter.

In a separate dish *mix* tomato paste, water, wine, vinegar, brown sugar, garlic, bay leaves, cinnamon sticks, cloves, cumin and raisins. *Pour* this mixture over meat and onions.

Cover and *bake* at 325 degrees for three hours. Do not stir. Just before serving, *stir* gently to blend.

Sprinkle each serving with toasted sesame seeds.

Serves 6

Photo at left: A backcountry camper admires the beauty of Mount McKinley as seen from a bluff near Wonder Lake.

Vegetarian Lasagne

*D*uring the Alaska Gold Rush, Italian emigrants traveled north to try their hand at panning for gold. During the long winter months, meat was often scarce for weeks at a time. Meatless dishes were common. If the prospectors had possessed recipes as good as Vegetarian Lasagne, they'd have forsaken the hunting and spent more time in the dining tent.

For best flavor, make the sauce a day ahead.

1	**cup minced onion**
1	**green pepper, minced**
½	**cup minced celery (with some leaves)**
¾	**tablespoon olive oil**
2	**cloves garlic, minced**
¼	**cup minced parsley**
2	**cups tomato sauce**
2	**cups whole tomatoes, cut up**
1	**6-ounce can tomato paste**
2	**teaspoons oregano**
2	**teaspoons basil**
1	**bay leaf**
½	**teaspoon pepper**
	dash cayenne
1	**teaspoon Worcestershire sauce**
	Parmesan cheese

Saute onion, green pepper and celery in olive oil. **Add** garlic and parsley and *saute* lightly. **Stir** in tomato sauce, tomatoes, tomato paste, oregano, basil, bay leaf, pepper, cayenne and Worcestershire sauce. **Simmer** for 1 to 2 hours over low heat until thick.

Prepare according to package directions:

8	**ounces lasagne noodles (whole wheat are tasty)**
1	**tablespoon vegetable oil**

Drain and *separate* noodles. *Grease* a deep-sided 9x13-inch baking pan or extend the sides of a regular pan with 2 inches of greased aluminum foil. *Preheat* oven to 350 degrees. *Layer* the following ingredients in order.

First layer:

⅓	**of the sauce**
½	**of the noodles**
2	**cups cottage or ricotta cheese**
2	**cups sliced fresh mushrooms**
1½	**cups sliced fresh zucchini**

Second layer:

⅓	**of the sauce**
½	**of the noodles**
1	**pound jack cheese, grated, or ½ pound each jack and mozzarella cheese, grated**
1	**cup finely grated carrots**
½	**cup sliced black olives**
1	**pound cooked, well-drained spinach**
⅓	**of the sauce**

Cover and *bake* at 350 degrees for 45 minutes. *Uncover* and *bake* for 30 to 45 minutes longer. Within the last 15 minutes of baking, *dust* with Parmesan cheese. *Let* stand about 20 minutes before cutting and serving.

Serves 12

Guests at Camp Denali and North Face Lodge enjoy a variety of Alaskana meals in a comfortable and spacious dining room. It is not unusual to watch caribou walking by outside the dining room as you are eating dinner.

Japanese Salad

$\mathcal{D}$enali National Park has many Japanese visitors every summer. Several avid Japanese photographers have captured Denali Park's wildlife on film and published books on the subject.

Winter is also a popular time for Japanese to visit Alaska. Tour groups head north to Fairbanks for the aurora borealis, also known as the "northern lights," which is supposed to bring good fortune to all who view it. This salad, light and tasty with an oriental touch, is very popular with visitors to Camp Denali.

¼	**cup lemon juice**
¼	**cup honey**
2	**oranges**
1	**8-ounce package cream cheese, well-chilled**
8	**servings of iceberg lettuce, washed and torn into bite-size pieces**
½	**cup roasted, unsalted cashews**

In a small saucepan, *heat* and *stir* lemon juice and honey until combined. *Set* aside to cool.

Grate rind of the two oranges. *Dice* cream cheese into ¼-inch cubes. *Dredge* cream cheese cubes in orange rind.

In a salad bowl, *toss* lettuce and dressing. *Add* cream cheese cubes.

Cut sections of oranges into halves. *Add* orange sections and cashews to salad and *toss* lightly.

Serves 8

Glacier Breakline Bread

The white and brown spirals in this bread resemble what is known as a breakline. This is when brown glacial currents and clear-water feeder creeks swirl together in the river bottomlands of Denali National Park. Camp Denali serves this delightful bread at dinner, and as an elegant sandwich bread for lunch.

3   cups lukewarm water
½   cup honey
2   tablespoons active dry yeast
6½   cups unbleached white flour
½   cup nonfat powdered milk solids
½   cup vegetable oil
2   teaspoons salt
½   cup bran
¼   cup molasses
2   tablespoons instant coffee granules
2½   cups whole wheat flour

Mix lukewarm water and honey. Add yeast. When yeast mixture is foamy, *add* 3½ cups white flour, powdered milk, vegetable oil and salt. Stir vigorously, about 200 strokes. Divide dough in half. To one half gradually *stir* in bran and 2 cups white flour. To the remaining dough, *stir* in molasses, coffee, whole wheat flour and 1 cup white flour.

Knead separately, adding additional white flour as necessary until doughs are smooth and elastic. Place doughs in separate oiled bowls, *cover* and *let rise* in a warm place until doubled in bulk. Punch down and divide each dough in half. Roll out one piece of light dough into an 8x12-inch rectangle. Repeat with a piece of dark dough. Place one dark dough atop a light dough and *roll* out together into a larger rectangle, about 10x15-inches, taking care to press out any air bubbles between layers. Roll up from the short side. Pinch seams together and place seam side down in a greased loaf pan. Repeat process with the remaining dough. Cover and *let rise* in a warm place until almost doubled. Bake at 350 degrees for 40 to 45 minutes.

Makes two 5x9-inch loaves

Russian Black Bread

The United States owns Little Diomede Island, which is located 2.5 miles from Soviet Union's Big Diomede Island. Early Eskimos traveled extensively between the islands to trade and subsistence fish and hunt. During World War II, the Soviet Union established the Iron Curtain, which prevented residents on Big Diomede from visiting their relatives on Little Diomede.

Russian Black Bread commemorates the "breaking of bread" fellowship that has resumed between these two nations. This dark bread is delicious with soup and cheese.

2	cups lukewarm water
1	tablespoon sugar
¼	cup molasses
2	packages active dry yeast
1	tablespoon instant coffee granules
3	cups rye flour
3	cup unbleached white flour
1	cup bran
¼	cup baking cocoa
1	tablespoon dried onions
2	teaspoons crushed caraway seeds
1	teaspoon crushed fennel seeds
¼	cup vinegar
¼	cup vegetable oil
2	teaspoons salt
1	teaspoon cornstarch
½	cup cold water

Mix lukewarm water, sugar and molasses. **Add** dry yeast. When yeast mixture is foamy, **add** coffee, 2 cups rye flour, 1 cup white flour, bran, cocoa, dried onions, caraway and fennel seeds, vinegar, vegetable oil and salt. **Stir** vigorously, about 200 strokes.

Gradually **stir** in 1 cup rye flour and 2 cups white flour until a kneadable dough develops.

Knead, adding white flour until dough is smooth but still slightly sticky. **Place** in an oiled bowl, **cover** and **let rise** in a warm place until doubled in bulk. **Punch** down and divide dough in half.

Shape each half into a round, tucking seams underneath. *Grease* two 9-inch cake pans or pie tins. *Place* each round in a pan. *Cover* and *let rise* in a warm place until almost doubled. *Bake* at 350 degrees for 40 to 45 minutes.

To glaze tops, *mix* cornstarch and cold water in a small saucepan. *Cook* over medium heat, *stirring* constantly until mixture boils, thickens and clarifies. As soon as bread is baked, *brush* mixture over tops of loaves and *return* to the oven for 2 to 3 minutes.

Makes 2 large round loaves

Each day, Nancy Bale bakes for as many as 100 guests and staff at Camp Denali and North Face Lodge.

Pioneer Ridge Rolls

Denali National Park's Pioneer Ridge extends nine miles from the north summit of Mount McKinley to Gunsight Pass, rising from 6,500 feet to 19,470. Brad Washburn named this ridge in 1945 to honor the first American pioneers who climbed this route. As this ridge is the base route for mountaineers, so this recipe is the base for a variety of breads baked fresh each day at Camp Denali. Try Onion-Herb Rolls, page 93, as a variation.

2 **cups lukewarm water**
½ **cup sugar**
1 **package active dry yeast**
3½ **cups unbleached white flour**
⅓ **cup nonfat powdered milk solids**
½ **cup softened margarine or butter**
2 **eggs**
1½ **teaspoons salt**
3 **cups flour**

In a large bowl, *mix* lukewarm water and sugar, *add* dry yeast. When yeast mixture is foamy, *add* white flour and powdered milk. *Stir* vigorously, about 200 strokes, then *add* margarine or butter, eggs and salt. Gradually *stir* in enough flour to form a soft dough.

Knead only until smooth. This dough should be soft, even a little sticky. *Grease* large bowl and baking pans or muffin tins. *Place* dough in oiled bowl, *cover* and *let rise* until doubled in bulk.

Punch down, *scrape* from bowl and *shape* into rolls as desired. *Place* ½-inch apart in baking pan, or in muffin tins. *Cover* and *let rise* in a warm place until very light and almost doubled.

Bake at 375 degrees for 20 to 25 minutes.

Makes about 3 dozen rolls

Onion-Herb Rolls

*T*hese Onion-Herb Rolls made with basil and oregano make wonderful companions to the Vegetarian Lasagne, page 86.

Prepare Pioneer Ridge Rolls dough, page 92. Set aside.

2   **tablespoons butter or margarine**
1   **large onion, finely chopped, or 6 green**
        onions, chopped
2   **cloves garlic, minced**
2   **tablespoons dried herbs, or ½ to 1 cup fresh**
        herbs. Choose from: basil, oregano, thyme,
        dillweed, marjoram, sage
1   **cup finely chopped fresh parsley**
1   **egg, beaten**
      vegetable oil
1   **egg, beaten**

Grease baking pans.

In a saucepan, *saute* butter, onion and garlic. *Drain* excess liquid and *add* herbs, parsley and one egg. *Blend* in food processor or blender to make filling smooth. *Set* aside.

After dough has risen once, *punch* down and *divide* in half. On a lightly-floured surface, *roll* out each half into a ¼-inch-thick rectangle. *Brush* lightly with vegetable oil and *spread* each with half the onion-herb filling.

Roll up, starting at the long edge. *Pinch* seam carefully to seal. *Cut* into 1-inch slices. *Place* about ½ to 1 inch apart in baking pans. *Cover* and *let rise* in a warm place until almost doubled. *Brush* with beaten egg.

Bake at 350 degrees for 20 minutes.

Makes 40 rolls

Strawberry Island Bread

$\mathcal{S}$trawberry Island, located in Glacier Bay National Monument, offers some of the best-eating wild strawberries you'll find anywhere. If a trip to Strawberry Island isn't in your immediate travel plans, substitute fresh or frozen strawberries from the local grocery store. Serve this fruitful bread for breakfast or brunch. Guests will say, "This is the best bread I've ever eaten!"

3	**cups unbleached white flour**
1	**tablespoon cinnamon**
1	**teaspoon baking soda**
½	**teaspoon salt**
4	**eggs**
2	**cups granulated sugar**
1	**cup vegetable oil**
20	**ounces cut-up, frozen strawberries, thawed**
1¼	**cups chopped nuts**

Preheat oven to 350 degrees. *Grease* two 5x9x3-inch loaf pans.

In a large bowl, *combine* flour, cinnamon, baking soda and salt; *mix* well.

In a separate bowl, *beat* eggs until fluffy. *Add* sugar, oil and strawberries, and *beat* again until well-mixed.

Add liquid ingredients to dry ingredients and *stir* only until blended. *Fold in* chopped nuts. *Pour* into loaf pans.

Bake at 350 degrees for 1 hour and 10 minutes. *Cool* in pans for 10 minutes before *turning* out onto wire racks. This bread slices best when chilled.

Makes two 5x9-inch loaves

Igloo Rye Bread

This sour rye bread, flavored with onion and dill, is good on picnics with cold cuts and cheese.

1¼ **cups lukewarm water**
1 **cup sourdough starter**
2 **tablespoons honey**
2 **tablespoons molasses**
2 **tablespoons dried onion**
2 **teaspoons dillweed**
1 **package active dry yeast**
1½ **cups rye flour**
1 **cup whole wheat flour**
½ **cup gluten flour***
¼ **cup buttermilk powder**
1½ **teaspoons salt**
2 **tablespoons vegetable oil**
2-3 **cups unbleached white flour**

Mix water, sourdough starter, honey, molasses, dried onion and dillweed. Add dry yeast. When yeast mixture is foamy, add rye flour, whole wheat flour, gluten flour, buttermilk powder, salt and oil. Stir vigorously, about 200 strokes. Gradually stir in white flour until a kneadable dough develops.

Knead until smooth and elastic. Place in an oiled bowl, cover and let rise in a warm place until doubled in bulk. Punch down and divide dough in half. Shape each into a ball, cover and let rest for about 10 minutes. Grease two French bread pans or baking sheets. Roll out each piece of dough into a 4x12-inch rectangle.

From the long end, roll each rectangle into an oblong loaf, pinching seams well and tucking under ends. Place on French bread pans or baking sheets. Let rise in a warm place until almost doubled. Slash diagonally 3 times with a serrated blade.

Bake at 350 degrees for 45 minutes.

Makes 2 long loaves

*Gluten flour helps this dough develop texture and rising power. It can be found at many health food stores. If unavailable, use ½ cup unbleached white flour.

Silverthrone Spice Drops

In 1945, the U.S. Army Cold Weather Test Party named a 13,220-foot peak in Denali National Park Mount Silverthrone, "because of its stately appearance," which aptly describes the regal taste of these cookies.

This recipe was originally given to Camp Denali by Louise Potter, author of several Alaska wildflower books, including *Roadside Flowers of Alaska* and *Wildflowers along Mt. McKinley Park Road*.

⅔ **cup margarine**
1½ **cups brown sugar**
2 **eggs**
2 **cups unbleached white flour**
⅔ **teaspoon baking soda**
1½ **teaspoons cinnamon**
1 **teaspoon cloves**
1 **teaspoon nutmeg**
½ **teaspoon allspice**
⅔ **cup raisins**
¾ **cup chopped walnuts**

Preheat oven to 350 degrees. *Grease* baking sheet.

Cream together margarine, brown sugar and eggs. In a separate bowl *sift* or *mix* flour, baking soda, cinnamon, cloves, nutmeg and allspice. *Add* dry ingredients to creamed mixture and *beat* until combined.

Stir raisins and chopped walnuts into mixture. *Drop* by teaspoonfuls onto baking sheet. *Bake* at 350 degrees for 8 to 10 minutes.

Makes 2½ dozen

Motherlode Cookies

*C*amp Denali is near Kantishna, a remote mining community. As a guest, you may want to try panning for gold in the nearby creeks. If you find a few flakes, take a break and dig into your lunch sack, where you'll discover the real motherlode in these cookies. Chances are you'll leave the pan high and dry as you head back to the kitchen for seconds.

These chewy, high-energy cookies are a favorite for hiking lunches.

½   cup margarine
1   cup peanut butter
1   cup brown sugar
½   cup granulated sugar
3   eggs
2   teaspoons vanilla
4½   cups old-fashioned rolled oats
2   teaspoons baking soda
⅔   cup plain candy-coated chocolate candies
⅔   cup chocolate chips
½   cup chopped nuts

Preheat oven to 350 degrees.

Cream together margarine, peanut butter, brown sugar and granulated sugar in a large bowl. *Add* eggs and vanilla and *cream* until light.

Mix oats and baking soda together thoroughly and *add* to creamed mixture. *Beat* until combined.

Stir in candies, chocolate chips and nuts. *Drop* by teaspoonfuls onto an ungreased baking sheet.

Bake at 350 degrees for 10 to 12 minutes.

Makes 2 dozen

Chee-choco Cupcakes

Chocolate lovers call these rich, delicious cupcakes Chee-choco after the recipe's two main ingredients—cream cheese and chocolate. Not to be confused with cheechako, a newcomer to Alaska.

1½ cups unbleached white flour
1 cup granulated sugar
1 teaspoon baking soda
¼ cup baking cocoa
½ teaspoon salt
¾ cup water
⅓ cup vegetable oil
1 tablespoon vinegar
1 teaspoon vanilla
8 ounces cream cheese, softened
1 egg
⅓ cup granulated sugar
  dash of salt
1 cup chocolate chips

Preheat oven to 350 degrees.

In a large bowl, *sift* together flour, sugar, baking soda, cocoa and salt.

In a separate bowl, *mix* water, oil, vinegar and vanilla. Add liquid ingredients to dry ingredients and *beat* for one minute.

In another bowl, *beat* together cream cheese, egg, remaining granulated sugar and salt until light and fluffy. *Stir in* chocolate chips.

Line cupcake tins with baking cups or *grease* and *flour* tins. Spoon cake batter evenly into cups, *topping* each with a spoonful of the cream cheese mixture.

Bake at 350 degrees for 20 minutes.

Makes 14 cupcakes

Muldrow Mud Cake

1½ cups strong coffee
¼   cup coffee liqueur or other flavor
5   ounces unsweetened baking chocolate
1   cup butter
2   cups granulated sugar
2   cups unbleached white flour
1   teaspoon baking soda
¼   teaspoon salt
2   eggs
1   teaspoon vanilla

Preheat oven to 275 degrees. Grease bundt pan or 10-inch springform pan (with a center ring), dust with sifted baking cocoa.

In a saucepan, heat the coffee and liqueur. Add chocolate and butter to the coffee mixture and heat until melted, stirring frequently. When chocolate-coffee mixture is smooth, add sugar and stir until dissolved. Cool until lukewarm.

Sift together the flour, baking soda and salt. Gradually add chocolate-coffee mixture to dry ingredients, beating well after each addition to avoid lumps in the batter. Add eggs and vanilla and beat at medium speed for 2 minutes. Turn into cake pan. Bake at 275 degrees for 1½ hours. When cool, frost with Chocolate Glaze.

Chocolate Glaze

4   ounces semisweet chocolate or chocolate
    chips
1   tablespoon butter or margarine
2   tablespoons milk, cream or strong coffee

Melt chocolate and butter in a double boiler. Add enough milk, cream or coffee to achieve a spreadable consistency. Pour or spread over cake while glaze is warm.

Serves 12

Uncooked Berry Pie

$\mathcal{F}$resh berry pies are more flavorful when prepared with this recipe. Camp Denali's specialty is made with local wild blueberries or a combination of crowberries and blueberries. When these berries are not available, try fresh peaches, strawberries or raspberries.

Prepare baked pastry or crumb crust

¾-1 **cup granulated sugar depending on tartness of berries or fruit**
3   **tablespoons cornstarch**
¼   **teaspoon salt**
¼   **cup water**
1   **tablespoon lemon juice (optional)**
2   **cups berries or sliced fruit**
1   **tablespoon butter**
2   **cups uncooked berries or fruit**

Combine sugar, cornstarch, salt, water and lemon juice. *Stir* in 2 cups berries.

Cook gently over medium heat, *stirring* frequently to prevent scorching. When mixture has thickened and cleared, *stir* in butter.

Cool to room temperature. *Spread* a small amount of cooled, glazed berries over the bottom of baked pie shell. *Add* 2 cups uncooked berries or fruit. *Pour* the remaining glaze over the top of the uncooked berries or fruit.

Refrigerate at least 2 hours or until set. *Top* with ice cream or whipped cream if desired.

Makes one 9-inch pie

Peppy Kernels

A nutritious hot cereal made from a blend of whole grains and seeds. You can mix the grains in quantity to be cooked as you need them. ''PKs'' make a filling breakfast when served with toasted wheat germ, brown sugar, raisins, cashews, yogurt and milk.

3   **parts old-fashioned rolled oats**
2   **parts rolled wheat flakes**
2   **parts bulgur wheat (cracked wheat)**
1   **part sesame seeds**
1   **part flax seeds**
1   **part hulled millet**
1   **part wheat or oat bran**
1   **part wheat germ**

Mix together and *store* in an airtight container.

Hot Cereal

1⅔   **cups water**
½   **teaspoon salt**
1   **cup Peppy Kernels**

Add salt to water and *bring* to a rapid boil. *Add* peppy kernels. *Cook* uncovered over low heat for 15 minutes, *stirring* occasionally. *Remove* from heat, *cover* and *let stand* a few minutes before serving.

Serves 4

Alaska Rainbow Lodge

laska Rainbow Lodge, 200 miles southwest of Anchorage, is a 17-minute floatplane flight northwest of King Salmon. You'll find the lodge on a bluff overlooking the Kvichak River, host of the largest runs of sockeye salmon in the world. Here each year, anglers catch some of the largest rainbow trout in Alaska, from 12 to 20 pounds.

The lodge has outstanding service and accommodations. Guests can choose completely furnished cabins or main guest rooms in the lodge. Each room is decorated in a different theme, has a queen-size and twin bed, is fully carpeted and sound-proofed, and has a luxurious bath and a sit-down shower. Electricity is available 24 hours a day and there is a personal VCR and television in each of the two cabins, with an extensive selection of video tapes available.

The main lodge is decorated with original oil paintings and Alaskan handicrafts, and has more than ample room for socializing. Owner Ron Hayes has an extensive library of first-edition hunting and fishing books available for guests to read. A fly-tying bench is near an open bar fully stocked with wine, beer, liquors, soft drinks, juices and flavored mineral waters.

The lodge books no more than 12 guests each week. This allows plenty of time to fish with other guests, make new friends and share adventures.

On your arrival, Sharon Hayes encourages you to fill out a questionnaire detailing your preferences on everything from drinks to meals, plus any medication they need to remind you to take.

Breakfast starts with a wakeup tray of juice and hot drinks delivered to your nightstand. At the dining table, your breakfast of choice is made to order.

Shore lunches include homemade soup and fresh-caught sockeye salmon grilled to perfection at streamside. The cook even remembered to pack my special thermos of Earl Grey tea. Lunch is always served on time, whether at the lodge or on the stream, an important factor for those requiring regular eating hours.

Evening meals are exquisite affairs, served on fine china and crystal. I felt quite special sitting at the long mahogany dining table. My place had been reserved with a personalized china nameplate.

Seafood night rivals the best restaurants in Anchorage or Seattle. For hors d'oeuvres, a brown sugar and salt-cured smoked sockeye salmon rates the best I have ever tasted. The main course is stuffed clams, Alaska shrimp and scallops, halibut, king crab and more. The quality food—flown in weekly—is prepared and served by a friendly and attentive staff.

The main lodge, with a view overlooking the Kvichak River, has lots of room for socializing.

Ron Hayes with a guest from Hawaii who just caught her first big pike.

Each evening after dinner, Ron reviews the best fishing opportunities available and listens carefully to what the guests want to fish for. He then merges the two into several selections for the next day's adventure.

The lodge operates three aircraft—a Beaver and two Cessna 206s. Scattered throughout the various fisheries are 24 riverboats and inflatables on 14 different streams, rivers and lakes. Equipment is constantly checked and repaired. Broken motors are brought in and replacements sent out immediately. All tackle, first-class equipment, is furnished.

Expect to enjoy some of the finest fishing opportunities in the Bristol Bay region, from char and pike to the majestic sheefish. Rainbow trout fishing is second to none, especially in the fall when guests delight in catching wild 'bows from 25 to 32 inches. The lodge adheres to a strict catch-and-release policy on trout, char and grayling. Silver and sockeye salmon fishing is excellent. Guides busily freeze and smoke catches as a courtesy for clients.

Owner Ron Hayes has guided and outfitted anglers throughout Alaska for over 30 years, and has flown over 25,000 hours in small aircraft. Sharon Hayes keeps lodge personnel motivated and guests happy. She takes everything one step beyond what is normally offered at full-service lodges. A gracious hostess, Sharon knows how to make her guests feel special. Because of the comfortable accommodations and availability of boats, a high percentage of Alaska Rainbow Lodge clients are couples. Repeat clientele know that they're a guest only once at Alaska Rainbow Lodge—after that, they're family.

Sharon Hayes, *Cook and Co-owner, Alaska Rainbow Lodge*

In 1976, high school senior Sharon Odd read a newspaper ad that changed her life, "Help Wanted: camp assistant/helper/cook at Alaska hunting lodge." She and her sister Holly, who was also looking for a new adventure, applied for the job.

Sharon's mother was less than enthusiastic about the girls' jaunt into the Alaska wilderness. She had checked out the ad, and told Sharon she was afraid that the girls might end up being white slaves. Coincidentally, Ron Hayes, the guide placing the ad, was from the Odd's hometown of Selah, Washington. The sisters dismissed the idea of a life in bondage. When they arrived in Anchorage, Ron's brother outfitted the two "city girls" with the necessary clothing and boots and flew them by bush plane to the lodge on the Sanford River in the Wrangell Mountains. Sharon and Holly soon learned new skills: skinning moose, caribou and sheep.

Sharon apprenticed under Ron's 72-year-old cook, Gertie, until she passed away. Sharon became head cook, working with Ron out of the remote village of Savoonga. Accommodations were primitive. When not in field camps they lived in the pool hall in Kotzebue, with neither a bathroom nor running water, and slept on pool tables. Shortly after, Ron asked Sharon to marry him and she accepted.

In 1981, Sharon and Ron Hayes left the hunting business and decided to build Alaska Rainbow Lodge on the banks of the Kvichak River near King Salmon. In the spring of 1982, they barged nine boxcars of building materials from Seattle. Eight people worked non-stop for six weeks to complete the lodge. The remainder of the season was spent preparing the interior of the lodge for the 85 guests already booked for the next season.

Sharon planned all the menus and did all the cooking during the first four years the lodge was open. Food was ordered several months in advance, and groceries were delivered by barge from Seattle each spring.

A food broker in Anchorage now ships the food once a week as bypass mail. Vegetables, meats and seafood are brought in by floatplane. Fresh herbs are grown in the lodge greenhouse.

Kitchen work at a wilderness fishing lodge can be quite demanding and stressful. "The cook at a fishing lodge is in a high-pressure position," Sharon said. "After the fishing, the meals are the most important to guests. Sometimes the meals may be even more important than the fishing. If the fishing is bad one day, serve the angler an excellent meal and he will cheer up and think about the next day's fishing opportunities.

"A high turnover of cooks can be quite a problem in the fishing lodge business," Sharon said. "Each season, many lodges have to replace cooks due to their incompatible temperaments with other kitchen staffers. Most of the conflict is due to poor management. At Alaska Rainbow Lodge, we encourage a strong team spirit or family spirit. As a result, we keep our cooks for a long time."

Sharon says that even the best laid plans can go astray. "Groceries can be delayed or guests may return late from fishing, requiring the dinner be put on hold. A sauce can be spilled, requiring a quick innovative substitute. Overall, the cooks who succeed in a fishing lodge environment have excellent people and managerial skills, show adaptability in the face of adversity, and show creativity in food preparation and presentation.

"For instance, our first chef was fresh out of culinary school. He had the training, but no practical, common sense. His Italian food was wonderful, but his roasts were terrible."

Sharon gives her cooks the latitude necessary for them to do their best in the kitchen. "Although the lodge has established entrees that are served each week, the salad, dessert and vegetable dishes are chosen by the cook, who interprets each recipe differently than either myself or the previous cook," she said. "A mutual compromise is reached between their ideas and what has worked for us in the past."

Sharon sees guests from all backgrounds and from around the world. She notes that people's tastes are changing to lighter, more health-conscious meals. "People don't consume as much food as in the past, and they avoid rich foods," Sharon tells us. "Breakfast consumption as a whole has gone down. Older guests prefer no-egg breakfasts. And smoked fish is the most requested item on the appetizer tray."

All meals are served family-style in a pleasing and inviting presentation. This breaks the ice, especially the first couple of days when guests are new to each other. By the end of the week, the guests have formed strong bonds with other guests and have joined the Alaska Rainbow Lodge extended family.

Ron Hayes, seated at far right, knows that client satisfaction contributes to the success of the lodge. At the last dinner of the week, he makes a special presentation to each guest.

Bristol Bay Smoked Salmon

$\mathcal{B}$ehind almost every cabin in Alaska is a fish smoker. Smoking fish has long been a way to preserve the summer's bounty. The natives call it "squaw candy," and it comes in a variety of tastes and textures. Our favorite is a little on the sweet side, moist and firm.

Alaska Rainbow Lodge will smoke your day's catch and have it ready for your trip back home.

Bristol Bay is home to the largest catches of sockeye salmon in the world. Bristol Bay was named in 1778 by Captain Cook in honor of the Admiral Earl of Bristol (England). The Bay extends 270 miles wide at the mouth, from Cape Newenham to the Alaska Peninsula and south to Unimak Island.

5	**cups brown sugar (4 handfuls)**
½	**cup salt (1 small handful)**
5	**sockeye or silver salmon fillets (or 2½ fish)**

Mix sugar and salt (10:1 ratio) together and *spread* on fish fillets. *Lay* fish flesh side down on screen in smoker.

Smoke fish for 1 to 1½ days. *Regulate* heat to 110 degrees and *smoke* for 12 to 13 hours, then two hours longer at 130 degrees to *dry* the fish.

Serves 24

Halfmoon Halibut

*H*alfmoon Bay is located on the north shore of Kvichak Bay, northwest of Naknek in the Bristol Bay region.

This dish is named not only for the bay, but for the cut of halibut. When cross-cut steaks are cut from halibut, they look like a moon with the bone in the center. When a smaller portion is desired, the full moon steak is cut in half, which is the traditional half moon steak.

For a free Alaska Halibut Cutting Brochure, contact the Alaska Seafood Marketing Institute, (907) 586-2902.

3   **eggs**
½   **cup canned milk**
½   **teaspoon dried dillweed**
1   **teaspoon garlic powder**
1   **teaspoon minced garlic**
½   **teaspoon seafood seasoning**
¾   **cup flour**
1   **cup finely crushed saltine crackers**
3   **pounds fresh halibut fillets or half moon**
     steaks, cut into smaller equal-size pieces
     olive oil

Preheat oven to 300 degrees.

In a bowl, *beat* eggs and canned milk together; *stir* in dillweed, garlic powder, minced garlic and seafood seasoning.

On a plate, *mix* flour and crackers together. *Dip* pieces of halibut in milk/egg mixture and *roll* in flour/cracker mixture.

Fry both sides of halibut in olive oil until golden brown. *Don't overcook!* *Stack* fish pieces in baking pan and *bake* in 300-degree oven for 15 minutes.

Serves 6—8

Stuffed Chignik Clams

1	dozen large-shell clams, in the shell
¾	cup chopped onion
1	14-ounce can mushrooms, drained & chopped
¼	cup butter, melted
3	tablespoons flour
1	teaspoon salt
	dash of pepper
2	tablespoons butter, melted
½	cup dry bread crumbs

Shuck, clean and *chop* clams. *Wash* shells thoroughly. *Dry* and *grease. Set aside.*

In a saucepan, *saute* onion and mushrooms in ¼ cup butter until tender. *Blend* in flour, salt and pepper. *Add* clams and *cook* until mixture is thick, *stirring* constantly. *Fill* greased clam shells with mixture.

Combine 2 tablespoons butter and bread crumbs; *sprinkle* on top of each filled shell. *Bake* in 400-degree oven for 10 minutes or until brown.

Serves 6

Friday is *"seafood specialty night"* at Alaska Rainbow Lodge. Entrees include Stuffed Chignik Clams, king crab, shrimp and a selection of other gourmet Alaska seafoods. Color photo appears on back cover.

Alaska Rainbow Lodge

Stuffed Chicken Kvichak

This is an elegant dish to serve your most special dinner guests. Serve with steamed rice and Vegetables Julienne on page 112.

4 **whole chicken breasts, filleted**
1 **cup chopped leeks**
½ **cup butter**
½ **cup dry white wine**
8 **ounces baby shrimp, cooked**
1½ **cups seasoned bread crumbs**
1½ **cups heavy cream**
½ **cup flour**
2 **eggs, beaten**
1 **cup bread crumbs**
   fresh parsley for garnish
   Tarragon Cream Sauce, page 111

Pound chicken breasts and *lay* flat between two pieces of waxed paper. *Chill* 2 to 3 hours.

To make stuffing, *cook* leeks in butter and wine until tender. *Add* baby shrimp and *remove* from heat. *Drain* two-thirds of the liquid. *Add* seasoned bread crumbs to leeks and *mix*. *Add* cream, *making* mixture the consistency of cooked, loose oatmeal. *Cool* to room temperature.

Lay out chicken breasts with the small end at the bottom and the wide end at the top. *Spoon* ¼ cup of stuffing onto the small end of the chicken breast. *Fold* in the wide ends. *Roll* up the chicken breast, over the stuffing, from bottom to top. *Fasten* with toothpick. *Roll* each chicken breast in flour, *dip* in beaten egg and *roll* in bread crumbs.

Preheat oven to 350 degrees. *Fry* stuffed breasts in shortening or butter on medium high heat until golden brown. *Place* breasts on rack with drip pan underneath, so oil doesn't soften bread crumbs.

Bake 30 to 45 minutes at 350 degrees.

To serve, *cut* three ½-inch diagonal slits across the chicken breast, *spoon* a stripe of Tarragon Cream Sauce on the plate, *lay* breast perpendicular on top of the stripe of cream sauce. *Spoon* another stripe of cream sauce along the top of the breast, perpendicular to the first stripe of sauce. *Garnish* with fresh parsley.

Tarragon Cream Sauce

¼ **cup finely chopped shallots**
2 **tablespoons tarragon**
1 **cup dry white wine**
2 **cups heavy cream**

Mix shallots, tarragon and wine in a saucepan. *Cook* over low heat for about 30 minutes until liquid has reduced to one-quarter in volume. *Add* cream and *cook* until liquid is reduced in half.

Serves 4

Alaska Rainbow Lodge received the Alaska Angler Lodge of the Year award for elegant meal preparation and presentation, as shown here with a serving of Stuffed Chicken Kvichak and Vegetables Julienne.

Vegetables Julienne

The long hours of sunlight during Alaska's summer produce huge quantities of vegetables, and Alaskans serve them proudly. This dish of julienned vegetables is pleasing to look at and delightful to taste.

Serve as a side dish with Stuffed Chicken Kvichak, page 110 (photo on page 111).

2	stalks celery
1	large carrot
1	medium to large red onion
1	small can water chestnuts, drained and sliced
1	small can baby corn, drained
1	small can sliced mushrooms, drained
1	large zucchini
1	large yellow summer squash
1	cup Chinese bean sprouts
½	pound snow peas
¼	cup olive oil
1	tablespoon freshly chopped garlic
1	teaspoon ground ginger
¼	cup soy sauce

Julienne all vegetables except corn and snow peas, *keeping* the vegetables in separate piles.

Heat oil, garlic and ginger. *Stir fry* each vegetable two minutes before *adding* the next, in the following order: celery, carrot, onion, water chestnuts, corn, mushrooms, zucchini, squash, sprouts and snow peas.

Add soy sauce. *Toss* lightly to coat vegetables.

Serve as a side dish with Stuffed Chicken Kvichak.

Serves 4

Dijon Onions

$\mathcal{S}$erve this wonderful side dish with prime rib.

4   large yellow onions
¾   cup butter, melted
¼   cup Dijon mustard
½   of a 3-ounce jar pimientos

Preheat oven to 350 degrees.

Clean onions and *cut* into quarters. *Arrange* onions in a 2-quart casserole dish. *Pour* butter over the onions, and *dot* with mustard. *Arrange* pimientos on the onions for color. *Bake* at 350 degrees for 35 to 45 minutes or until golden brown.

Serves 8

Alaska Rainbow Lodge owner Ron Hayes dishes up some fried jack salmon to two guests on the bank of a remote Alaska river. Fresh-caught fish complemented with side dishes prepared earlier at the lodge create a memorable wilderness shore lunch.

Alaska Rainbow Lodge

Cream of Broccoli Soup

This tasty warmer-upper is best served hot after a few hours of fishing or as a precursor to a wild game meal. The cooks at Alaska Rainbow Lodge prepare this soup in the morning and dish it up in a wide-necked thermos for guides to serve with shore lunches.

For the best taste, use broccoli fresh from your garden as soon as it becomes available. Broccoli grows well in Alaska, however, if lodge owners wait too long to harvest their broccoli, moose help themselves to the bounty, devouring the entire plant down to its root stubs.

1	teaspoon finely chopped onion
2	tablespoons butter
3	tablespoons flour
1	teaspoon onion salt
	dash of pepper
1	cup pureed cooked broccoli
2	cups heavy cream
2	cups milk

Saute onion in butter. Blend in flour, salt and pepper. Cook over low heat, stirring constantly, until smooth. Stir in broccoli and bring to a boil. Boil for one minute, stirring constantly. Remove from heat. Gradually stir in cream and milk. Heat on low until soup reaches serving temperature.

Serves 6

Peninsula Pasta

The Alaska Peninsula is a beautiful wilderness. When viewed from afar, glaciers, volcanoes and mountains often exhibit multi-layered hues of white, orange and green, which are the primary colors of this recipe. Alaska Rainbow Lodge often packs this dish freshly-made each morning in shore lunches for anglers fishing the Peninsula for salmon or char.

1	**pound dry tri-colored pasta noodles (white/green/orange)**
1	**small can black olives, drained and chopped**
1	**small can sliced mushrooms, drained and chopped**
1	**small can baby corn, drained and coarsely chopped**
2	**medium tomatoes, quartered and chopped**
½	**cup marinated artichoke hearts, diced**
2	**packages zesty Italian dressing—prepare as directed on package**
	salt and pepper

In a 2-quart saucepan, *cook* noodles. *Drain* and *cool.*

In a large salad bowl, *place* noodles, olives, mushrooms, corn, tomatoes and artichoke hearts. *Pour* Italian dressing over ingredients and *toss.* *Add* salt and pepper to taste.

Refrigerate a few hours before serving.

Serves 8

Pedro's Pineapple Casserole

This dessert was named in honor of prospector Felix Pedro, who discovered gold in a valley 10 miles northeast of Fairbanks. Pedro's find started the 1902 gold stampede to the Fairbanks area. Your guests will stampede to the table when you serve this casserole with its golden chunks of pineapple and cheese. When you need a side dish or dessert in a hurry, this dish is quick to fix with ingredients on hand.

2   **14-ounce cans crushed pineapple**
4   **tablespoons all-purpose flour**
½   **cup granulated sugar**
2   **cups grated Cheddar cheese**
1½ **sleeves Ritz crackers**
½   **cup butter**

Preheat oven to 350 degrees.

Mix pineapple, flour, sugar and cheese together in a 2-quart casserole dish. *Crumble* Ritz crackers and *sprinkle* over the top. *Dot* with butter. *Bake* at 350 degrees for 30 minutes. *Serve* hot.

Serves 8

Photo at left: Alaska Rainbow Lodge, considered to be one of the most elegant lodges in the state, is a lesson in contrast to the stereotypical view that a fishing lodge is a run-down shack with only beans and fish on the menu. (Color photo on back cover).

Tundra Trifle

*T*his spongy angel food cake, moistened by fruit juice, best commemorates the tundra, a unique berry-laden landscape that is widespread throughout Alaska.

This beautifully elegant dessert is perfect to serve for company.

1   **angel food cake, baked**
1   **16-ounce can peaches**
1   **16-ounce can apricots**
2   **bananas, sliced**
1   **cup fresh or frozen blueberries**
3   **kiwi fruit, peeled and sliced**
1   **cup fresh or frozen raspberries**
1   **tablespoon rum or amaretto**

Cut angel food cake into six pieces.

Drain liquid from peaches and apricots. *Set aside.*

Tear one piece of cake into chunks, *place* in bottom of a large, deep, glass serving bowl. *Layer* with peaches.

Place alternating layers of cake chunks and fruit in bowl in the following order: apricots, bananas, blueberries, kiwi, ending with raspberries on the top.

Mix fruit juice with rum or amaretto. *Drizzle* liquid over the top and *poke* with a knife. *Drizzle* again with liquid. *Keep* refrigerated.

Serves 6

Lemon Glacier Sorbet

This lemon sorbet is as refreshing as a spring breeze across Lemon Glacier, reportedly named for John Lemon. In 1879, Lemon was placer mining with James Hollywood on Lemon Creek, which drains Lemon Glacier. In 1880, John joined the Edmund Bean party of prospectors who blazed a trail over Chilkoot Pass to the headwaters of the Yukon River.

Lemon sorbet is a beautiful and refreshing accompaniment to fish. It may be served on the side or for dessert.

½   cup lemon juice
½   cup orange juice, freshly squeezed
3   cups water
1   cup granulated sugar
       thin lemon slices
       fresh mint leaves for garnish

Mix lemon juice, orange juice, water and granulated sugar in a 2-quart sauce pan. Heat on top of the stove until sugar is dissolved. Pour into ice cream maker container and freeze several hours, stirring intermittently.

When frozen, scoop sorbet balls with ice cream scoop and place on individual glass plates. Garnish each with a thin slice of lemon and a sprig of mint leaf.

Serves 6—8

At the entrance to Denali West Lodge, Sherri Hayden offers Chris Batin freshly baked cinnamon rolls.

Denali West Lodge

*E*ach year, hikers, rafters, anglers and adventurers look forward to tossing their cares aside and indulging in the blissful tranquility of Denali West Lodge.

A bluff near the lodge's front door offers a front-row seat to Nature's finest performances. Guests sit back with eyes closed, enjoying the cool breezes whispering through the emerald-green spruce and white birch trees. Waves from Lake Minchumina lap, with metronome regularity, at the multi-colored gravel shoreline, while loon laughter echoes against the scenic backdrop of Mount McKinley, North America's tallest mountain.

Denali West Lodge sits at the base of the Kuskokwim Mountains, in that never-never land between Alaska's major cities: Anchorage to the south, and Fairbanks to the north. The sprawling growth of either city makes no inroads into the heart of this remote environment. At Denali West Lodge, you will never see tour buses, motor homes and campers—the nearest highway is over 100 miles away. Instead, you'll find a rolling sea of unbroken forests with the glacier-crowned panorama of the Alaska Range looming in the distance. During the Great Ice Age this area was a lush forest while most of North America was covered under an endless sea of glaciers.

*J*ack and Sherri Hayden have owned and managed Denali West Lodge for over a decade. Jack is a professional bush pilot and guide, who has climbed Mount McKinley. He has extensive experience in gold mining and long-distance dog sled racing. He is also an experienced log-home builder and spent several years building the hand-hewn log lodge, with its spacious dining room, adjoining kitchen and separate guest quarters.

Sherri Hayden is a competent wilderness cook, not only in menu selection and preparation, but in cooking skills. She uses a wood-burning stove to prepare sheefish chowder and a wide array of freshly baked breads and desserts. Coping with the wide-scale temperature variations of a wood-burning stove requires special knowledge and constant attention to detail. The extra care shows. Her oven-cooked delights gently caress the palate with the delicate, nutty tinge of fresh birch wood, unattainable when foods are baked in conventional ovens.

Denali West is a family-run lodge, and anglers enjoy the slow but punctual pace. Meals are presented in a relaxed, unhurried atmosphere, where natural sights always have top priority. A moose in a nearby meadow, or an eagle on the lakeshore may result in clients

Float planes allow accessibility to remote, wilderness areas that provide outstanding dining scenery.

showing up for dinner a half-hour late, an allowable excuse at Denali West.

The lodge offers a variety of eco-tourism experiences and wilderness adventures for families and small groups. Hikers delight in photographing wildlife and exploring the moraines left by ancient glaciers in Mystic Pass. Choose a flightseeing tour of Denali National Park, visit an Athabascan village, or explore the remote bays of nearby Lake Minchumina in a riverboat or canoe.

Lace agates are a treasured find for rockhounds, who look for the beautiful specimens along the gravel bars. Don't forget to carry your goldpan, because this is a historical mining area.

*A*ngling adventure is but a stone's throw away. This is 'big river' country where the Yukon, Kuskokwim, Holitna, Hoholitna and the Nowitna reign in splendor. The scenery and wildlife viewing are outstanding. Anglers from around the world visit Denali West Lodge to fish for salmon, northern pike, lake trout and sheefish. You'll fish areas with no crowds, so there is no need to rush to be on the water at first light. If you insist, however, keep in mind that you'll miss some good breakfasts and the only thing better than the fishing at Denali West is the cooking.

Author Adela Batin admires an agate she found on a gravel bar in the Nowitna area. This area is rich in geological finds.

Sherri Hayden, Cook and Co-owner, Denali West Lodge

When I first met Sherri Hayden, she gave me a big smile, a warm handshake and welcoming words of genuine, down-home hospitality. Sherri's caring, thoughtful attitude is why Denali West Lodge guests feel like part of the Hayden family.

A wise man once said that good things come in small packages. This maxim applies to the Hayden's family-owned and operated small business. The log lodge, part of their home, is nestled into a hillside of white birch trees, up the trail from Lake Minchumina. Sherri and her husband, Jack, built the lodge themselves after a great deal of struggle and sacrifice.

Sherri came to Alaska from Bellevue, Washington, in 1976. She wanted to live a life different than typical suburbia, but wasn't sure what that different life was to be. Sherri's story is one of how a person can excel in any field if he or she has the incentive and the determination.

Sherri remembers her first visit to Jack Hayden's gold camp. His brother flew her out to base camp, which was no more than a tent and a two-burner camp stove. The brothers left for the afternoon, saying they would return for dinner around 6 p.m. Sherri was flabbergasted. She had never cooked a meal in her life and could not figure out what to fix, or how. She found canned meat, but no fresh fruits or vegetables. Sherri sat down and cried. When Jack returned, he did the cooking and Sherri washed the dishes.

However, the Alaska bush life grew on Sherri. Her best memory of that summer was when she and Jack walked down the creek with a fishing rod, frying pan, onions and a jar of oil. Sherri said there was nothing finer than grayling cooked alongside the stream! Soon Jack asked Sherri to marry him, and she accepted.

The next summer, Jack acquired an inexpensive wood burning stove. He made an "oven" out of a white gas can by cutting a hole in the top for a door. He put a welding rod across the width for a rack, and sat it atop the wood stove to tap its heat source. One of Sherri's adventurous projects was to make a three-layer chocolate birthday cake in the oven, using three small cast-iron skillets. By the time the stove got hot enough to heat the oven, it was time to take the oven off and reload the stove with wood! After the lengthy baking process, Sherri frosted and decorated the cake. As they cut into it, everyone laughed as they realized every layer had fallen, and Sherri had just filled them in with frosting!

The following year, Jack and Sherri worked in another mining camp, where Sherri finally learned to cook. She said cookbooks, two freezers, refrigerators, a propane range, and a patient, encouraging crew made her lessons pleasurable.

Nowitna River Sheefish

The Nowitna National Wild and Scenic River is in the central Yukon River valley. The river is an excellent hotspot for catching sheefish. The species is called "tarpon of the north," due to its acrobatic nature once hooked.

The sheefish has a delicate flavor, and anglers prize its white, flaky meat. Sheefish are available only in arctic and subarctic areas of the world, and are occasionally sold in seafood specialty shops. If this fish is unavailable in your area, substitute whitefish, grayling, cod, burbot, northern pike, catfish, mahi-mahi or pollock.

¾	**cup butter, melted**
1	**cup dry white wine**
⅔	**cup lemon juice**
2	**cloves garlic, crushed**
1	**tablespoon lightly crushed fresh thyme**
½	**teaspoon freshly ground pepper**
1	**tablespoon chopped fresh parsley**
2	**tablespoons chopped fresh chives or green onions**
1	**10 to 12 pound sheefish, cleaned and scaled**
2	**tablespoons cornstarch**

In a bowl, *combine* butter, wine, lemon juice, garlic, thyme, pepper, parsley and chives or green onions.

Place sheefish in a large baking pan. *Pour* sauce over fish and *marinate* in a cool place for several hours.

Cover dish with oiled foil and *bake* at 450 degrees for about 10 minutes for every inch of thickness of fish. Don't overcook! *Place* fish on serving platter, *covering* platter to keep fish warm. In a small amount of cold water, *blend* in cornstarch until dissolved. *Pour* sauce in saucepan, *add* cornstarch; *stirring* constantly over medium heat until thickened. *Pour* over fish and *serve*.

Serves 12—14

Photo at right: Adela Batin holds an interior Alaska sheefish. The sheefish is one of the finest fish in the arctic.

Chilchitna Chicken Enchiladas

Salsa De Chile

½	cup chopped onion	½	tsp. dried oregano
1	clove garlic, minced	¼	tsp. cumin
2	tbsp. olive oil	1	tsp. salt
1	tbsp. flour	2	cups tomato puree
¼	cup chili powder	1	bouillon cube

Saute onion and garlic in oil until tender. Add flour, *cook* one minute, then *add* rest of ingredients. Simmer 10 minutes. Will keep several days in refrigerator.

Makes 2 cups

Chicken Filling

½	cup chopped onion	1	cup Salsa De Chile
2	tbsp. butter		(recipe above)
2	cups chicken, cooked	1	cup sour cream
	and chopped		

Saute onion in butter until tender. Remove from heat; add chicken and Salsa De Chile, *blending* well. Fold in sour cream.

Enchiladas

12   corn tortillas
      oil for frying tortillas
2   cups chicken filling (recipe above)
2   cups cream or evaporated milk
1   cup chicken stock or canned broth
1½   cups grated jack cheese

Fry tortillas in oil for two seconds per side to soften. Spread chicken filling on tortillas, *roll* and *place* seam side down in baking dish. Mix cream or evaporated milk with broth and *pour* over enchiladas. Sprinkle with cheese and *bake* at 350 degrees for 25 minutes or until heated through.

Serves 6—8

Cathedral Spires Potatoes

A highlight of a visit to Denali West Lodge is a flightseeing tour of the Cathedral Spires and surrounding glaciers in Denali National Preserve. You'll remember the experience for a lifetime. The small peaks of these whipped potatoes, slightly browned against a baking dish of white, are the culinary equivalent to this spectacular sight.

6	**medium potatoes, peeled, boiled and drained**
1	**8-ounce package cream cheese, softened**
¼	**cup finely chopped onion**
¼	**cup butter**
2	**tablespoons flour**
2	**eggs**
	salt and pepper

Preheat oven to 350 degrees.

Mash potatoes and cream cheese together. **Add** onion, butter, flour and eggs; *whip* until well-blended. **Add** salt and pepper to taste.

Drop potato mixture by spoonfuls in 9x13-inch baking dish to form small peaks. **Bake** at 350 degrees for 20 to 25 minutes or until golden brown.

Serves 6

Jack Hayden attests to the outstanding pike fishing in nearby Lake Minchumina, as well as along the tributaries, sloughs and lakes of the Yukon River system.

Succulent Sheefish Soup

At Denali West Lodge, the sheefish is one of the most sought-after species of sportfish. Anglers practice catch and release on most of the sheefish they catch, as a 20-pound sheefish can be 15 to 20 years old. The Nowitna offers good populations of sheefish, and anglers occasionally delight in keeping one so Sherri can prepare this wonderful recipe.

6	medium potatoes, peeled and quartered
3	cups water, reserved from boiled potatoes
7	chicken bouillon cubes
2	leeks, chopped
4	green onions, chopped
4	tablespoons butter
3	tablespoons flour
1-2	cups sheefish, cooked, deboned and flaked
3	cups Nowitna River Sheefish sauce (poured off the baked sheefish, page 124)
1	cup sour cream
1½	cups evaporated milk or half and half
	dash pepper
	parsley for garnish

In a large pot, *cover* potatoes with 4 cups water and *boil* until tender. *Remove* potatoes to a separate bowl and *mash*. *Set* aside. *Heat* 3 cups potato water, *add* bouillon cubes; *stir* until cubes dissolve.

In a small saucepan, *saute* leeks and green onions in one tablespoon butter until tender, not brown. *Add* rest of butter and flour, *stir* to form a paste; *cook* until bubbly. *Add* to large pot, along with mashed potatoes, fish and sheefish sauce. *Stir* and *simmer* for 10 minutes. *Add* sour cream and evaporated milk. *Heat but do not boil*. *Season* with pepper to taste. *Serve* garnished with parsley.

Serves 10

Minchumina Mandarin Salad

A short distance from the front doorstep of Denali West Lodge is nine-mile-long Lake Minchumina, which means "clear lake" in the Tanana Indian dialect. Sherri picks some of the ingredients of this salad fresh from her garden that overlooks this lake, often while anglers are on the water trying their luck for northern pike.

¼   **cup almond slices**
1   **tablespoon granulated sugar**
¼   **head lettuce, torn into bite-size pieces**
¼   **bunch romaine lettuce or fresh spinach,**
      bite-size pieces
2   **stalks celery, chopped**
2   **green onions (with tops), thinly sliced**
1   **7-ounce can mandarin oranges or pineapple**
      chunks, drained

Cook almonds and sugar over low heat, *stirring* constantly until sugar is melted and almonds are coated. *Cool* and *break* apart. *Store* at room temperature.

Place lettuce, romaine, celery and onions in a plastic bag. *Pour* dressing into bag. *Add* orange segments (or pineapple chunks). *Close* bag tightly and *shake* until salad greens and orange segments are well-coated. *Add* almonds and *shake.*

Dressing

¼   **cup vegetable oil**
2   **tbsp. sugar**
2   **tbsp. wine vinegar**
1   **tbsp. snipped parsley**
      or mint leaves

½   **tsp. salt**
    dash of pepper
    dash red pepper
    sauce

Place oil, sugar, wine vinegar, parsley (or mint leaves), salt, pepper and red pepper sauce in tightly covered jar. *Shake* and *refrigerate.*

Serves 4—6

Innoko Noodle Salad

If you take a topographical map and find the Innoko River to the west of the Kuskokwim Mountains, you'll discover the area is jam-packed with oxbows, or U-shaped ponds, that were once the main body of the river itself. When the river changes course, it leaves these noodle-shaped bodies of water that usually offer good fishing for pike.

Sherri packs this salad in anglers' shore lunches. Because there is no mayonnaise in this salad, nor any lettuce to wilt, it is especially convenient for hot summer days.

2   tablespoons sesame seeds, toasted
½   cup slivered almonds, toasted
½   head green cabbage, chopped
3-4 green onions, sliced
1   package chicken-flavor ramen noodles,
      crushed

Mix dressing recipe below and *set* aside.

In a salad bowl, *mix* together sesame seeds, almonds, cabbage, onions and ramen noodles. *Pour* dressing over salad. *Toss* and *refrigerate* overnight.

Dressing

2   tablespoons granulated sugar
½   cup vegetable oil
3   tablespoons wine vinegar
½   teaspoon salt
½   teaspoon pepper
1   package of ramen seasoning from noodles

In a tightly-covered jar, *mix* sugar, oil, vinegar, salt, pepper and ramen seasoning. *Shake* and *refrigerate.*

Serves 4—6

Kantishna Cranberry Salad

The Kantishna country is known for its gold mines, as well as a healthy supply of lowbush cranberries. In August, you can easily find these tart morsels, glistening like red rubies in the morning sun.

4   cups lowbush cranberries
1   cup granulated sugar
1   6-ounce package flavored gelatin (raspberry, cherry or strawberry)
2   cups boiling water
1   8-ounce can crushed pineapple
1   cup coarsely chopped walnuts

Combine berries and sugar in a bowl. *Set* aside. *Stir* gelatin in water until dissolved. *Cool* and *add* to cranberry mixture. *Stir* in pineapple and walnuts. *Chill* until gelatin is firm.

Serves 10—12

Variation

1   6-ounce package flavored gelatin (raspberry, cherry or strawberry)
1   cup boiling water
1   13½-ounce can crushed pineapple
1   16-ounce can jellied cranberry sauce
½   cup coarsely chopped walnuts

Dissolve gelatin in boiling water. *Drain* pineapple, *reserving* juice. *Add* extra water to juice to make one cup. *Stir* into gelatin. *Chill* until thickened, but not set. *Cut* cranberry sauce into cubes. *Stir* cranberry sauce cubes, drained pineapple and walnuts into gelatin. *Chill* until firm.

Serves 10

Bearpaw Buns

*I*t's easy to judge the size of an Alaska brown bear by the size of its track. For instance, a front paw track that is over eight inches wide belongs to a 10-foot bear. And it's equally easy to judge the hunger of returning anglers by how quickly they remove their fishing gear when the Minchumina breezes carry the hot-from-the-oven goodness of these buns to their cabin.

For a special treat, Sherri makes sandwiches with these buns for shore lunches.

2	tablespoons dry yeast
¼	cup warm water (85-105 degrees)
¾	cup honey
¼	cup vegetable oil
1¼	cups hot water
1¼	cups evaporated milk
3½-4	cups whole wheat flour
1	tablespoon salt
2	cups millet
3½-4	cups white flour
1	egg, beaten
¼	cup milk
	sesame or poppy seeds

Dissolve yeast in warm water. In a large bowl, *stir* honey, oil, hot water and evaporated milk together. Mix in dissolved yeast and *stir* in whole wheat flour until a thick, pasty batter is formed. Beat well with a spoon (100 times). *Cover* and *let rise* for 50 to 60 minutes, until double.

Fold in salt and millet. Fold in additional white flour until dough comes away from the sides of the bowl. Knead on a floured board about 10 to 15 minutes until dough is smooth. Use more flour as needed to keep dough from sticking. *Let rise* until double.

Twist off dough in 2-inch diameter balls. Knead each until smooth and *place* on a cookie sheet so that they won't touch when they rise. *Let rise* 20 minutes. Mix egg and ¼ cup milk together to make an egg wash. Brush egg wash on rolls before baking. Sprinkle sesame seeds or poppy seeds on top if desired. Bake 25 minutes at 375 degrees.

Makes 24—30 buns

Cama'i Muffins

*I*n central Yupik language, cama'i means "A warm Alaska hello." When guests arrive at Denali West Lodge, Sherri always has a plateful of these snacks on the table as a way of welcoming guests to the lodge.

1	**cup oatmeal**
1	**cup buttermilk or soured milk**
⅓	**cup margarine or vegetable oil**
½	**cup brown sugar**
1	**egg**
1	**cup all-purpose flour**
1	**teaspoon baking powder**
½	**teaspoon baking soda**
1	**teaspoon salt**
½	**cup raisins**

Preheat oven to 400 degrees. *Grease* muffin tins.

In a mixing bowl, *soak* oatmeal in milk for 15 minutes.

Add margarine or oil, brown sugar and egg to oatmeal mixture and *stir* until well-blended.

Sift together dry ingredients: flour, baking powder, baking soda and salt. *Stir* lightly into oatmeal mixture. Do not overmix. *Stir* in raisins. *Fill* muffin tins ⅔ full. *Bake* at 400 degrees 20 to 25 minutes, or until golden brown.

Makes 12 muffins

Temperatures at Denali West Lodge often reach into the 90s, at which time the guests and staff take to mountain biking into Lake Minchumina for a quick and fun cool-down.

Another refreshing activity the Haydens enjoy is waterskiing on Lake Minchumina.

Kaksurok Carrot Cake

*K*aksurok Mountain is located in the Igichuk Hills on the Arctic Slope, and in Inupiak Eskimo dialect means "flat top." This delicious cake, with its icing spooned onto the top of each slice, reminds me of this mountain in early September, when the first dusting of snow powders the upper elevations.

1½ **cups granulated sugar**
1½ **cups cooking oil**
4 **eggs, beaten**
2 **teaspoons vanilla**
2½ **cups flour**
2 **teaspoons salt**
2 **teaspoons baking soda**
2 **teaspoons cinnamon**
½ **teaspoon ground cloves**
½ **teaspoon grated nutmeg**
3 **cups grated carrots**
½ **cup chopped nuts**

Preheat oven to 300 degrees. *Grease* and *flour* 9x13-inch cake pan. In a large bowl, *mix* sugar, oil, eggs and vanilla. *Sift* flour, salt, baking soda and cinnamon together and *stir* into oil/egg mixture until well-blended. *Fold* in carrots and nuts; *pour* into cake pan. *Bake* 1 hour at 300 degrees.

Icing

1 **8-ounce package cream cheese, softened**
1 **teaspoon vanilla**
¼ **cup butter, softened**
1½ **cups powdered sugar**
2 **tablespoons milk**
⅓ **cup chopped nuts**

Blend cream cheese, vanilla, butter, powdered sugar and milk until creamy smooth. *Stir* in nuts. *Slice* carrot cake while still warm and *serve* with icing spooned over top of each slice.

Serves 10—12

Coffee Creek Streusel

$\mathcal{C}$offee was a mainstay for Alaska prospectors in the late 1800s. It was often more important than what many jokingly refer to as the prospector's three major food groups: tobacco, jerky and liquor. There are seven Coffee Creeks throughout Alaska, named either because the streams' water resembled strongly brewed coffee, or because the water from that particular stream made the best coffee. Whatever the reason, the importance of coffee to early-day prospectors is well-documented, and for modern anglers heading out to prospect for fish, there is no finer accompaniment than a thermos of hot coffee and several slices of this coffee cake.

1½	**cups flour**
3	**teaspoons baking powder**
¾	**cup granulated sugar**
½	**teaspoon salt**
¼	**cup shortening, softened**
½	**cup milk**
1	**egg**
1	**teaspoon vanilla**

Mix filling recipe below and *set* aside. *Preheat* oven to 375 degrees. *Grease* and *flour* 9-inch round cake pan. *Combine* flour, baking powder, sugar and salt. *Cut* in shortening. *Beat* milk, egg and vanilla together and *combine* thoroughly with dry ingredients. *Pour* two-thirds of cake mixture into cake pan. *Top* evenly with filling and *add* remaining cake mixture. *Bake* at 375 degrees for 30 minutes.

Filling

2	**tablespoons margarine or butter, melted**
½	**cup brown sugar**
2	**tablespoons flour**
2	**teaspoons cinnamon**
½	**cup walnuts, chopped**

Combine ingredients and *set aside.*

Serves 4—6

Carl and Kirsten Dixon in front of Riversong Lodge.

Riversong Lodge

iversong Lodge caters to a variety of fishing clientele, from the occasional dabbler to the most elite fly fisherman. The lodge is located on the Yentna River, about 70 miles (a 40-minute flight) from Anchorage.

Although the lodge exudes a country atmosphere, special events at Riversong offer sophisticated elegance made even more appealing by the location.

We spent a day floating Lake Creek and caught a variety of salmon, trout and char. Near the end of the float, our guide put ashore on a gravel bar where tarps and tables had been neatly arranged. Here we enjoyed a wine-tasting party. Smoked salmon, shish kabob, various cheeses, marinated vegetables, fresh fruits and desserts covered the table. We sampled the fare between casts and caught trout from nearby pools. Riversong Lodge is a unique and fun way of enjoying the Alaska wilds.

The cost of providing such service is not cheap. Food must be flown in at 20 cents a pound. Equipment and supplies must also be barged up the Yentna, taking a minimum of 20 hours. The effort produces client satisfaction that brings Riversong guests back year after year.

Why the name Riversong? Owner Carl Dixon said he sat down one day on the bank of Lake Creek to think of a name.

"One of my favorite pastimes is to listen to Lake Creek run by," he said. "There was a play named Riversong, and also a song by that name. It was a natural."

*D*ixon says most of his guides have worked for him at least three years. He keeps his quality staff by offering incentive and educational programs. Dixon himself is as close to a perfect guide as you'll find. He knows where the fish are, meets the needs of clients, and cares for the resource.

Expect rustic-yet-comfortable sleeping accommodations at Riversong. The woodstove-heated cabins are spacious and comfortable. The main lodge has a lounge area, electricity and all the modern conveniences, which makes it the place for after-hours socializing.

Dixon is open and honest about his lodge. "We don't pretend to have a premier lodge in a trophy area," he

Kirsten's garden overlooks the Yentna River.

said. "We do offer anglers value for their dollar and easy, hassle-free access from Anchorage. The ideal stay for fishing is three days, unless you're floating Lake Creek for salmon, then plan to spend six."

Riversong is a good choice if you're passing through Anchorage, and want a lodge environment with good fishing at an affordable price.

Kirsten, a gracious hostess, provides a dining atmosphere with plenty of country charm. Here, guests enjoy their meal in Riversong's greenhouse dining room.

Kirsten Dixon, *Cook and Co-owner, Riversong Lodge*

Kirsten Dixon lives a life that many people only dream of experiencing. Along with her husband, Carl, she oversees the operation of Riversong Lodge. Hers is a rags-to-riches story, with the riches defined as the personal satisfaction of serving clientele the best food possible in the Lake Creek area.

The success they now enjoy did not come easily. Kirsten worked in Anchorage as a critical care nurse. There she met Carl, an audiologist. After a brief courtship, they were married in 1981. The couple shared similar philosophical views, and although they both were making a good living, they began searching for a livelihood they could enjoy together.

Carl was especially enamored with the Lake Creek area, so the couple purchased land with a cabin at the mouth of Lake Creek. From that tiny cabin they built a lodge, one that was in harmony

with Nature. They sold their home in Anchorage to help finance their move, run ads and photocopy fliers for direct mail to potential anglers. It was nip and tuck for a while, but they eventually built a fishing clientele.

Kirsten always liked to cook. She remembers her first request for a Christmas present was a "Galloping Gourmet" cookbook. Her cooking hobby proved invaluable when they opened the lodge, because she was the lodge's only cook. Her recipes were well-received by guests, and she soon began writing regular cooking columns for several Alaska publications and a cookbook on the lodge.

Kirsten considers herself a New Age country cook. Many of her recipes require herbs and vegetables she grows in the garden near the lodge. "Gardening and cooking go hand in hand," she said. "I harvest the bounty of fresh produce, and plan all my meals around the vegetables.

"I didn't want to give up the kitchen work, but the increase in clients required additional cooks." Kirsten kept an extensive recipe card file, and instructed the newly hired cooks in her New Age style. Today, the cooks still work from original recipe cards, with each cook adding special touches.

"Our food is not deep fried, Cajun or gourmet," Kirsten says. "We don't serve veal medallions because not only are they expensive, but they don't come from the surrounding land. We pride ourselves on using the organic foods we grow right here. We raise chickens and harvest salmon from the river. We'll use beef occasionally, but don't serve wild game to our clients."

Kirsten is dedicated to client satisfaction. Her attention to detail shows in the meals and creates smiles on clients' faces. "I'd rather have another employee for the upcoming season than a new coat," she says. Kirsten is a true pioneer in Alaska fishing lodge cuisine.

Yentna Filo Salmon

2	teaspoons butter
4	shallots, minced
1	pound salmon fillet, skinned and deboned
1	cup heavy cream
3	ounces cream cheese
¼	teaspoon salt
	pinch of nutmeg
	pinch of cayenne pepper
1	large sheet of paper same size as sheet of filo
1	pound filo dough
¼	cup butter, melted for brushing
1	egg, beaten
1	pint sour cream
1	tablespoon lemon juice
¼	teaspoon dillweed

Heat butter in a small frying pan. Add shallots and saute lightly; remove from heat and set aside. Check to be sure that all the bones and skin from the salmon are removed. Place salmon in a blender or food processor and grind it thoroughly, while slowly adding the heavy cream. When the salmon is well-ground, add cream cheese, salt, nutmeg and cayenne pepper; blend well. Transfer salmon mixture to a bowl and add sauteed shallots.

With a pair of scissors cut the paper into the shape of a free-form fish. Use this shape as a pattern to cut 16 sheets of filo dough into the fish shape.

Lightly grease a large baking sheet. Lay out eight of the fish-shaped filo sheets on the baking sheet, one on top of each other, brushing each sheet with melted butter. Spread the salmon mixture on the filo, leaving a one-inch margin around the edge. Cover the mixture with eight more sheets of filo, each brushed with butter. Seal the edges with butter and a bit of beaten egg applied with your fingers. Fold the edges over ½ inch to seal the fish completely. Brush the entire top of the fish with egg.

Bake at 375 degrees for 30 minutes or until golden brown. Cool the filo fish about 10 minutes before serving. Mix sour cream, lemon juice and dillweed. Cut filo fish into serving size pieces and add a dollop of sour cream mixture on top of each.

Serves 4—6

Fiddleheads & Crab

The lush, fiddlehead fern forests line the pathway through which the Yentna River flows. Riversong country is rich with these beautiful ferns that overflow the banks into the river. Look for fiddleheads that are tightly coiled, very young. Never eat them raw—they need to be at least blanched because they contain a toxin that will cause a tummyache. There are other ferns that resemble fiddleheads, so make sure you know what you are picking. The brown, papery skin should be peeled off, but it won't hurt if a little is left on. One medium grated zucchini may be substituted for the ferns.

20-25 blanched fiddleheads, drained and patted dry (or substitute 1 medium zucchini, grated)
2   teaspoons salt
4   quarts water
3   tablespoons butter
1   clove garlic, crushed
1   pound fresh, cooked crab meat
1   tablespoon freshly squeezed lemon juice
     salt and pepper to taste
2   cups shredded Cheddar cheese
     lemon slices or red pepper rings for garnish

Blanche the fiddleheads in salted water for five minutes. (If using grated zucchini, omit this step).

Pat ferns very dry with paper towels so dish doesn't get runny. Saute ferns in butter and garlic, *coating* all sides for 5 to 8 minutes (2 minutes for zucchini).

Place in an au gratin dish or 1½-quart, low-sided, oven-proof casserole. Spread crab meat across the top. Sprinkle with lemon juice, salt and pepper to taste. Add the cheese on top and *bake* at 300 degrees until the cheese is melted and bubbly. Serve with lemon slices or red pepper rings arranged on the top.

Serves 4

Skwentna Winter Chicken

This chicken recipe is easy to prepare. If you would like to use Alaska game, substitute Ruffed Grouse (white meat) for the chicken. The sauce is wonderful and different. Kirsten serves it with an accompaniment of brown rice, topped with sauteed winter vegetables (onions, celery and bell peppers). You can make the rice and apricot sauce ahead of time, go skiing for an hour, and come back to finish the dish.

1	**cup orange marmalade**
1	**cup red wine**
1	**cup water**
½	**cup orange juice**
1	**cup pureed apricots**
1	**tart apple, peeled, pared and diced**
2	**tablespoons red current jelly**
2	**tablespoons brown sugar**
2	**tablespoons cornstarch**
¼	**cup cold water**
3	**tablespoons olive oil**
3	**boneless whole chicken breasts, cut into ½-inch strips**
½	**cup flour for dredging**
¼	**cup brandy**

Combine marmalade, wine, water, orange juice, pureed apricots, apples, jelly and brown sugar in a saucepan on the stove. *Mix* the cornstarch with cold water and *add* to the sauce. *Cook* and *stir* until thickened. *Heat* the oil in a frying pan or wok over medium-high heat until hot. *Dredge* the chicken strips in flour and *saute* in the oil until golden. *Remove* chicken, *pour* the oil from the skillet and *wipe* clean. *Return* the chicken, *add* the brandy; *simmer* 2 minutes. *Stir* in the apricot sauce, *spooning* over the chicken strips to coat.

Serves 6

Chulitna Moosemeat Stew

*I*n winter the style of eating changes at the lodge. They no longer have the lush salads of summer, but rely on long-lasting staples. Kirsten cooks big one-pot meals that simmer all day on the woodstove. Riversong rarely has beef in the winter because moosemeat is so plentiful, but this recipe is equally good made with moose or beef. Kirsten likes to make it thick and serve it with a big bowl of rice. Accompaniments are shredded Cheddar cheese, sour cream and hot corn bread. She serves moose stew to the racers on the Iditaski Race, but state laws require beef to be served to commercial guests.

6   strips bacon, cut into 1-inch pieces
2-3   pounds moosemeat or lean beef, cut in
        2-inch cubes
      salt and pepper
10   small onions, peeled
2   medium potatoes, well-scrubbed and cubed
3   tablespoons all-purpose flour
1½   cups dry red wine
1   cup beef broth
3   tablespoons brandy
2   cloves of garlic, pressed
1-2   strips of orange peel (make sure you wash
        the orange well to remove any chemical
        residue)
1   teaspoon marjoram
1   teaspoon fresh thyme (½ teaspoon if dried)
1   medium-size onion, studded with 3 cloves
1   pound medium-size mushrooms
4   large carrots, peeled and cut ½-inch thick

In a large frying pan on medium heat, *cook* bacon until brown and crumbly. With a slotted spoon, *remove* bacon from pan and *place* in a deep casserole dish. *Reserve* pan and bacon drippings.

Sprinkle meat with salt and pepper. **Add** meat cubes to the pan, a few pieces at a time, and *cook* over medium heat until brown on all sides. *Remove* meat cubes from pan and *add* to casserole. To the remaining pan juices, *add* white onions. (The easiest way to peel small onions is to drop them whole into boiling water for a few minutes, remove and peel). *Cook* onions until light brown. *Set* aside.

Add flour to the remaining pan juices. *Cook* until bubbly, *stirring* frequently. *Pour* in wine and brandy, *stirring* until sauce is thick. *Add* garlic, orange peel, marjoram and thyme. *Pour* sauce over meat in casserole. *Tuck* clove-studded onion down in liquid.

Bake in 325 degree oven for 2½ hours. During the last half-hour of cooking, *add* mushrooms and carrots, *cooking* until tender. *Remove* the studded onion.

Serves 6

Variation

If you prefer rich undertones, *add* a touch more brandy and mushrooms. If you like orangey undertones, *use* more orange peel. *Use* good-quality red wine.

Rainbow trout are plentiful in Lake Creek and draw anglers from around the world to test their fly fishing skills in catching these colorful acrobats.

Amanda's Vegetable Pie

This pie has endless variations with different types of vegetables and herbs added for flavoring. Kirsten uses a potato crust, although carrot crusts are good, too. She likes to serve this dish with a spicy condiment like chutney. This dish is named after her daughter, Amanda, who loved it as a baby.

3   cups grated raw potatoes
½   teaspoon salt
2   eggs, beaten
3   tablespoons dehydrated onion
1   teaspoon lemon pepper

Preheat oven to 400 degrees. *Grease* a 9-inch pie plate.

Place the grated potatoes in a colander resting in a bowl. Mix in salt and *allow to stand* at room temperature for 15 minutes. Water will *drain* out of the potatoes and into the bowl. *Squeeze* the potatoes to release extra water. *Remove* to a clean, dry bowl.

Blend eggs, onion and lemon pepper into the potatoes. *Pat* the potato mixture into the pie pan, *building* the crust up the sides of the pan with your fingers. (*To remove* excess liquid from potato crust, *blot* with paper towel.)

Bake for 35 to 45 minutes in 400-degree oven until crisp.

Vegetable Filling

1   cup chopped onion
1   clove garlic, crushed
3   tablespoons butter
1   head cauliflower
      or broccoli
¼   teaspoon thyme
½   teaspoon basil
½   teaspoon

1   cup grated Cheddar
      cheese
2   eggs
¼   cup half-and-half or
      cream
      lemon pepper
      paprika

Lower oven temperature to 350 degrees.

In a frying pan, *saute* onion and garlic in butter until both are light brown. *Cut* cauliflower or broccoli into flowerettes. *Remove* stems. *Add* thyme, basil, salt and cauliflower (or broccoli) to frying pan and *cook*, covered, for 10 minutes.

Spread half of the cheese into the baked potato crust, then *add* the sauteed onion, garlic and cauliflower (or broccoli), and the rest of the cheese.

Beat eggs in a small bowl or measuring cup, *add* half-and-half. *Blend* well. *Pour* this custard slowly into the pie crust (too fast and it will spill). *Sprinkle* with lemon pepper and paprika for color. *Bake* in a 350-degree oven for 25 to 35 minutes until set.

Serves 4—6

Riversong Lodge set up this wine tasting on a gravel bar of a nearby river. Lodge guests tested the newest wines on the market, provided by a co-sponsoring distributor in Anchorage. Between samplings of wine, hors d'oeuvres and desserts, we fished for rainbow trout. Everyone enjoyed the harmonious combination of wilderness and civilization. We had no cares in the world as we floated the river back to the lodge.

Chelatna Asparagus Puff

The headwaters of Lake Creek begin at Chelatna Lake in the Alaska Range. The creek is the main source of water for the lodge's garden, which grows tender green asparagus under the midnight sun. The best garment to wear for asparagus harvesting is an Alaska tuxedo: an olive drab jacket with patches on the elbows, patch pockets on hips and chest, and doused heavily in mosquito repellent.

1	pound asparagus
4	tablespoons butter
2	tablespoons chopped onion
½	teaspoon granulated sugar
1	teaspoon salt
2	tablespoons water
6	eggs
⅓	cup heavy cream
	fresh ground pepper
1½	cups grated muenster cheese

Preheat oven to 425 degrees.

Cut asparagus into one-inch pieces. Melt 2 tablespoons butter in a saucepan, saute onion until soft and golden. Add asparagus, sprinkle with sugar and ½ teaspoon salt, and toss for one minute. Add water, cover and steam cook for 1 to 2 minutes. Remove cover and cool slightly.

Beat until frothy: eggs, cream, ½ teaspoon salt and pepper to taste. Melt 2 tablespoons butter in an ovenproof 10x10-inch baking dish. Pour in the egg mixture and cook about three minutes over medium heat until the bottom is set. Arrange the asparagus and onions in a single layer on top of the eggs. Bake uncovered at 425 degrees for five minutes. Remove from the oven, cover asparagus with grated cheese, and bake an additional 10 minutes.

When the eggs have puffed and the cheese has lightly browned, the dish is done. Serve immediately.

Serves 4

Riversong Sourdough Starter

The Yukon Gold Rush started in 1897, but there were miners living in Alaska and searching the backcountry for gold long before that. For these men, a sourdough pot often meant the difference between eating tasty fresh biscuits or going without for many months. Good starters were highly coveted by early cooks. Things aren't quite so drastic for modern Alaskans, but it is still a good idea to keep a sourdough starter going in the kitchen.

Some people are hesitant to keep sourdough, because they worry about keeping it going. Good news—it can be stored in the freezer for up to three months without ever having to think about it.

Just remove the starter from the freezer, let it thaw slowly in the refrigerator for 24 hours, add equal parts of warm water and flour (usually one cup each). Let the mixture stand overnight, and it will be ready to go. There's no mystique to sourdough, and it's not difficult to keep up.

The best container for sourdough storage is a regular **plastic** 2-quart pitcher with a lid and a pour spout. **Never use a metal container.** If you are able to get two containers exactly alike, this makes it easy to pour the sourdough from one container into a clean one periodically. Stick a piece of masking tape on the front of the pitcher and write on it the last date the starter was added to. Just switch your starter into a clean pitcher whenever it begins to get real crusty and gooey on the sides of the container.

Use the following method for starting sourdough:

1 **1¼-ounce packet dry yeast (1 tablespoon)**
1½ **cups warm water**
2 **cups white flour**

Add yeast, warm water and flour to a 2-quart pitcher; stir it up but don't worry about getting all the lumps out.

Cover the container with a lid, but *ensure* the spout is open so the starter can get air. Yeast are living organisms, remember!

Set the starter in a warm area of the kitchen, near the stove but not so close that it will get too hot. The perfect temperature is 85 degrees Fahrenheit. The starter should be in a place free from drafts. If the sourdough happens to bubble over, quickly *clean* it up; it can make a ''gluey'' mess. *Keep* the sourdough warm for three to five days, *stirring* once or twice a day. You should begin to *smell* the yeast fermenting. *Store* the starter in the fridge, but *return* it to room temperature before using.

If you aren't using your starter frequently, *stir* it once a week and *replenish* it by adding 1 cup of water and 1 cup of flour. Whenever you use the starter, *add* back to the pot an equal amount of flour and water. If you start to get too low on your starter, *take* a tablespoon of starter, 2 cups of flour and 1½ cups of warm water; *add* them together and *set* aside for a day or two. If a liquid forms on top of your sourdough, just *stir* it in. If your sourdough turns red or orange, *throw* it away and *start over.*

There are many sourdough variations. You can *add* honey, whole wheat flour, rye flour or potato water to your starter. Besides using sourdough in bread and pancakes, Riversong uses it in cookies, pies, cakes and even main dishes.

Now that you have your own sourdough starter, try these recipes.

Variation

When making starter, if water from boiled potatoes is used and approximately 1 tablespoon sugar is added, dry yeast can be omitted and ''natural yeast'' will begin to grow in the starter. This will take a longer time before it's ready to use—about 1 to 2 weeks.

Kirsten's Sourdough Bagels

1	packet active dry yeast
¼	cup warm water
2	eggs, room temperature
1	cup sourdough starter
1	teaspoon salt
2	tablespoons granulated sugar
3	tablespoons vegetable oil
3-4	cups all-purpose flour
4	quarts water

Grease a large bowl and *grease* and *flour* a large baking sheet. *Sprinkle* yeast over the warm water. *Let* soften for several minutes. In another large bowl, *beat* eggs. *Stir* in the sourdough starter, salt, sugar, oil and yeast mixture. *Add* enough flour to make a firm dough. *Knead* the dough for 8 to 10 minutes or until smooth. *Place* the dough in greased bowl and *cover* with oiled plastic wrap. *Set* in a draft-free place for 2 to 2½ hours or until doubled in size.

Punch the dough down and *knead* a few times, then *divide* the dough into 12 balls. *Press* out the center of each ball with your thumb. *Turn* the dough in your hands to make the bagel larger and *set* on the baking sheet. *Let rise* 20 minutes.

Preheat the broiler. *Bring* the water to a boil in a large pot. Under the broiler, *brown* the bagels on each side, one to two minutes. (*Watch* bagels carefully while broiling, as they will burn easily). Gently *lift* each bagel into the boiling water, being careful not to overcrowd. *Boil* about two minutes on each side. Bagels will turn over in the boiling water by themselves. *Drain* bagels on paper towels.

Place the bagels back on the baking sheet and *bake* for 25 to 30 minutes or until golden brown in a 375-degree oven. *Serve* with Alaska honey and whipped butter.

Makes 12 bagels

Alaska Sourdough Pizza

*S*moked salmon makes this popular dish into an Alaska Extravaganza. Serve as an entree, or make the pizza in a rectangle, cut into squares and serve as hors d'oeuvres. Other unique Alaska toppings include reindeer sausage or pepperoni, moose burger or moose sausage.

⅔   **cup milk**
1   **teaspoon active dry yeast**
⅓   **cup warm water**
1½   **cups sourdough starter, room temperature**
1   **teaspoon salt**
1½   **tablespoons granulated sugar**
3   **tablespoons olive oil**
3 - 4 **cups all-purpose flour**
2   **cups homemade pizza sauce**
1½   **pounds mozzarella cheese, shredded**
½   **pound smoked salmon, sliced in thin strips**
½   **onion, thinly sliced**

Heat milk in a small saucepan over medium heat. Do *not* *boil*. *Set* aside. *Add* the yeast to the warm water in a glass measuring cup. *Let* the mixture soften for five minutes. In a large bowl, *combine* sourdough starter, salt, sugar, oil, milk, and yeast mixture. *Stir* in enough flour to make a firm dough. *Knead* for 8 to 10 minutes until the dough is elastic and shiny; *place* in a greased bowl. *Cover* the bowl with oiled plastic wrap or moist towel. *Let rise* for 2 hours.

Separate the dough into two balls. *Roll* out into 12- to 14-inch rounds, and *crimp* the edges up. *Spread* with pizza sauce and *top* with cheese. *Arrange* the salmon strips and onion slices evenly across the top. *Bake* 25 minutes at 400 degrees or until the crust is brown.

Makes 2 medium-size pizzas

Cheechako Chocolate Cake

This cake is favored by cheechakos and old time Alaskans because of its hint of sourdough, coffee and chocolate, which are often referred to as the three major food groups of the Alaskan sportsman. A cheechako is an individual unaccustomed to Alaska ways. An old Alaska campfire tale has it that cheechako was a term originated in the Gold Rush days of the early 1900s. A couple of Alaska Natives described two prospectors from Chicago who did everything wrong. The Natives took delight in calling the incompetent newcomers "chee-cha-ker," which was as close as they could come to pronouncing "Chicago."

1½	**cups white flour**
⅓	**cup powdered milk**
1	**teaspoon baking soda**
½	**teaspoon salt**
1	**cup sourdough starter, room temperature**
1	**cup water**
2	**teaspoons freeze-dried coffee**
1	**teaspoon vanilla**
4	**ounces (4 squares) bitter chocolate**
½	**cup butter, softened**
2	**cups granulated sugar**
3	**eggs, separated**

Butter the sides and *line* the bottoms of three 8-inch cake pans with waxpaper. *Set* aside. *Mix* flour, milk, soda and salt; *set* aside. In a separate bowl, *mix* starter, water, coffee and vanilla; *set* aside. *Melt* the chocolate on very low heat, *stirring* frequently.

Preheat oven to 350 degrees. *Cream* together the butter and sugar, *beating* until light and fluffy. *Beat* in the egg yolks one at a time. *Add* the melted, cooled chocolate and *beat* rapidly until well-blended. Continue to *beat* and alternately *add* the flour mixture and the sourdough mixture, ½ cup at a time. *Set* aside when the mixtures are well-blended. Next, *beat* the egg whites until they form stiff peaks. *Fold* the egg whites very gently into the batter. *Pour* the batter into the prepared cake pans. *Bake* at 350 degrees for 40 minutes or until the center is done. *Remove* the cakes and *cool* on a rack. *Frost* with your favorite frosting.

Serves 16

Sourdough Pancakes

*A*nglers regularly request Riversong's sourdough pancakes before starting their fishing day. When fresh-picked wild blueberries are added to the pancakes, there's not a better breakfast you can enjoy in the northcountry.

1½	**cups all-purpose flour or half white/half whole wheat**
2	**teaspoons baking powder**
½	**teaspoon baking soda**
½	**teaspoon salt**
1	**tablespoon sugar**
1	**egg, room temperature**
1	**cup sourdough starter, room temperature**
1	**cup milk**
3	**tablespoons vegetable oil**
1	**Granny Smith apple, peeled and thinly sliced**

Stir together flour, baking powder, baking soda, salt and sugar. *Set* aside. In a separate bowl with spout, *beat* egg. *Stir* in starter, milk and oil. *Add* the dry ingredients until just moistened. *Stir* in apple slices.

Place a griddle over medium-high heat until a drop of water "skitters" across the griddle, then *pour* ½ cup of batter onto the preheated surface. *Cook* one to two minutes on each side.

Serves 4

Blueberry Pancakes

To prevent "blue batter," do not mix blueberries into batter. Instead, *sprinkle* fresh blueberries on top of pancake batter after you pour batter on the griddle.

Matanuska Muffins

$\mathcal{M}$atanuska Valley, in southcentral Alaska, is a world-renowned agricultural area famous for growing huge vegetables and 50-pound cabbages. These bountiful breakfast muffins symbolize the bounty of the Matanuska Valley.

1	large tart apple, peeled
½	stick butter, softened
½	cup granulated sugar
2	large eggs
1½	cups flour
1	teaspoon baking powder
1	teaspoon baking soda
½	teaspoon salt
¼	teaspoon ground cardamom
1	cup rolled oats
½	cup finely chopped walnuts
1	cup grated Cheddar cheese
¾	cup milk
1	small apple, peeled and cored
½	stick butter, melted
2	tablespoons granulated sugar
1	tablespoon cinnamon

Preheat oven to 400 degrees. *Butter* muffin tins. Finely *chop* tart apple into 1/8-inch cubes; *set* aside.

Cream butter and sugar together in a large bowl. *Add* eggs and *beat* well. In a separate bowl, *sift* together flour, baking powder, baking soda, salt and cardamom. *Stir* into butter/sugar mixture. *Stir* in oats. *Add* apple cubes, walnuts and cheese to mixture. *Stir* in milk, *mixing* lightly. *Fill* muffin tins two-thirds full. *Cut* second apple into 12 thin slices the same diameter as the muffin tins. *Brush* the apple slices with butter and roll in sugar/cinnamon mixture. *Place* one apple slice on batter in each cup, *top* with batter to three-quarters full and *sprinkle* with remaining sugar/cinnamon mixture. *Bake* for 25 minutes at 400 degrees. *Cool* on a wire rack.

Makes 12 large muffins

Alaska Wilderness Safaris

*T*he Alaska Peninsula is often touted as the premier place for sportfish variety and numbers. This part of Alaska doesn't receive the world-wide acclaim given to other areas because getting there is an adventure in itself. Weather, as well as the long flying distance from King Salmon, Anchorage and Dillingham keep the Alaska Peninsula watersheds from receiving much if any fishing pressure.

While only a handful of fishing lodges are currently operating on the Alaska Peninsula, Alaska Wilderness Safaris offers a wilderness fishing adventure unlike anything else available in the state.

Alaska Wilderness Safaris operates from a modern tent camp on the Pacific side of the Alaska Peninsula, about a 75-minute flight southeast of King Salmon.

Manager J.W. Smith offers tent camps that provide maximum comfort in a wilderness environment. He uses Eureka Bombshelters, the premier in Alaska tents: roomy, spacious and virtually guaranteed not to blow apart in high winds. Each tent is equipped with table, towels, cots with comfortable air mattresses, linen and bedding, things you don't usually find in mobile or even permanent tent camps. The dining tent is nearly 18 feet long and 10 feet wide, with plenty of head room. There are two cook tents complete with propane stoves, sinks and meal preparation equipment, which are all flown or boated in at the beginning of the each season. There is even a separate tent with a built-in shower stall and hot running water.

Smith locates his camps on the banks of super-productive salmon and char rivers. In late August, the rivers are blackened with salmon entering on the incoming tide. Other streams within easy boating distance of camp offer equally outstanding fishing.

Fishing is not restricted to camp or boat access. Smith has bush pilot extraordinare Mark Krupinski handling the fly-outs. Because of the extreme weather conditions on the Peninsula, a pilot has to be well-skilled in bush flying. Krupinski is a former Air Force flight instructor and reconnaissance pilot who can handle a small plane with precision and skill. He uses a Super Cub on wheels to land you on remote river bars where you can fish a clearwater spring and tributary teeming with hundreds of char. There are so many salmon in the stream, if you walked through the water the salmon would jump out onto the banks.

The food is classy. Dawn Smith does an excellent job of supervising the meal preparation. Breakfast items from cereal to eggs and bacon are your choice. Steaks, chicken, turkey and salads with plenty of fruit and baked

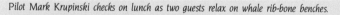

Pilot Mark Krupinski checks on lunch as two guests relax on whale rib-bone benches.

Dining tents capable of seating 12 are custom-made by Eureka to withstand the occasional cyclone-force winds prevalent on the Alaska Peninsula. Guests stay in comfortable 8x10-foot tents.

Mount Chiginigak

goods round out the menu. Evenings around the firepit are memorable as you sit on eight-foot-long whale rib bone benches, relax and socialize with camp companions.

*T*he Peninsula offers much to see and appreciate. Weather permitting, ask the pilot to take you on a flightseeing trip of the area. Tour Mount Chiginigak, a 6,995-foot volcano, or the glaciers north of camp. There are wilderness sections of river that anglers seldom fish, and you can drop in and sample them for an hour before trying somewhere else. Such fishing and access is only possible with wheeled planes and veteran bush pilots. Or choose to fly to remote beaches and search for Japanese glass fishing floats that are coveted by collectors.

When you consider what you're receiving for your money, a week's stay is a bargain. The logistics of dining, fishing and adventuring on your own in this area would be cost prohibitive. Besides, it's worth the price just to sample the cooking and take in the view, which ranks among the best Alaska has to offer.

It was love at first sight when Dawn saw Alaska in 1988. She, her husband, J.W., and a couple of friends made a memorable 80-mile float down the Aniak River. Now she spends summers in Alaska cooking for Alaska Wilderness Safaris. This is her dream-come-true, and her only complaint is not getting to fish as much as she'd like!

Dawn developed her cooking skills under a Cordon Bleu-trained chef. An avid reader of cookbooks and cooking magazines, she loves to experiment with new recipes.

Alaska Wilderness Safaris operates within a National Wildlife Refuge. The entire camp must be flown in at the beginning of the season and flown out at the end. Groceries are flown in weekly. There is no refrigeration, so meat comes frozen and dairy products come in insulated boxes. In camp, food is stored in large coolers in the shade. Dawn has never had trouble with food spoilage.

Dawn's kitchen is a tent. She has hot and cold running water and an apartment-size range that runs on propane. "The most challenging part of cooking in camp is preparing meals for up to 16 people on the small range. To compensate for the small oven we often grill beef rib-eye or salmon steaks over the campfire," Dawn says.

With no electricity, Dawn keeps in good shape beating and mixing things by hand, especially the pecan cheesecake!

Dawn enjoys preparing dishes people don't expect to see coming out of a tent kitchen, such as Cornish game hens, Spinach Timbales and Red Wine Biscuits.

Being limited to a weekly grocery delivery can spark one's creative cooking juices. Variations and substitutions keep the menu interesting, and offer new ideas for recipes.

Dawn spends her winters in Kileen, Texas, either building custom flyrods, tying fishing flies, fishing Texas hill-country creeks and rivers, or photographing the countryside. Dawn has a Bachelor of Arts in photojournalism, with a minor in biology.

When she is not in the kitchen, Dawn Smith can usually be found in the main tent tying flies for clients. In the photo above, she is putting the final touches on a Dawn's Firecracker, an excellent fly for Dolly Varden char.

Cream Cheese-Scallion Spread

$\mathcal{S}$erve this delicious spread in the center of Red Wine Biscuits, page 167, with Bristol Bay Smoked Salmon, page 107, or Igiugig Lox, page 282, and Kirsten's Sourdough Bagels, page 149.

1	**8-ounce package cream cheese, softened**
2	**tablespoons milk**
⅓	**cup minced scallions**

Beat cream cheese at medium speed with an electric mixer until smooth. Gradually *add* milk, *beating* until light and fluffy. *Stir* in scallions. *Refrigerate* overnight.

Makes 1¼ cups

Near the main camp, streams are teeming with chum and pink salmon. A fish a cast is commonplace, with plenty of wilderness solitude.

Wide Bay Salmon

$\mathcal{W}$ide Bay, on the Pacific Ocean side of the Alaska Peninsula arm, is a popular spot for camp guests to fish for fiesty silver salmon, fresh from the ocean. Broiling is a quick and easy way to prepare this rich Alaskan delicacy.

1	**large silver salmon fillet**
½	**cup mayonnaise**
1	**teaspoon tarragon**
1	**teaspoon seasoning salt**
½	**teaspoon black pepper**
1	**onion, sliced into rings**

Grease a large flat baking pan. *Clean* and *fillet* salmon (you can leave the skin on). *Place* fillet skin side down in pan. *Spread* mayonnaise generously on salmon. *Season* with tarragon, salt and pepper. *Garnish* with onion rings.

Broil for 15 minutes or until cooked through.

Serves 6—8

Alaska Wilderness Safaris base camp is located near salt water, so fresh salmon are readily available and served as often as requested by guests. These silver salmon fillets are ready for the oven.

Chiginigak Chicken

M ount Chiginigak is a commanding presence over the remote base camp operated by Dawn and J.W. Smith. A clearwater stream teeming with salmon meanders just a few yards from the camp before emptying into a nearby saltwater bay. Dawn prepares meals in a cook tent with plenty of ventilation. When the breezes come in off the ocean, anglers a half-mile upstream have caught the wonderful aroma of this recipe and hurried back to camp, afraid they might miss out on dinner!

4	**chicken breast halves, deboned and skinned (may substitute Ruffed Grouse)**
½	**teaspoon freshly ground black pepper**
½	**cup all-purpose flour**
4	**tablespoons butter**
1	**cup sliced fresh mushrooms**
2	**tablespoons lemon juice**
¼	**cup dry white wine**
3	**medium cloves garlic, minced**
3	**tablespoons chopped fresh parsley**

Place chicken between two sheets of plastic wrap and *pound* to ½-inch thickness. *Sprinkle* with pepper and *coat* with flour. *Melt* 2 tablespoons butter in a large skillet and *brown* chicken over medium heat for about 5 minutes, until lightly golden. *Remove* from skillet; *keep* warm.

Add remaining butter to skillet; *saute* mushrooms until tender. *Return* chicken to skillet. *Add* lemon juice, wine and garlic. *Simmer* 7 to 10 minutes until sauce thickens slightly. *Top* with parsley.

Serves 4

Herbed Cornish Hens

The char, rainbow, grayling and salmon fishing is spectacular on the Alaska Peninsula. But after a few days of eating fish in this wilderness paradise, even the most dedicated angler will smack his lips when elegant Cornish game hens preside over the dinner table. Compliments abound as diners cut into this tender, juicy bird. Asparagus spears make a tasty accompaniment.

4	**Cornish game hens**
4	**small onions**
	tarragon
¾	**cup butter, melted**
¾	**cup dry white wine**
½	**teaspoon salt**
¼	**teaspoon pepper**
	all-purpose flour for dredging

Preheat oven to 450 degrees.

Remove giblets from hens and *reserve* for some other use. *Rinse* hens in cold water, *pat* dry. *Place* an onion in the cavity of each hen; *sprinkle* outside of each hen with tarragon.

In a small bowl, *combine* butter, wine, salt and pepper.

Dredge hens in flour. *Place* in a baking dish; *pour* wine mixture around hens. *Place* in 450 degree oven, and *reduce* heat to 350 degrees. *Roast* uncovered until tender, about 45 to 60 minutes, *basting* occasionally.

Serves 4

Pilot Point Pork Chops

1   **cup fresh bread crumbs**
¼   **cup all-purpose flour**
¼   **teaspoon salt**
¼   **teaspoon black pepper**
2   **egg whites**
1   **tablespoon water**
4   **pork chops, ¾-inch thick, excess fat trimmed**
1   **large garlic clove, crushed**
2   **tablespoons butter**
4   **tablespoons olive oil**
1   **small onion, chopped**
⅓   **cup dry white wine**
½   **cup beef broth**
1   **bay leaf**

Place bread crumbs on a large plate. On another plate *combine* flour, salt and pepper. *Place* egg whites in a bowl, *add* water and *beat* lightly.

Pat chops dry, *rub* both sides with garlic. *Dredge* in flour mixture; *shake off* excess. *Dip* in egg whites; *coat* with bread crumbs. *Place* on platter, *refrigerate* 15 minutes to 1 hour.

Preheat oven to 350 degrees. In a large skillet, *melt* butter and oil over moderately high heat until bubbling. *Add* chops and *cook* until browned and crisp, about 3 minutes on each side. *Transfer* to a roasting pan.

Reduce heat under skillet to medium. *Add* onion and *cook* until soft and beginning to brown, about 5 minutes. *Add* wine, *simmer* until reduced to 2 tablespoons. *Add* beef broth and bay leaf and *simmer* 2 minutes. *Pour* around chops.

Cover roasting pan tightly with foil. *Bake* at 350 degrees for 20 to 25 minutes or until meat is white when cut next to the bone. *Transfer* to a warm platter. *Discard* bay leaf and *pour* onion sauce over meat. *Serve* hot.

Serves 4

Spinach Timbales

When your anglers come home empty-handed, you can put a smile back on their faces with this appetizing recipe that is much like a crustless quiche, but with more vegetables. Serve it as a side dish, or as an entree for lunch with fruit salad and bread.

½   **cup cream**
4   **eggs**
½   **teaspoon paprika**
     dash lemon juice
1   **cup vegetable or chicken stock**
½   **teaspoon salt**
     dash nutmeg
1   **cup cooked spinach, well-drained**
½   **cup grated smoked Swiss cheese**
     hollandaise sauce for garnish

Preheat oven to 325 degrees.

Combine cream, eggs, paprika, lemon juice, stock, salt and nutmeg. *Whisk* until combined. *Stir* in spinach and cheese.

Butter six individual half-cup molds or muffin tins. *Fill* two-thirds full with timbale mixture. *Place* molds or muffin tins into a larger baking pan containing an inch of hot (not boiling) water. *Lay* a piece of foil over the top, but do not seal the edges.

Bake at 325 degrees for 40 to 50 minutes or until a knife blade inserted in the center comes out clean. *Garnish* with hollandaise sauce.

Serves 6

Shishmarev Salad

This bold, flavorful salad honors Captain Glieb Shishmarev, an Imperial Russian Navy explorer. Shishmarev is well-known for his arctic Alaska expeditions. From 1817 to 1820, he explored the Alaska coastline from Norton Sound to Unalaska and the Aleutian Islands—not an easy task, as anglers familiar with the cyclonic weather in this region can attest.

2	medium cloves garlic, minced
1	small yellow onion, quartered
1	teaspoon Dijon mustard
1	teaspoon dried dill
½	teaspoon salt
½	teaspoon pepper
¼	teaspoon chili powder
1	cup basalmic vinegar
¾	cup extra-virgin olive oil
¼	cup water
2	heads Boston or bibb lettuce
1	avocado, chopped
1	tablespoon lemon juice
4	roma or 8 cherry tomatoes, sliced

In a quart jar, *combine* garlic, onion, mustard, dill, salt, pepper, chili powder, vinegar, oil and water. *Shake* well, *refrigerate* two hours to overnight.

Wash and *dry* lettuce. *Toss* avocado with lemon juice. *Tear* lettuce and *place* in a salad bowl. *Add* tomatoes and avocado to lettuce. *Shake* vinaigrette well, *pour* over salad, *toss* and *serve*.

Serves 4

Ring of Fire Pepper Biscuits

$\mathcal{D}$awn serves these peppery biscuits once a week under the smoking countenance of Mount Chiginigak, a 6,995-foot active volcano near the Alaska Wilderness Safaris base camp.

Mount Chiginigak is one of many volcanoes in what geologists call the "ring of fire," a series of volcanoes encircling the Pacific Rim area. The mildly hot flavor of these biscuits commemorates this geological attraction.

1¾ cups all-purpose flour
2 teaspoons baking powder
1 teaspoon granulated sugar
½ teaspoon salt
¼ teaspoon baking soda
1½ tablespoons coarse ground black pepper
¼ cup shortening or melted butter
¾ cup buttermilk

Preheat oven to 450 degrees.

In a large bowl, sift together flour, baking powder, sugar, salt and baking soda. Stir in black pepper. Cut in shortening or butter to fine crumb stage. Add buttermilk and stir until dough clings together. Knead on lightly-floured board 10 to 12 strokes. Roll out until ½-inch thick and cut with biscuit cutter. Place biscuits on ungreased baking sheet. Bake at 450 degrees for 10 to 12 minutes.

Makes 1 dozen

Red Wine Biscuits

These colorful biscuits are especially tasty when served with Cream Cheese-Scallion Spread.

2½ **cups all-purpose flour**
1 **teaspoon salt**
3 **teaspoons baking powder**
⅓ **cup sugar**
1½ **teaspoons pepper**
½ **cup dry red wine**
½ **cup vegetable oil**

Preheat oven to 450 degrees.

In a medium-size bowl, *combine* flour, salt, baking powder, sugar and pepper; *mix* together with a fork. Using a wooden spoon, *form* a well in the center of flour mixture. Add the wine and oil and *mix* just until a dough is formed.

Divide dough into 24 pieces. *Roll* each piece into a 3-inch log. *Press* the ends together to form a ring.

Place 1½ inches apart on ungreased baking sheet and *bake* at 450 degrees for 10 to 12 minutes, or until bottoms are golden.

Spoon a bit of Cream Cheese-Scallion Spread, page 158, into the center of each biscuit ring.

Makes 2 dozen

Photo at left: J.W. Smith with a September Dolly Varden char. Anglers catch and release from 20 to 100 fish per day at Smith's outpost fishing camps.

Bear Bread

*D*uring mealtime at the Alaska Wilderness Safaris base camp, don't be surprised to see one of the guides run out of the tent, grab a shotgun, and fire a few shots into the air to scare off the bears trying to sneak into the food tent. The guides reenter the dining tent and resume eating, while guests new to Alaska sit there with gaping mouths. Make plenty of this beer bread, as it disappears fast, whether to hungry anglers or brown bears.

3	**cups all-purpose flour**
¼	**cup granulated sugar**
1	**tablespoon baking powder**
1	**teaspoon salt**
1	**12-ounce can beer**
½	**cup butter, melted**

Preheat oven to 350 degrees. *Grease* an 8½x4½x2½-inch loaf pan.

In a large mixing bowl, *sift* together flour, sugar, baking powder and salt. *Pour* in beer and *stir* until mixed. *Pour* batter into greased loaf pan. *Pour* butter over the top.

Bake at 350 degrees for 45 to 50 minutes until golden brown. *Remove* from oven, *leave* the loaf in the pan on a cooling rack for 15 minutes. *Remove* from pan, *invert* loaf and allow to *cool*.

Makes 1 loaf

Nut Island Cheesecake

Nut Island, in Sitkalidak Strait south of Kodiak, was given this descriptive name by the U.S. Coast and Geodetic Survey in 1928 because of the nutlike shape of the island.

Alaska has no nut trees, so guests of Alaska Wilderness Safaris are lucky that their hosts, Dawn and J.W. Smith, hail from Texas. Every summer they bring fresh Texas pecans to make this wonderful dessert.

Crust:

⅓	cup butter, melted
1½	cups graham cracker crumbs
⅓	cup granulated sugar
½	cup finely chopped pecans
¼	teaspoon cinnamon

Filling:

3	8-ounce packages cream cheese, softened
1½	cups granulated sugar
3	eggs
2	cups sour cream
1	teaspoon vanilla
1	cup finely chopped pecans

Combine melted butter, graham cracker crumbs, sugar, pecans and cinnamon; *press* into a 9-inch springform pan.

Cream the cream cheese and sugar. *Add* eggs one at a time, *beating* after each. *Stir* in sour cream and vanilla, *blending* well. *Stir* in pecans and *pour* into pan. *Bake* at 475 degrees for 10 minutes. *Reduce* heat to 300 degrees and bake 50 minutes or until done. *Turn* off heat and *allow* to cool in oven with door ajar for one hour.

Serves 16

Larry Suiter, owner of Freebird Charters, with a 90-pound Kenai king salmon.

Freebird Charter & Fish Camp

*I*n the mid 1970s, the Kenai River was becoming known worldwide as the premier king salmon fishery in southcentral Alaska. A number of lodges boomed along the banks of this turquoise-hued river. One of the first to offer full-service lodging and accommodations for anglers was Freebird Charter & Fish Camp.

The lodge just south of the Kenai Keys was an idyll of Alaska fishing indulgence. Owners Larry and Sheary Suiter held the philosophy that the Kenai was more than just a meat fishery for big kings. They were one of the first to provide a well-rounded itinerary of everything the Kenai River had to offer—from viewing the nesting birds on islands in Skilak Lake to exploring the seldom-fished backeddies in the upper river for rainbow and char. In the evenings, anglers were pampered with exquisite dining and Alaska hospitality.

This dedication to providing a well-rounded Kenai River experience helped Freebird Charters grow from a one-boat operation to several boats and cabins. It wasn't long before clients had to book a year or two in advance to ensure a spot during the short summer season.

*F*reebird's success was the result of the Suiters' close working relationship. Larry spent years learning the Kenai River and developing fishing skills that made him one of the most successful guides on the Kenai. After a long day of guiding clients, Larry spent the evening hours finding the best holes and learning about the Kenai fishery, an investment that eventually paid off. He produced fish for clients when other guides were throwing their hands up in despair.

Sheary's part in the operation was no less important. She believed that fishing was only a single highlight of the total experience of the Kenai River fishing scene. A happy angler is a well-fed angler, so she devoted long hours to developing recipes and meals that exceeded the area's finest restaurants. Exquisitely prepared salmon, deer roasts, desserts and breakfasts, as well as fresh-baked breakfast goods served on the boat during the fishing day kept anglers coming back, year after year.

Larry saw that state restrictions placed on the Kenai fishery in the 1980s would not allow him to provide the first-class service he wanted for his clients. They sold the lodge in 1985, but the meals, camaraderie, service and fishing they offered are still topics of discussion for anglers experienced in the world's best sportfishing.

As pioneers, Larry and Sheary Suiter set the standard that many Alaska fishing lodge operators now follow, and Freebird has earned a place in the history books as one of Alaska's top fishing lodges.

After experiencing a thrilling morning of catching the huge Kenai kings, guests enjoy a brunch of strawberry waffles, bacon and sausage at the lodge.

While living in Oregon, Sheary decided she didn't want to be a dental hygienist all her life. Larry wanted to come to Alaska to pursue his dream of being a fishing guide. They struck a deal: she would help Larry achieve his goals in exchange for the opportunity to pursue hers: writing. She worked all summer so she could take the winter off to write. During that time she wrote and had her first two books published: young adult romance novels.

"When we lived on the river," says Sheary, "I spent long winter hours pouring over recipe books and magazines. I tested recipes on Larry as well as at a few elaborate dinner parties for friends in Soldotna. It amazed me when I received compliments for my cooking, because when I was growing up it was not something I was dedicated to. In fact, my family was floored when I told them I would be operating a lodge and doing all the cooking. As a

teenager, I was determined that I would not be a cook-and-clean housewife, secretary or teacher. In a round-about way, I became all of the above. I was secretary extraordinaire for Freebird. I cooked and cleaned, and I taught the clients about life in Alaska, its fauna and habitat.

"The main reason I was successful was that I am extremely organized. Each day's kitchen activities were outlined the night before, like giving a dinner party. Right down to the final 15 minutes before serving, each step, planned in exact order, was crossed off as it was completed (for that wonderful feeling of satisfaction).

"I planned each week's main entrees by referring to previous menus recorded in a notebook. I also checked client file cards to see which dishes returning guests had specifically requested last time they were at the lodge. I loved to surprise them with their favorite dishes.

"Everyone appreciated my tasty and eye-appealing meals," said Sheary. "I liked receiving compliments for my efforts."

Sheary sums it up this way, "There is a lot about Freebird Charter & Fish Camp on the Kenai River that I miss. It's a time and place that is gone forever except in the hearts and minds of the guests with whom we shared those six seasons. But the one sure thing about life is that things always change, and so did Freebird."

Freebird Smoked Salmon Dip

*T*his recipe is a great way to use left-over cooked salmon. Serve this delicious appetizer with crackers.

1   **8-ounce package cream cheese, softened**
    dash hot sauce
½   **cup sour cream**
¼   **cup butter or margarine, softened**
2   **teaspoons horseradish**
1   **tablespoon lemon juice**
½   **teaspoon salt**
½   **teaspoon pepper**
½   **teaspoon garlic powder**
1   **tablespoon snipped parsley**
1   **teaspoon grated onion**
¼   **teaspoon dried dillweed**
8   **ounces smoked salmon or one 7¼-ounce can**
    salmon with skin and bones removed
    liquid smoke flavoring

Combine cream cheese, hot sauce, sour cream, butter or margarine, horseradish and lemon juice; *beat* together. *Stir* in salt, pepper, garlic powder, parsley, onion and dillweed. *Add* flaked salmon. If unsmoked canned salmon is used, *add* liquid smoke flavoring to taste. *Mix* and *cover*; *chill*.

Makes 2½ cups

Duck Lake Delights

*A*laska topographic maps show at least 24 uses of the word "duck" to describe creeks, lakes and bays, including a Duck Lake on the Kenai Peninsula.

No matter where you acquire your ducks, this marinade creates tasty appetizers out of them all, from shovelers to mallards. Sheary prefers the longer marinade time for full flavor enhancement.

To make the most of these wild treasures, Sheary fixed this appetizer for guests so they could try a taste of Alaska.

6 - 8 wild duck breasts
    water for soaking duck breasts
1   tablespoon baking soda
1   tablespoon salt
½   cup soy sauce (tamari)
½   cup red wine
2   tablespoons sugar
2   teaspoons finely chopped onion
2   cloves garlic, crushed
1   teaspoon powdered ginger
2   small bay leaves, crushed

Remove wild flavor from the duck breasts by soaking the breasts for 2 to 3 hours in water, baking soda and salt.

Mix soy sauce, wine, sugar, onion, garlic, ginger and bay leaves to form the marinade. **Marinate** the breasts at least 30 minutes, preferably overnight (up to 24 hours).

Broil the breasts 15 to 20 minutes, four inches from heat, *basting* with the marinade sauce every few minutes. **Cook** medium rare. **Slice** thin.

Serves 8—10

Barbequed Salmon

*S*ockeye salmon is an abundant harvest on the Kenai River. In the winter, Sheary would bake, broil or poach the salmon that had been frozen, but in the summer, she preferred fresh fillets cooked on the grill. When guests asked for serving suggestions for their take-home catch of salmon, she demonstrated the following barbeque technique. Serve fish with hot rice and stir-fried vegetables.

Serving-size fillets (8 ounces each) of sockeye, silver or king salmon, marinated in Sterling Secret Sauce, page 179

Preheat gas grill to medium. (Instructions are for gas grills, but are easily applied to charcoal grilling.) *Place* serving-size marinated fish fillets on grill, skin side down.

Close hood of grill, *cook* steaks 7 to 12 minutes, depending on thickness, or until spatula slides easily between fillet and skin. *Turn* fillet, *placing* it back on top of the skin, and *baste* well with preferred sauce. Bottled BBQ sauce is quick and delicious, especially on sockeye salmon. For variety, try the Tarragon-Butter Sauce, page 179.

Cook another 7 to 12 minutes, basting frequently, until fish can be flaked easily with a fork. *Turn* again and *baste* once more. *Garnish* fish with stuffed olives, lemon wedges and sprigs of parsley.

Freebird Charter & Fish Camp

Soldotna Salmon Bake

Soldotna, a small town on the Kenai Peninsula, is the hub for anglers fishing the famous Kenai River for sockeye salmon and the world's largest strain of chinook, or king salmon. Most anglers keep their catch and freeze a supply for winter. This is a quick and easy recipe for preparing left-over cooked salmon.

3   tablespoons butter
3   tablespoons flour
1   teaspoon salt
    dash of pepper
2   cups milk
2   cups cooked salmon, flaked
4   cups cooked and sliced potatoes
½   cup mayonnaise
½   cup shredded sharp cheese
1   teaspoon Worcestershire sauce
1   teaspoon prepared mustard
    paprika

Preheat oven to 350 degrees.

In a saucepan, melt butter and blend in flour, salt and dash of pepper. Gradually add milk and cook, stirring constantly until thickened. Flake salmon and add to mixture. In a shallow baking dish, arrange salmon in alternate layers with potatoes.

Mix mayonnaise, cheese, Worcestershire sauce and mustard. Spread on top of mixture in baking dish. Sprinkle with paprika. Bake at 350 degrees for 30 minutes.

Serves 4

Venison Roast

2   two-pound venison, moose or caribou roasts
    salt
    pepper
    garlic powder
    onion powder
    Salad Supreme
    oregano
    marjoram
    thyme
    basil
    dry mustard
    mild chili powder
3   tablespoons flour
3   tablespoons au jus mix
1   large oven-browning bag
1   cup red wine
1-2 cups water
4   potatoes, scrubbed and quartered
4   carrots, cut into small sticks
3   yellow onions, quartered
1   package dry onion soup mix
2   bay leaves

Preheat oven to 350 degrees. *Sprinkle* roasts generously with salt, pepper, garlic powder, onion powder, Salad Supreme, oregano, marjoram, thyme and basil. *Sprinkle* lightly, on one side only: dry mustard and mild chili powder. *Place* flour and au jus mix into large oven-browning bag; *shake* bag to coat inside. Gradually *add* red wine, *shake* to form gravy-like liquid. Add 1 to 2 cups water for desired amount of gravy.

Place oven bag in 9x13x2-inch baking dish. *Add* roasts, potatoes, carrots and onions. *Sprinkle* dry onion mix soup over roasts, *add* bay leaves.

Close bag with tie, *poke* four small air vents in the top and *bake* at 350 degrees until cooked medium, about 1½ hours. *Remove* from oven and *let stand* 15 minutes. *Slice* roasts into thin slices and *serve* with the gravy and vegetables.

Serves 4—6

Hungry Angler Casserole

*D*uring those cool fall days when Larry was out fishing or hunting for their winter meat supply, Sheary prepared this robust casserole in time for Larry's return. It is also a great meal to serve at streamside. Place the Dutch oven on the coals to simmer before fishing a hatch, and the casserole will be piping hot and ready when all have returned. Serve with hot Goldstream Cornbread, page 297, or Russian Black Bread, page 90.

¼ **cup vegetable oil**
⅓ **cup thinly sliced onion**
½ **cup slivered green pepper**
½ **cup sliced celery**
1 **cup thinly sliced carrots**
1 **pound boneless pork shoulder, cut into 1-inch**
    cubes (or salt pork, bacon or ham)
1 **cup diced tomato (or stewed tomatoes)**
3 **cups water**
1 **teaspoon salt**
    dash of pepper
1½ **cups lentils, well-rinsed**
1 **large bay leaf**
    few grains ground cloves

In a large pot, *heat* oil over medium-high heat; *cook* onion, green pepper, celery and carrots in oil until tender. *Remove* vegetables from pan with a slotted spoon.

Brown pork, *adding* more oil if necessary. *Drain* off fat.

Add vegetables, tomato, water, salt, pepper, lentils, bay leaf and cloves to pork. *Bring* to a boil, *reduce* heat, *cover* and *simmer* for one hour, *stirring* occasionally. *Add* more water if it seems too dry.

Serves 6

Sterling Secret Sauce

*T*his secret sauce is what made barbequed salmon the guests' favorite at Freebird Charter & Fish Camp. Use it to marinate salmon fillets before barbequeing on the grill.

> **soy sauce**
> **brown sugar**
> **water**
> 3 **cloves garlic, crushed**

Fill any container half-full with soy sauce. **Add** brown sugar until liquid fills two-thirds of container. *Fill* remaining one-third of container with water and garlic. Let *set* for one day. *Marinate* salmon fillets in secret sauce at least one hour before barbequeing or broiling.

Tarragon-Butter Sauce

½ **cup butter, melted**
2 **teaspoons lemon juice**
2 **teaspoons seasoned salt**
½ **teaspoon marjoram**
1 **teaspoon tarragon**
¼ **teaspoon garlic powder**
½ **teaspoon lemon peel**
  dash of cayenne

Combine butter, lemon juice, salt, marjoram, tarragon, garlic powder, lemon peel and cayenne. *Stir* and *baste* on salmon while barbequeing.

Makes enough sauce for three pounds of salmon fillets

Tustumena Tomatoes

*W*hen you need to prepare a delightfully light, yet tasty vinaigrette salad, or a colorful garnish for the Super Hole Macaroni Salad, page 181, try this recipe. And if you have trouble pronouncing the name, remember you have to "trust a me na" when it comes to Tustumena.

2	**medium tomatoes**
3	**tablespoons wine vinegar**
1	**teaspoon crushed oregano leaves**
¼	**teaspoon pepper**
¼	**teaspoon dry mustard**
½	**teaspoon onion salt**
1	**garlic clove, crushed**
½	**cup olive oil**
	leaf lettuce, romaine lettuce or fresh spinach
4	**green onions, finely chopped**
1	**tablespoon dried parsley**

Slice tomatoes and *place* in a shallow baking dish. **Mix** together vinegar, oregano, pepper, mustard, onion salt, garlic and olive oil in a jar with a tight lid and *shake*. **Pour** dressing over tomatoes. **Cover** tomatoes and *refrigerate* at least two hours.

Arrange lettuce or spinach leaves around Super Hole Macaroni Salad, page 181, and *place* tomato slices on top of leaves. *Sprinkle* the tomatoes with the green onions and parsley, and *drizzle* the vinaigrette dressing over the tomatoes.

Serves 4

Super Hole Macaroni Salad

*F*ootball fans have their Super Bowl, and Kenai king anglers have their Super Hole—a long deep stretch in the upper Kenai River that yields big kings, including my 56-pound International Gamefish Association world line-class record that appears on the cover of our book, *"How to catch Alaska's Trophy Sportfish."*

This salad, like Super Hole, will keep you coming back for more. Sheary packed this salad for boat lunches because she knew that Super Hole anglers won't give up their fishing spot to return to the lodge for lunch.

3 cups medium macaroni (shell or elbow)
2 quarts water, salted
2 cups cubed Cheddar cheese
1 cup chopped celery
½ cup chopped green pepper
¼ cup chopped red pepper
¼ cup chopped onion
1 cup sour cream
1 cup mayonnaise or salad dressing
¼ cup milk
½ cup sweet pickle relish
4 teaspoons apple cider vinegar
1½ teaspoons prepared mustard
¾ teaspoon salt
 green pepper rings for garnish

Cook macaroni in 2 quarts of boiling salted water until tender. *Drain. Cool. Toss* macaroni with cheese, celery, green and red peppers and onion. In a separate bowl, *combine* sour cream, mayonnaise and milk. *Stir* in relish, vinegar, mustard and salt. *Add* to macaroni, *toss* and *cover. Chill* several hours. *Garnish* with green pepper rings.

When served as a dinner salad, *garnish* with Tustamena Tomatoes, page 180.

Serves 12

English Muffin Bread

$\mathcal{S}$heary served this bread for breakfast, still warm from the oven, with Kenai Cranapple Jam, page 189. It also makes great toast. Guests never fail to appreciate homemade bread and this recipe is so simple, you can serve it often by baking extras for the freezer. It requires no kneading and rises only once, right in the pan.

	cornmeal
3	cups whole wheat flour
2	packages dry yeast
1	tablespoon granulated sugar
2	teaspoons salt
¼	teaspoon baking soda
2	cups milk
½	cup water
3	cups unbleached flour

Grease two 8½x4½x2½-inch loaf pans and *sprinkle* with cornmeal. In a large bowl, *combine* whole wheat flour, yeast, sugar, salt and baking soda.

Heat milk and water on the stove or in microwave until very warm (120 to 130 degrees). Add liquids to dry mixture, *beat* well. *Stir* in unbleached flour to make a stiff batter.

Grease hands. *Divide* dough in half and *place* into loaf pans. *Sprinkle* tops of loaves with cornmeal. *Cover, let rise* in warm place for about 45 minutes.

Bake at 400 degrees for 25 minutes. *Remove* from pans immediately and *cool* on wire racks. Recipe can be doubled.

Makes 2 loaves

Lowbush Cranberry Nut Bread

The low-lying hillsides overlooking the Kenai River are collectively called the "Cranberry Capital of Alaska." Forget the cranberries growing at eye level: those are the highbush variety. Lowbush cranberries are lower than a snake's belly (don't worry...there are no snakes in Alaska), which means you find them hugging the ground. These ruby-red berries are what you need in this treasure chest recipe of flavorful delights.

2	cups all-purpose flour
1½	teaspoons baking powder
½	teaspoon baking soda
1	teaspoon salt
¼	cup shortening or butter, softened
1	cup granulated sugar
¾	cup orange juice
1	tablespoon grated orange rind
1	egg, well-beaten
1	cup lowbush cranberries
½	cup chopped walnuts

Grease a 9x5x3-inch loaf pan. *Preheat* oven to 350 degrees.

Sift together flour, baking powder, baking soda and salt. In a separate bowl, *cream* together shortening or butter and sugar. *Stir* in orange juice, orange rind and egg. *Pour* into dry ingredients and *mix*. *Stir* in cranberries and walnuts. *Pour* into loaf pan and *bake* at 350 degrees for one hour until crust is golden brown and a toothpick inserted in center comes out clean. *Remove* from pan and *cool* on rack.

Makes 1 loaf

Sunrise Cinnamon Bread

A favorite morning boat snack for Sheary's guests. Along with a thermos of hot coffee, it made waiting for those 7 a.m. Kenai kings a pleasure!

2	**packages dry yeast**
½	**cup lukewarm water**
2	**cups milk (or 1 cup scalded water, then add 1 cup evaporated milk)**
1	**cup butter**
1	**cup granulated sugar**
4	**eggs, beaten**
2	**teaspoons salt**
8	**cups flour**
	butter, melted
	granulated sugar
	cinnamon

Grease four 8½x4½x2½-inch loaf pans and large bowl.

Soften yeast in lukewarm water. *Scald* milk, then *stir* butter and sugar into milk. *Cool. Stir* in yeast. *Add* eggs and salt to mixture. *Add* half of flour and *mix* until smooth. **Work** in rest of flour until soft but not sticky (will not be as stiff as bread dough). *Place* in large greased bowl, *cover* with cloth and *let rise* until double. *Punch* down.

Cut dough into small pieces. *Roll* liberally in melted butter, then in sugar and cinnamon. *Place* in loaf pans, *push* pieces gently together and *add* more until pans are half-full. *Let rise* until dough reaches the top of pans. *Bake* at 350 degrees for 30 to 40 minutes.

Makes 4 loaves

Skilak Surprise

Anglers who have fished Skilak Lake during a storm can attest to how deceiving this greenish-blue water can be. The same holds true with this dessert. Don't let the green color fool you. It's a taste treat you'll enjoy.

1	cup flour
½	cup butter
¾	cup finely chopped nuts
1	cup powdered sugar
1½	cups non-dairy whipped topping
1	8-ounce package cream cheese, softened
3	cups milk
2	3½-ounce packages instant pistachio pudding

Preheat oven to 375 degrees. Blend together flour, butter and nuts. Pat on bottom of a 9x13-inch ungreased pan. Bake at 375 degrees for 20 minutes. Cool.

Mix together powdered sugar, whipped topping and cream cheese. Spread on top of first layer. Beat together milk and pistachio pudding until well-blended, 1 to 2 minutes. Spread pudding on as third layer. Refrigerate 4 to 6 hours. Top with additional non-dairy whipped topping.

Serves 6—8

Rhubarb-Peach Cobbler

*L*ocating a good supply of rhubarb is a sure bet in Alaska: almost everyone has a plant or two in the yard. If you usually find rhubarb's flavor too tart, this recipe may just change your mind.

1½   **cups all-purpose flour**
3   **tablespoons sugar**
2   **teaspoons baking powder**
¼   **teaspoon baking soda**
½   **teaspoon salt**
¼   **cup butter or margarine**
1   **cup plain yogurt**
1   **teaspoon vanilla**
1   **29-ounce can sliced peaches, reserve syrup**
¾   **cup granulated sugar**
2   **tablespoons cornstarch**
¾   **teaspoon cinnamon**
    dash salt
3   **cups rhubarb, cut into 1-inch pieces**
1   **teaspoon vanilla**

In a large bowl, *stir* together flour, sugar, baking powder, baking soda and salt. *Cut in* butter or margarine until mixture resembles coarse crumbs; *set* aside.

In another bowl, *mix* yogurt and the first teaspoon of vanilla; *set* aside. *Drain* peaches, *reserving* ⅓ cup syrup. In a saucepan, *mix* the ¾ cup sugar, cornstarch, cinnamon and dash of salt. *Stir* in reserved syrup. *Add* rhubarb. *Cook* and *stir* until thickened and bubbly. *Cook* and *stir* two minutes longer. *Add* peaches and second teaspoon vanilla; *return* to boiling. *Turn* fruit mixture into 3-quart casserole. *Add* yogurt mixture to flour mixture, *blending* well. Immediately *drop* eight mounds of dough on top of hot fruit. *Bake* in a 400-degree oven for 30 minutes. Serve warm with vanilla ice cream.

Serves 8

Blueberry Filling & Topping

2	cups Alaska blueberries
¾	cup water
¼	cup granulated sugar
	dash of salt
¼	teaspoon cinnamon
1	teaspoon lemon juice
1	tablespoon cornstarch
1	tablespoon cold water

Rinse and *pick* over blueberries to remove leaves and woody stems.

In a saucepan, *combine* blueberries, water, sugar, salt and cinnamon. *Cook* and *stir* over medium heat five minutes. *Stir* in lemon juice. *Blend* cornstarch and cold water; *stir* into fruit. *Cook* until thick and bubbly.

Serve as a filling or warm topping for Bountiful Blueberry Crepes, page 188. *Cool* and *spread* on top of Arctic Cheesecake, page 257.

Makes 2 cups

Sheary's Rhubarb-Peach Cobbler, recipe page 186, is best served warm with a generous scoop of ice cream.

Bountiful Blueberry Crepes

*C*repes reach perfection when prepared with wild blueberry filling, page 187. It doesn't matter which variety of blueberry. In Alaska, there is bog blueberry, Alaska blueberry, early blueberry, dwarf blueberry and thin-leaved blueberry—all candidates for this tasty breakfast dish. And best of all, they are a natural source of Vitamin C.

¾   **cup all-purpose flour**
¾   **cup milk**
3   **eggs**
¼   **cup water**
½   **teaspoon salt**
2   **tablespoons butter, melted and cooled**
4   **tablespoons butter, melted, for cooking**
       powdered sugar

To make crepes, *blend* together very quickly in a blender flour, milk, eggs, water and salt. *Add* cooled butter and *blend* again quickly. *Let stand*, covered, for at least an hour.

When ready to cook, *heat* a small omelet pan. *Pour* in a small amount of melted butter, *tilting* pan until bottom is well-coated. *Pour* batter directly from blender to pan, *swirling* pan to coat with a thin layer of the batter. *Cook* the crepe over moderately high heat until the underside is browned, *flip* and *brown* the other side.

Fold each crepe in thirds and stack on an oven-proof plate in a low-temperature oven until all the crepes are made.

Fill with Blueberry Filling, page 187, Kenai Cranapple Jam, page 189 (heated until runny), Raspberry Sauce, page 298, applesauce or whipped cream. *Roll* and *sprinkle* with powdered sugar.

Makes 7 large crepes

Kenai Cranapple Jam

The Kenaitze Indian tribe called the Kenai Peninsula "Yaghanen," an ancient word meaning "the good land."

Lowbush cranberries grew abundantly right outside the back door of Freebird Charter & Fish Camp. Sheary served Cranapple Jam year-round with her English Muffin Bread, page 182, and gave the jam as a delicious and colorful holiday gift.

If you heat the jam in the microwave for a couple minutes, you have instant Cranapple Syrup. It's exceptionally good served with crepes, page 188, Sourdough Pancakes, page 152, or Fog Island French Toast, page 245.

4   **cups lowbush cranberries**
2   **cups apple juice**
1   **package pectin**
7   **cups granulated sugar**

Boil cranberries and apple juice, then *add* pectin. *Return* to a boil, then *add* sugar and *boil* for one minute. *Pour* immediately into hot, sterile jars and *seal*.

Makes 10 half-pints

To lessen the tedious chore of cleaning freshly picked lowbush cranberries, try this invaluable tip passed along by one of Freebird's frequent guests, Mrs. Chris Hovey of Anchorage.

Rather than struggle with pans of water to separate berries from leaves, she spreads an old bath towel on the kitchen counter, nap side up, dumps a cup or two of berries onto the towel, and with the palm of her hand, gently rolls the berries over to either side of the towel; the leaves and stems magically stay put, sticking to the textured nap.

Princeton Hall

*I*f you hanker to experience the finest in saltwater fishing and outdoor recreation amid thousands of miles of scenic beauty, look no farther than the portal to adventure known as Admiralty Island, home port of the Princeton Hall. Fully appreciating Admiralty's potential is much like looking at a vista through opaque glass: You can make out its beauty, but the details are obscure.

It is easy to understand why this island was designated a national monument in 1978 by presidential proclamation. Old coastal rain forests blanket a mainland of glacially carved rock and snow-capped mountains. Sitka blacktail deer graze in alpine pastures and on sandy, shell-covered beaches. Whales perform a marine ballet in misty fjords and secluded bays. Deep-sea rods strain under the weight of 100-pound halibut, and coho salmon aggressively inhale bait and plugs. Sea-run cut-throat and rainbow trout swirl the surface of a wilderness lake, coaxing you into a ''just one more cast'' scenario that may last for hours.

Thanks to the years of charter experience of Dale Anderson, it doesn't take long to appreciate the wonders of Admiralty and its surrounding beauty. Dale owns and operates Admiralty Tours and uses the 65-foot Princeton Hall as a floating lodge.

$\mathscr{B}$uilt in 1941 by the Presbyterian Church in Sitka, Alaska, the Princeton Hall carries with her quite a history. Originally built to be a "mission boat," she replaced an earlier boat, The Princeton, which was lost on a reef in 1938. A family named Hall financed the construction of the new vessel, thus its name, Princeton Hall. Shortly thereafter, the boat was appropriated by the U.S. Navy for military use as a patrol boat operating in the dangerous Icy Straits. It led convoys carrying supplies and transporting prisoners of war through the mine fields. In 1944 the boat was sold back to the church, which operated it as a mission boat for another 15 years. In 1958 the boat was sold into private ownership and in 1981, Juneau attorneys Bill and Kathy Ruddy decided to restore the vessel. It took three shipwrights almost three years of hard labor and more than $500,000 to restore the Princeton Hall. Dale currently operates the vessel for sport anglers interested in experiencing southeast Alaska sportfishing in style.

The Princeton Hall offers comfortable accommodations for six anglers plus crew.

Photo at right: Anchor in a secluded harbor, listen to the seabirds, watch the wildlife and the setting sun. Photo below: Whales are common in the fiords and secluded bays of Southeast Alaska.

When he's not skippering the Princeton Hall, Dale Anderson delights in exploring remote areas of Alaska by float plane. This intertidal glacier is located in Glacier Bay National Park.

She has a large salon with a television, VCR and hot showers. The menu offers Alaska specialties such as "coq au vin" steak, bouillabaisse made from fresh Alaska seafood, and sourdough bread, as well as old standbys of grilled salmon, halibut and steamed king and Dungeness crab. The on-board freezer is available to save the best of your catch for shipping home. Two skiffs with outboards are available for shore excursions to walk on the beach, view and photograph the wildlife or explore each new cove for abundant freshwater fishing opportunities. Fishing is excellent for fresh-from-the-sea coho and pink salmon, and Dolly Varden char. Anglers can expect to catch halibut ranging from 30 to 200 pounds, as well as sea-bright king salmon, rockfish and ling cod. Cutthroat and rainbow trout are also available to the fly fisherman looking for remote streams.

Anglers the world over have delighted in experiencing the many wonders of Admiralty Island aboard this "floating lodge." Anchor in a secluded harbor, be served a gourmet dinner, watch the wildlife and the setting sun, listen to the seabirds, and drink in the intoxicating beauty of the coastal rainforest. You'll soon realize why the Princeton Hall is a favorite choice among anglers. For more information on Princeton Hall, see page 304.

Dale Anderson, *Cook and skipper, Princeton Hall*

Dale Anderson is truly a jack of all trades. This 40-year-old Juneau resident has worked as a real estate salesman; owned and operated two camera and jewelry stores, a custom picture framing shop and art gallery; and is an art conservator (restores old paintings).

But Dale's first love is sharing Alaska with others. As skipper and head cook of the Princeton Hall, Dale stays busy from 5 a.m. to 9 p.m, catering to the needs of each party of six anglers.

"Meals are very important aboard the Princeton Hall because they reflect the overall quality of the trip," he said. "One can't have a perfect experience in the Alaska wilderness without good eating."

Anglers can expect a constant stream of fresh seafood aboard the Princeton Hall. "We catch our own seafood the day we serve it," he said. "Fresh crab, salmon or halibut are usually brought on board a few hours before the evening meal."

Dale's cooking skills started at his mother's apron strings. "My mom was an excellent cook," he remembers. "I always helped prepare family meals. But when I managed Admiralty Inn, I fully learned the nuances of making a memorable meal presentation."

Most of his food preparation and presentation style comes from working with over a dozen fine chefs associated with Admiralty Inn and Admiralty Tours.

As part of his presentation, Dale anchors the boat each evening in a scenic wilderness area. He has many secret spots, each with its own special beauty or attractions. "Guests are mesmerized by the glaciers looming around them," he said. "They observe the huge ice chunks calving and crashing into the ocean, and look over the side of the boat to watch the seals and salmon. "I enjoy taking guests to a location away from the crowds, personally serving them meals and telling them about the area's wonders," Dale said.

"The closer we travel to Glacier Bay National Park, the fewer trees we observe—until there is nothing but rock and ice and our choice of 16 tidewater glaciers. It's a trip back through time, from the current age to the remnants of the Ice Age. Best of all, we enjoy eating off the bounty of the land and sea during the entire voyage."

Dale plans his meals around the pre-trip questionnaire he sends to his clients, in which they list likes and dislikes, and indicate any dietary considerations. Dale says, "I tailor the menu to fit the individuals, as well as ask them each day what they would prefer. For instance, they may be on a low-fat diet, but decide to splurge one night and ask for some deviled butter. They devour it," he says with a smile. Dale says that when surrounded by such impressive beauty and good fishing, people eat heartily. And when they eat heartily, that means he's doing his job. For him, there is no finer reward.

Big Dipper Crab

The Big Dipper means several things to Alaskans: it's an integral part of the design in our state flag, it aids sportsmen in finding the North Star during the winter months, and it describes a wonderful dip for Dungeness crab found in southeast Alaska waters. Dale Anderson harvests these crab in virtually all the sheltered coves where he anchors each evening, and serves them fresh within the hour to his guests.

1	**cup sour cream**
1	**8-ounce package cream cheese, softened**
3	**green onions, chopped**
¼	**green pepper, chopped**
¼	**teaspoon salt**
¼	**teaspoon lemon pepper**
¼	**teaspoon garlic salt**
1½	**cups Dungeness crab, cracked and cleaned**

Blend together sour cream and cream cheese until smooth. **Pour** into a saucepan and *stir* in onions, green pepper, salt, lemon pepper, garlic salt and crab. **Heat** on low heat until warm or hot. **Serve** dip in a fondue dish to keep warm. This is also good as a cold dip.

Makes 3 cups

Dungeness, king or snow crab is harvested fresh each evening to serve guests aboard the Princeton Hall.

Buttered Up Dungeness

There is only person who can eat more crab than Dale Anderson, and that is his good friend and fishing buddy, Don Jergler. For many years running, Don and his friends have come to enjoy God's Creation and partake of the bounty of the sea. You ought to see the smile come across Don's face when the skiff returns with pots teeming with Dungeness. Dale keeps the saucepan hot to satisfy the demand for more deviled butter as Don and company devour the crab.

This is one of those meals where you need to roll up your sleeves and go for the gusto!

1   **cup butter**
1   **pinch cayenne pepper**
2   **pinches lemon pepper**
2   **teaspoons Dijon mustard**
2   **teaspoons wine vinegar**

In a saucepan *melt* the butter, *stir* in cayenne and lemon pepper, mustard and vinegar. *Set* aside while steaming the crab.

Serves 4

Steamed Crab

water for boiling crab
2   **bay leaves**
    Spike
    Dungeness crab, cleaned and cracked

In a large deep pot, *boil* enough water to steam the crab, *leaving* room at the top so the pot does not boil over once the water gets rolling. **Add** a couple of bay leaves and, to your taste, a portion of a spice called "Spike." When the water is at full boil, *place* the crab in the pot and *boil* for 9 minutes.

Serve immediately with deviled butter on the side.

Icy Strait BBQ Halibut

*D*ale has a reputation for guiding anglers to barn-door-sized halibut of 100 to 200 pounds. A fish this size will yield anywhere from 60 to 140 pounds of boneless, white fillets that more and more people are preferring over steak. This is enough halibut for a block party barbeque when you return home. Dale says if you use this recipe, "Be certain you've saved a few fillets for yourself, because there won't be any leftovers."

5	**pounds of halibut fillets**
2	**sticks of butter**
2	**onions, sliced**
2	**tomatoes, diced**
2	**tablespoons pressed garlic**
1	**lemon**
5	**tablespoons fine white wine**
3	**tablespoons grated Parmesan cheese**
1	**cup fresh mushrooms**
2	**tablespoons butter**
	dash of garlic powder
1	**tablespoon white wine**

Cut the fillets into serving portions and *place* on a piece of heavy duty foil large enough to fold it over the top and seal so that the juices from the fish can steam the fillet while cooking. Slice the butter. Place butter slices, along with the sliced onion, tomatoes and garlic, on top of the fillets. Squeeze the juice of the lemon over the top. Sprinkle with the wine and Parmesan cheese.

Seal the foil over the fish and *place* in your preheated BBQ grill. Dale likes to add a few green sticks of alder to the hot coals just before putting the fish on.

Let the fish simmer over the coals for about 10 to 12 minutes, then *open* the seal on the foil to allow a touch of the unique alder-smoke flavor to seep into the fillet. Cook with the foil open for another 8 to 10 minutes.

This is the most critical time, because the cook must *test* the fillet to make sure it is perfect for those who have gathered to savor the moment. The key is to not over-cook...let the fish *cook* just until it loses its shiny translucence and is white throughout.

While the fish is cooking on the grill, *prepare* the fresh mushrooms, *sauteing* them in two tablespoons butter. **Add** a dash of garlic powder and a tablespoon of wine. *Top* fish with the lightly sauteed mushrooms.

Have the rest of the meal preparation completed, be-cause you need to *serve* this immediately, hot and steaming.

Serves 10—12

The advantage of living aboard a floating lodge such as the Princeton Hall is that anglers can fish whenever they want just by walking up to the railing and dropping their line over the side.

Poor Man's Lobster

The East Coast's claim to fame is lobster, which isn't available in Gulf of Alaska waters. With the right preparation, the meat of the halibut produces a variety of tastes. This recipe, claims Dale, can fool lobster aficionados into thinking they have just tasted fresh "Alaska lobster." Substitute burbot when halibut is unavailable.

½   **cup granulated sugar**
¼   **cup salt**
4   **quarts water**
4   **pounds fresh halibut, cut into 2-inch squares**
    fresh chopped parsley or dill
    salt and pepper
    melted butter

In a large pot, *dissolve* sugar and salt in water and *bring* to a rolling boil. *Place* the halibut chunks into the water all at once. When they rise to the surface, *remove* from the water, *drain* and *keep* in warming oven until ready to serve. Allow fish to cook until transparent look is gone.

Dust with fresh chopped parsley or dill, salt and pepper. *Serve* with a melted butter flavored to your tastes, Pepper Point Butter, page 26, Deviled Butter, page 195, Drawn Butter, page 211, or a seafood cocktail sauce.

Serves 6—8

20-Fathom Halibut

This recipe begins with a fresh-caught halibut hauled up from at least 20 or more fathoms (120-feet-plus for you landlubbers). For many anglers, the only way to prepare deep-water halibut is deep fried in beer batter. Expect your guests to go overboard when it comes to second and third requests for more halibut. Dale likes to serve these crispy golden nuggets alongside baked potato wedges and fresh corn on the cob.

2   cups all-purpose flour
1½ teaspoons salt
½   teaspoon lemon pepper
¼   teaspoon garlic powder
1   tablespoon paprika
1   tablespoon parsley flakes
2   tablespoons butter, melted
1   12-ounce bottle of beer
4   eggs, separated
3   pounds fresh halibut, cut into 2-inch squares
    grease or cooking oil for frying fish
    flour

Sift together flour, salt, lemon pepper, garlic powder and paprika. Stir in parsley, butter, beer and egg yolks. Let stand 1½ hours at room temperature. Whip egg whites until stiff. Fold stiff egg whites into the batter.

Heat grease or cooking oil in a deep fryer. The grease needs to be maintained at 300 to 325 degrees. Flour individual pieces of fish and dip into the batter. This will help the batter stick to the fish while frying. Drop the pieces into hot grease and fry a few at a time for approximately 4 to 5 minutes or until golden brown and the pieces float to the surface. Drain fried fish on paper towels.

Serves 6

Shaker Spinach Toss

Small king salmon are referred to as shakers. When hooked, they thrash the surface of the water while shaking their heads—not too much, but just enough to alert the angler. This behavior describes the necessary technique to properly toss this simple, yet tasty salad. This salad complements fresh Alaskan seafood such as Dungeness crab, scallops or famous Frederick Sound shrimp.

6	cups fresh spinach, torn in bite-sized pieces
4	oranges or tangerines, peeled and sectioned
6	slices bacon, crisp-cooked, drained and crumbled
1	cup peanuts, chopped

In a salad bowl, *combine* torn spinach, orange sections, bacon and peanuts. **Add** desired portion of either a French or Italian dressing over the orange-spinach mixture, *tossing* lightly to mix.

Serves 5—6

The scenery in southeast Alaska is perhaps the most spectacular in the world. Tall, jagged mountains and deep-blue lakes are encircled by lush forests of Sitka spruce and Lodgepole pine. Gin-clear streams flow from the mountaintops where snowfields linger most of the summer.

Southeast Huckleberry Pie

*R*ed and black huckleberries, along with blueberries and bilberries, are closely related fruits belonging to the heath family. The huckleberries are located primarily in southeast Alaska. To make this delicious pie, look for berries growing in open meadows and on the rocky hillsides of Hoonah Sound and Chatham Strait.

Prepare your best pastry for a two-crust 9-inch pie. Set aside.

2	tablespoons cornstarch
¼	cup water or fruit juice
1	cup granulated sugar
5	cups fresh Chatham Strait red huckleberries
3	tablespoons grated lemon peel
½	teaspoon nutmeg
	dash of salt
1	tablespoon lemon juice
2	tablespoons butter

Mix cornstarch with water or fruit juice until very smooth, then *blend* in the sugar until dissolved.

In a separate bowl, *combine* huckleberries, lemon peel, nutmeg and salt. *Stir* in the cornstarch mixture and *let stand* 15 minutes before putting it into the pie shell.

Line a 9-inch pie plate with pastry and *fill* with huckleberry mixture. *Sprinkle* with lemon juice and *dot* with butter. **Cover** pie with top crust or a lattice. **Cut** slits for escape of steam. **Seal** edges well so juices don't run out.

Bake pie in 450-degree oven for 10 minutes, then *reduce* heat to 350 degrees and *bake* for 35 to 40 minutes.

Remove from the oven, *cool* until sauce sets up. *Serve* with a scoop of honey vanilla ice cream on the side.

Makes one 9-inch pie

Blue Mouse Cove Delight

According to Dale, Blue Mouse Cove in Glacier Bay National Park is aptly named because there is so much ice in the water and on the beaches even the mice are blue from the cold. Dale, however, is never blue when he enters this cove. He's happy because he is about to collect a bucket full of tiny, sweet, succulent fruit from a secret patch.

Picture yourself lounging on the aftdeck of the Princeton Hall, having just finished a savory meal of fresh Alaska seafood, and Dale shares this secret delight with you—fresh wild Alaska strawberries, served with cream and chocolate—as you watch the sun slip behind the glacier-rimmed peaks.

2   **ounces of semi-sweet chocolate, chopped into small pieces**
2   **cups heavy cream**
2   **tablespoons powdered sugar**
4   **cups wild Alaska strawberries**

Line a baking sheet with wax paper. In a small microwave bowl, *melt* the chocolate in the microwave oven at medium power for 30 seconds. *Stir* and *microwave* for another 30 seconds, or until melted.

Spread chocolate as thin as possible on the prepared baking sheet. *Place* in the freezer until chocolate is hard, about 15 minutes. Meanwhile, in a medium bowl, *whip* the cream with the powdered sugar just until cream has thickened.

Peel the chocolate off the wax paper; *crumble* or *sliver* the chocolate with a knife.

Rinse and *dehull* berries. *Spoon* the berries into six dessert dishes or wine glasses. *Top* with the thick cream and *garnish* with the chocolate slivers. *Serve* immediately or *refrigerate* for up to 30 minutes.

Serves 6

Admiralty Omelet

Admiralty Island is one of the top-ranking islands for fresh and saltwater fishing within the Alexander Archipelago. This omelet ranks first for breakfast requests among Princeton Hall guests, and it gets them rarin' to go for a full day of fishing in Admiralty Island waters.

1	**tablespoon butter**
3	**eggs, briskly beaten with whisk**
½	**cup crabmeat or smoked salmon**
	sour cream
3	**tablespoons fresh mushrooms**
2	**tablespoons chopped scallions**
¼	**cup white or yellow cheese**

In a small omelet pan *melt* butter over medium heat. R*otate* the pan as you *add* the eggs so they spread evenly. P*lace* seafood, a touch of sour cream, mushrooms and part of scallions on half of the egg mixture. F*old* the omelet over, *sprinkle* cheese and the remaining scallions on top, and *allow* cheese to melt.

S*erve* immediately.

Serves 1

Painter Creek Lodge

here are several reasons why anglers return often to the Painter Creek wilderness area. They can wet a line in a seldom-fished stream, or walk on mountaintops that have previously known only the footprints of caribou and wolves. Salmon blacken the bottoms of rivers and brown bear tracks criss-cross nearby sandy beaches. Glaciers surround active volcanoes that vent wisps of steam like smoke signals. Nearby mountaintops—scarred an ash-brown from a series of volcanic eruptions since the turn of the century—are skirted with lush-green wraps of inpenetrable alder brush.

This area remains a remote wilderness because Painter Creek has a complex line of defenses that keep out all but the most determined anglers. Untrekable expanses of muskeg and swamp prevent foot or all-terrain-vehicle traffic from the closest city, King Salmon, over 120 miles to the north. Conflicting weather patterns—from the Pacific Ocean on one side and the Bering Sea on the other—create dangerous flying conditions. Within minutes, a clear sky can metamorphose into drizzle, fog and zero visibility. But the old saying, "All is calm in the eye of the storm," pertains particularly to Painter Creek. Situated between two protective mountain ranges, Painter Creek often basks in the sun while the surrounding areas experience some of the most inclement weather on the Alaska coast.

*D*on't expect to see drop-in fishermen at Painter Creek Lodge. The lodge uses the only gravel runway in the area, and nearby creeks are too treacherous for float plane landings. With the lack of landing strips, pilots from King Salmon and Anchorage hesitate to venture into this area. The area has an interesting history. In 1923, R.H. Sargent, of the U.S. Geological Survey, named the stream after his cook, Al Painter.

In the 1960s, companies exploring for oil and precious metals built the main structure and equipment sheds to serve as a base for an exploration camp. The story has it that test drilling at Yantarni Bay opened up a vein of volcanic magma. That site was eventually abandoned, along with the exploratory operation in the area.

Several Alaskan investors purchased the camp in the early 1980s and named it Painter Creek Lodge. After extensive remodeling, the complex now consists of a spacious main lodge, equipment sheds and several modern guest cabins with indoor plumbing. A gravel road for four-wheelers and trucks winds a mile through tundra and cottonwood stands to Painter Creek.

Author Adela Batin enjoys a mid-day break with country music superstar Johnny Cash and son John Carter Cash. John is relating a colorful rendition to the two about the big king he caught.

Several riverboats transport guests to Painter Creek and connecting rivers for fishing. The lodge also uses wheeled-equipped aircraft to fly clients to the remote beaches of the Gulf of Alaska or Bering Sea to fish for chum and silver salmon. Many anglers choose to stay in one of several remote camps, or to float one of the area's rivers for a variety of fish species, or to take a sightseeing trip to the hot springs at the base of Mount Chiginagak. Perhaps the most popular fishing/adventure destination is a journey into Aniakchak Crater.

"We land on a 2½-mile-long lake in the center of the 2,000-foot-deep, six-mile-wide crater," says lodge manager Joe Maxey. "Anglers can expect to catch char, Dolly Varden and sockeye salmon, plus explore explosion pits, cinder cones and hot springs." He says there's no immediate fear of the volcano erupting. The last recorded activity was a minor eruption in 1935.

The area is also home to Alaska-Yukon moose and brown bear, and some of the largest concentrations of waterfowl in North America. Expect to see caribou migrating through camp, or lynx chasing ground squirrels on the trail outside the lodge. It's common to see caribou, moose and brown bear around the lodge.

Maxey relates an interesting story about uninvited guests the lodge occasionally receives. "We were talking with the guests in one of the cabins, when one of the guide's dogs began barking. The guide opened the window, yelled at the dog to stop barking, and we resumed our discussion. But the dog kept barking. When the guide opened the door and looked outside, he saw a large brown bear eating the dog's food. The bear, seeing the guide in the doorway, grabbed the dog's dish in his mouth and ran off into the brush."

Painter Creek invigorates the soul like no other. The magnitude of its beauty can only be surpassed by the severity of its inclement weather, which allows no second chances for the foolhardy. One can't help wishing for Painter Creek to stay "as is" for generations to come. It is a last bastion for the free spirit to enjoy true wilderness sportfishing adventure at its finest.

For more information on Painter Creek, see page 305.

Robert Griffith, *Chef, Painter Creek Lodge*
Barbara Griffith, *Baker, Painter Creek Lodge*

Barb grew up along the Oregon coast, and began fishing at age three. Always active in the outdoors, she began hunting at eight years old.

In 1975, mutual friends in Eugene, Oregon, introduced Barb to Bob Griffith, who shared her love of the outdoors and cooking. Their dates were always dinner dates where they would cook for each other.

Bob, tired of working as a logger, got into the cooking business through his brother, an executive chef at Lake Tahoe. At his brother's invitation he moved to California as sous chef at Smith River Inn, where they had good fishing. Bob spent the summer there, but went back to logging in Oregon to make more money. To keep his hand in cooking, he continued chef duties on Sundays.

Hearing that cooks in Alaska made a lot of money, Bob headed north. His move to Alaska took him to some of the finest hotels. In Sitka, he worked for two years as a dinner chef at the Sheffield Hotel.

In 1979, Bob moved to Anchorage and was a dinner cook at the Sheraton Hotel, where he helped open Josephine's, a premier fine dining restaurant. Very talented people on the kitchen staff taught him northern Italian cuisine. After short work stints in both Fairbanks and Valdez, Bob returned to Anchorage and ran the kitchen at the Crow's Nest in the Hotel Captain Cook.

In 1981, Bob invited Barb to move to Anchorage. They married, bought a house and settled down. At the Hotel Captain Cook, Bob worked under Jens Hansen, a master chef from Denmark. Barb, who had never cooked professionally but had experimented with recipes, sharpened her culinary skills by doing prep work for Bob at the Crow's Nest.

When the oil spill hit Prince William Sound in 1989, Bob and Barb headed for Valdez, where they cooked for 1,000 people twice a day, plus packed lunches. They cooked on navy ships converted to clean-up ships for the oil spill.

Bob and Barb began working for Painter Creek Lodge in July 1991 as chef and baker, respectively. They wanted to be around people with interests similar to theirs—fishing and hunting. Having successfully hunted Alaska big game, including a near-record caribou, Barb now has her sights set on an assistant guide's license.

The Griffiths enjoy lodge life. "However," says Bob, "I had to get used to being in contact with guests. As a restaurant chef, I never talked to the people I cooked for. I felt self-conscious at first, but now I enjoy the interaction. It's good for the ego to get positive feedback from the people eating your food. It's nice to know they're enjoying their meal."

Bob and Barb also enjoy the fact that management gives them a free hand. Bob suggested using the economical bypass mail system to transport food to the lodge. This system circumvents regular mail routing and guarantees delivery within 36 hours. At 20 cents a pound for shipments over 1,000 pounds, it is the most cost-effective way to fly in food. A food shopper in Anchorage buys fresh produce and mails it to the lodge once a week.

The lack of stress at Painter Creek Lodge is particularly attractive to Bob and Barb. "Everyone here is on vacation," Barb says. "It's always a happy, relaxed environment. People are here because they want to be. For us, too, working here is like being on vacation. It's much easier to cook for 10 clients at a time than 1,000 people!"

The following guest comments were taken from the Painter Creek Lodge guest book:

"To all of you at Painter Creek,

I can't describe in words the overwhelming sense of gratitude I have for you as hosts to my first introduction to one of the last frontiers. Every day Alaska gently demanded respect from me and I have never been so humbled. There is a most unusual combination of serene and savage power here that I can only imagine what it must be like to live here — to tap the pulse.

Thank you all for the laughs and food and flight and warmth. Where else but in this wilderness could one take a steaming hot shower with a belly full of hot food?

Love to you here — Hope to see you again. That little tent of blue which prisoners call the sky."

Cathi E. Figg

"Probably the best vacation of my life! The food is outstanding, the scenery truly breathtaking, and the fishing without comparison."

Bryan Taylor

Shelikof Salmon Bits

Shelikof Strait is the 20-mile-wide water passage between the Alaska Peninsula and Kodiak Island. It extends 150 miles southwest from the Barren Islands. The strait was named for Grigori Ivanovich Shelikov, a Siberian shipbuilder and merchant. Shelikov has justly been called the founder of the Russian colonies on this continent. He formed several partnerships in the fur trading business. They led to his expedition across the Pacific in 1783 to establish a permanent settlement to protect and advance the interests of Russian fur hunters and traders. His expedition led to the first permanent Russian settlement of Alaska in 1784.

Much to the delight of anglers, Shelikof Strait hosts large runs of salmon that enter the many streams along the Alaska Peninsula. At day's end, anglers savor their freshly-caught salmon prepared in this manner.

1	**teaspoon dried parsley flakes or dillweed**
1½	**teaspoons lemon pepper**
1½	**teaspoons seasoning salt**
1	**cup all-purpose flour**
1	**2-pound salmon fillet**
2	**eggs, beaten**
1½	**cup bread crumbs**
	vegetable oil
	ranch dressing
	hollandaise sauce

Mix parsley flakes or dillweed, lemon pepper, seasoning salt and flour in a bowl. Cut salmon into bite-size pieces, trimming off gray (fatty) flesh.

Roll salmon bits in flour; dip in beaten egg; roll in bread crumbs. Refrigerate for one hour.

Heat oil to medium-high and deep fry fish. Drain salmon on paper towels. Serve hot with ranch dressing or hollandaise sauce for dipping.

Serves 4—6

How to Cook Fish

Fish is a very delicate meat and should be treated that way in handling and cooking. The most effective way to maintain color, flavor and moisture in fish is to either poach or bake it.

Poaching Fish

When poaching fish, use a court bouillon made by boiling carrots, onions, celery and herbs in the poaching water. Some favorite herbs for fish are dill, basil, bay leaves and thyme. When poaching fish, place the fish in a sieve or perforated pan before submerging. This makes it easier to retrieve the fish from the water.

It is important to not overcook the fish. *Bring* the water to a boil. *Submerge* the fish—an 8- to 10-ounce portion about 1 to 1½ inches thick—and *reduce* heat. *Steep* the fish uncovered for 5 to 6 minutes before checking with a fork. You should be able to separate the muscle fibers without breaking up the portions. Remember, fish will continue to cook after it is removed from the water so it is better to undercook than overcook. Always use fresh ingredients and again, *don't overcook*. All the spices and sauces in the world won't cover up overcooked food.

Baking Fish

Coat bottom of cookie sheet with butter. *Roll* fillets in butter, *season* to taste with herbs and spices. *Pour* enough white wine around the fish to create steam while fish is baking. *Place* fish in 500-degree oven for 8 to 10 minutes.

When baking fish, the key is to use high heat. Whether baking steaks or fillets, it's important to keep moisture in the fish. Use white wine and drawn butter under the fish to keep it moist and add flavor. Drawn butter, page 211, works well because it has a higher burning point than whole butter, and a more distinctive flavor. When cooked, the fish should be firm but not dry. Muscle fibers should separate easily with a fork, and the meat should have a translucent appearance. It is best to undercook the fish a bit, since the residual heat will continue to cook the fish after it is removed from the oven.

Orange-Glazed Arctic Char

1	**large orange**
½	**cup dry white wine**
½	**cup all-purpose flour**
½	**teaspoon seasoning salt**
½	**teaspoon dillweed**
1	**9-ounce arctic char fillet**
2	**tablespoons olive or vegetable oil**
1	**teaspoon flour**

Squeeze juice from orange into cup; *strain* juice to remove seeds. *Add* equal amount of wine and *stir. Set* aside.

Mix flour, seasoning salt and dillweed in a paper sack. *Cut* fillet in half. *Add* fillet pieces and *shake* to coat. *Heat* oil in skillet and *fry* fillets until golden brown on one side; *turn* over.

Pour juice/wine mixture over browned side of fish. *Cover* pan and *steam cook* fish no longer than one minute. *Remove* fish, *place* on serving dish and *keep* warm.

Simmer liquid until it thickens, *adding* one teaspoon flour if necessary. *Stir* continuously until it becomes a nice glaze. *Dip* spoon into glaze and *turn* over. If the back of the spoon is glazed, the sauce is thick enough.

Pour orange glaze over fish fillets.

Serves 2

Drawn Butter

Put butter in pan and *melt* on low heat until butter separates. When the milk solids come to the surface, *skim* off with ladle. *Let sit*; any remaining solids will settle on the bottom. *Ladle* off clear oil. *Cook* with the clear oil, which is the drawn butter.

Dough Guides

$\mathcal{D}$ ough Guides are more than just a tasty little bread. At Painter Creek Lodge, they often serve as a tongue-in-cheek indicator for real-life guides. Guides carefully watch how clients approach these breads. If the client tears them apart in an angry fashion, the guide knows he had better place the client into some good fishing, or risk being torn apart by the client. Fortunately, at Painter Creek the fishing is usually good, and anglers only tear apart dough guides in a hurry so they can layer them with jam and butter or dip them in honey.

2   **cups warm water**
2½   **packages dry yeast**
2   **tablespoons granulated sugar**
1   **teaspoon salt**
2   **tablespoons vegetable oil**
5-5½ **cups white all-purpose flour (or half**
       wheat, half white)
       vegetable oil for frying

Grease a large bowl and cookie sheet. *Pour* warm water into another bowl. *Stir* yeast, sugar and salt into warm water until dissolved. *Stir* in oil. *Add* flour, one cup at a time, *mixing* thoroughly between additions. *Knead* dough on a floured board at least 10 minutes. *Place* in a greased bowl and *let rise* until double. *Beat* down and *shape* into balls. *Flatten* each ball and *place* about 1½ inches apart on a greased cookie sheet and *let rise* until half again in size.

Fill deep fryer half-full with vegetable oil and *heat* to 300 degrees. Carefully *lift* dough guide and *place* in hot oil. *Cook* until golden brown, *turn* and *cook* other side until golden brown, being careful to cook thoroughly but not burn.

Drain on paper towels and *serve* hot.

Makes 24

Photo at right: The evening meal at Painter Creek Lodge is a joyful, yet informative, recap of the day's angling experiences at varied locations.

Aniakchak Surprise Bread

A highlight of Painter Creek Lodge is a visit to Aniakchak Crater, a six-mile-wide dormant volcano that requires an entire day to explore. Take your fishing rods on this adventure, because you'll find a surprise in the crater. Surprise Lake, located in the crater's center, offers good fishing for char and sockeye salmon. Another surprise is when you open your lunch and find this wonderful carrot-pineapple bread made by Barb Griffith. For a unique treat, warm the bread on the hot cinders in this volcanic caldera.

3	**cups flour**
1	**teaspoon cinnamon**
1	**teaspoon baking soda**
1	**teaspoon salt**
½	**teaspoon baking powder**
1	**cup granulated sugar**
1	**cup brown sugar**
1	**cup vegetable oil**
1	**tablespoon vanilla**
3	**eggs**
1½	**cups crushed pineapple, drained**
1½	**cups shredded carrots**

Preheat oven to 350 degrees. *Grease* and *flour* two loaf pans. *Set* aside.

Sift together the flour, cinnamon, baking soda, salt and baking powder in a bowl.

In another bowl, *beat* together the white and brown sugars, oil, vanilla and eggs. *Stir* in pineapple and carrots. *Add* dry ingredients and *blend* well.

Bake at 350 degrees for one hour or until toothpick inserted in center comes out clean.

Makes 2 loaves

Spike Camp Bread

*P*ainter Creek pilots reach remote fishing spike camps by landing their bush planes on wilderness saltwater beaches. Due to weight limitations of the aircraft, anglers can only pack must-have items. While the menu for the night usually includes freshly grilled silver salmon, the cooks pack lots of this chocolate-banana bread for dessert and on-stream snacks when anglers need quick energy to battle acrobatic silver salmon.

3	eggs
1	cup vegetable oil
1	tablespoon vanilla
1	cup granulated sugar
1	cup brown sugar
3	cups flour
1	teaspoon cinnamon
¼	teaspoon cloves or nutmeg
1	teaspoon baking soda
½	teaspoon salt
¼	teaspoon baking powder
2	one-ounce squares bakers chocolate, melted
2½	cups mashed over-ripe bananas (6 bananas)
½	cup chopped walnuts

Preheat oven to 350 degrees. *Grease* and *flour* two 8½x4½x2½-inch loaf pans. *Set* aside.

In a large bowl, *beat* eggs and *blend* in oil, vanilla and sugars. *Beat* well.

Sift together flour, cinnamon, cloves or nutmeg, baking soda, salt and baking powder. *Stir* dry ingredients into mixture alternately with chocolate and bananas. *Beat* well. *Stir* in nuts. *Pour* into loaf pans and *bake* at 350 degrees for one hour, or until toothpick inserted in the center comes out clean.

Makes 2 loaves

Chocolate Pecan Pie

1   tablespoon soft margarine or butter
2   cups minced pecans
12   ounces chocolate chips
4   eggs
1   cup pancake syrup
2   teaspoons flour
½   teaspoon salt
2   teaspoons vanilla
½   cup pecan halves

Preheat oven to 350 degrees.

Spread butter on the sides and bottom of a 9-inch deep dish pie pan. *Cover* the sides and bottom of pan with the minced pecans.

Melt the chocolate chips in the top of a double boiler over hot water (not boiling).

In a deep bowl, *combine* eggs, syrup, flour, salt and vanilla and *beat* well. *Stir* in melted chocolate and *beat* with an electric mixer at high speed until well-blended. *Pour* into prepared pie pan, *decorate* top with pecan halves.

Bake at 350 degrees for 30 to 40 minutes. *Serve* warm or cold, *topped* with whipped cream.

Serves 8—10

Tony Oswald, at right, gives pointers to anglers rebuilding their inventory of flies depleted by the aggressive Dolly Varden char and silver salmon at Painter Creek.

Cicely Apple Crisp

*C*icely, the fictional town in the television series "Northern Exposure," actually does exist in Alaska. But it's not in the form of a town. Lake Cicely is two-tenths of a mile long, and is about 10 miles southwest of Kodiak. There's nothing fictional about the taste of this sour cream apple crisp; surprisingly simple, yet delicious.

Filling:

6	**cups peeled and sliced apples (5 large apples)**
1	**cup sour cream**
1	**cup granulated sugar**
3	**tablespoons cornstarch**
1	**teaspoon cinnamon**
2	**eggs**

In a large bowl, *mix* together apples, sour cream, sugar, cornstarch, cinnamon and eggs. *Set* aside.

Topping:

3	**cups quick oats**
1	**cup granulated sugar**
½	**cup brown sugar**
1	**cup sliced almonds**
1	**cup butter, melted**

Mix together oats, sugars and nuts. *Pour* in melted butter and *stir* until all dry ingredients are coated. *Pour* filling into 9x9-inch baking dish. *Spread* evenly with topping. *Bake* at 350 degrees for one hour.

Serves 6—8

Kachemak Bay Wilderness Lodge

*O*n the shore of China Poot Bay, about 40 minutes by boat from Homer, is Kachemak Bay Wilderness Lodge. Surrounded by huge spruce trees and tidepools teeming with life, the lodge offers guests the opportunity to enjoy the natural wonders of Alaska.

Kachemak Bay Lodge is an Alaska adventure lodge, where fishing is only one of many "commune with Nature" activities. Hike into the high glacial mountain country, watch mountain goats and black bear, and bask in the cool mist of a cascading waterfall. Photograph huge coastal brown bear at McBride's Chenik Brown Bear Wilderness Camp, or explore the myriad tidal pools filled with bright sea anemones, shrimp, crab and nine edible mollusks including blue mussels. Dolly Varden and salmon are caught from nearby spits or from charter boats.

The lodge, owned by Diane and Mike McBride, has earned awards from The Hideaway Report, as well as being listed as "America's Best Wilderness Lodge" in *America's Best* 100. The McBrides have hosted dignitaries and celebrities from around the world, including Prince Ranier and a German count and countess.

The attractions are many. From the time you set foot on the dock, the lodge radiates "Alaskana." Driftwood, glass Japanese fishing floats, and hemp ropes and colorful flower boxes lead you along trails to the main lodge, a handsome log structure meticulously maintained. A stone fireplace and convenient nearby are focal points for guests wanting to learn more about the natural wonders of the area.

A fresh fruit basket, wine, chocolates and fresh flowers welcomes your arrival. Accommodations include private cabins with electricity, modern bathrooms, telephone, solarium and hot tub. The sod-roofed Finnish sauna will soothe your body and soul at day's end.

The bed in our room was unique. Four entire driftwood trees, complete with the roots, had been turned upside down to form a poster bed. The root system of the trees supported the ceiling of the bedroom. To form a canopy, a fish net was strung between the posts, and starfish and shells were intertwined in the net. This was rustic elegance at its finest.

Meals at Kachemak Bay are as delightful as the surroundings. Desserts garnished with wild blueberries or salmonberries, fresh-baked breads, seafood quiches and soups are served in an elegant dining room overlooking the bay. Conversational topics vary from sightings of marine creatures to tours taken via kayak around the

Guest cabins are rustic, yet comfortable and uniquely decorated with items from the surrounding area. Sleeping in this driftwood four-poster canopy bed created a sense of resting in Nature's nest.

Kachemak Bay Wilderness Lodge has earned two international awards for excellence in service and accommodations, including the honor of being, "America's Best Wilderness Lodge."

Few lodges offer the dining room decor that exists at Kachemak Bay Wilderness Lodge. Mike and Diane McBride have spent over 20 years adding to and refining this room. The large picture window allows guests to dine while watching the continuously changing view caused by the tides. Photo by David Robbins.

shoreline cliffs. Diane and Mike are walking storehouses of information, adding their observations after 20 years of watching nature unfold at Kachemak Bay. In 1981, the McBrides started the Center for Alaskan Coastal Studies, an educational facility chartered to educate others about preserving Alaska waters, marine life and coastal forest ecology.

Mike is a master guide, licensed skipper, bush pilot and naturalist with strong expertise in marine biology. He was elected into the Royal Geographical Society and Explorers Club for leading wilderness expeditions in Antarctica, the Arctic, Africa, Siberia and Polynesia.

Diane's extensive knowledge of the land and sea, strengthened by her biological expertise and teaching career, combines well with her culinary talents.

*V*iewing brown bears at their Chenik Bear Camp is one experience you'll cherish for a lifetime. In this sub-arctic, coastal, tundra environment, watch as the huge runs of salmon enter the area streams, and the large brown bears chase and catch them. Sows and newborn cubs are always popular photo subjects. The panorama is graced with volcanoes and high alpine glaciers, with fields and meadows filled with purple lupine and ivory cow parsnip.

Mike and Diane cater to each individual's needs and desires, making sure the avid angler gets taken to a private hot spot for salmon, and the photographer is shown the best spots for wildlife viewing. For more information on Kachemak Bay Wilderness Lodge, see page 303.

Diane McBride, Cook, Co-owner, Kachemak Bay Wilderness Lodge

"In 1970, Mike and I bought acreage on China Poot Bay, a few miles by boat from Homer," Diane said. "We began building our first cabin. Being without electricity and indoor plumbing required a pioneer spirit and mental fortitude to persevere, especially when all the comforts of home could have been ours a few miles away in Homer. In the dark hours of winter I feared boating the high seas between the lodge and Homer Spit. I told myself to take things one step at a time. When I did, the seas didn't seem so bad."

Their first clients came in late 1970, and Diane did all the cooking and housekeeping. They had tiny cabins, outhouses, a wood stove and kerosene lanterns for light. Fortunately, the clients loved it. They finished the lodge in 1978.

As the lodge grew, so did its clientele. Diane learned to prepare to perfection not only the seafood Mike harvested from nearby Kachemak Bay, but fresh-baked breads and desserts. When cooking chores became too overwhelming, Diane hired a professional chef to assist her with meal preparation.

"My criteria was, and still is, that the chef has to be a better cook than me," says Diane. "It's not an immodest statement. Our guests anticipate a certain type of food preparation and style here, and my chefs have to understand that philosophy and make it happen. During the last two decades, master chefs from Switzerland and gourmet chefs from across the United States have worked at the lodge. Each brought his or her own expertise to the Kachemak Bay experience."

Kachemak Bay's reputation for gourmet meals is partly based on using fresh Alaska seafood, including Dungeness and tanner crab, large tiger shrimp and halibut. Diane believes meals must not only be tasty, but presented in a colorful manner.

"One time," she says, "our chef served halibut, cauliflower and baked potato; all white foods on a white plate. When I saw it, I knew it was a disaster. I scrambled at the last minute to add lemons, parsley and tomato for color. No matter how good the recipe, the meal will flop without the proper color, texture and presentation."

The lodge has won awards for its superb dining and its ecological focus. Diane now primarily manages the lodge and personnel, but rises early to bake all the breads and muffins. She enjoys meeting new people and sharing with them the ecological wonders of the bay. A naturalist and licensed skipper, Diane guides clients on fishing trips, sea otter and bird rookery observation trips, and nature hikes. "We call Kachemak Bay the 'equal opportunity bay,'" says Diane. "Fifty percent of the people working on the water are women— commercial fishermen and boat skippers. Here the women are the guides and the men do the cooking."

Alaska Shrimp

$\mathcal{T}$he shrimp in Diane McBride's world-famous seafood dishes are harvested from the waters around Kodiak Island. The large tiger shrimp are 20 count to the pound, while the smaller pink shrimp are 30 count to the pound. Both marine crustaceans have a delicate flavor that keeps guests begging for more.

1 **cup olive oil**
1 **teaspoon soy sauce**
1½ **teaspoons minced fresh garlic**
   dash of chili powder
1 **teaspoon chopped fresh parsley**
1 **dozen large Alaska shrimp**

Combine olive oil, soy sauce, garlic, chili powder and parsley to form marinade.

Peel large shrimp and *place* in marinade for one hour. *Fry* for one minute. *Serve* with steamed rice.

Serves 2

Mike McBride shows a crab trap with an afternoon's bounty. The McBrides delight in sharing all aspects of the area's riches with guests from around the world.

Halibut Cove Florentine

Halibut Cove, five miles north of China Poot Bay, is an artist community established by Clem and Diana Tillion. Diana is best known for her Japanese-style watercolors, painted with sepia-toned octopus ink.

In the summer, the population of Halibut Cove increases by several hundred people and includes artists and commerical fishermen. Halibut Cove is actually an island called Ismalof Island. The quaint community features a restaurant, boardwalk, several art galleries and charming Cape Cod-style buildings.

1	tablespoon butter for baking dish
2	10-ounce packages frozen chopped spinach, thawed slightly
½	cup white wine
	salt
	pepper
4	halibut fillets, ½-inch thick
1	can cream of shrimp soup
½	stick margarine
	Parmesan cheese
	paprika

Preheat oven to 350 degrees.

Butter the bottom of an 8x8-inch baking dish. *Spread* thawed and separated spinach in the baking dish. *Pour* in white wine and *sprinkle* salt and pepper over spinach.

Place halibut fillets on top of spinach and *pour* undiluted soup over fillets. *Dot* with margarine and *sprinkle* with Parmesan cheese and paprika.

Bake 20 minutes at 350 degrees.

Serves 4

Roasted Alaska Duck

During the late fall, Kachemak Bay Lodge offers specialized waterfowl hunts to select hunters who wish to better acquaint themselves with the life history and migratory habits of many species of Alaska waterfowl. This is not a shoot-all-you-can experience, but an enlightenment where you learn of the inter-connectedness between man and this wonderfully beautiful coastline. When a few waterfowl are taken for close-up examination and study, they are then prepared in a manner that exemplifies this quest.

4   **wild ducks, plucked and cleaned**
1   **cup white wine**
½   **cup sugar**
1   **tablespoon wine vinegar**
     juice from 2 oranges
½   **cup orange liqueur**
     grated peel of 1 orange
¼   **cup orange peel in julienne strips**
½   **teaspoon salt**
¼   **teaspoon pepper**
     degreased pan juices

Preheat oven to 425 degrees. *Place* ducks in a roasting pan. *Roast* ducks, uncovered at 425 degrees, *basting* with white wine every 10 minutes. *Cook* until moderately well done, tender and juicy, 30 minutes to one hour, depending on size and age of ducks. *Save* pan juices, *refrigerate* to congeal grease.

In a saucepan, *combine* sugar and wine vinegar and *cook* over medium-low heat, *stirring* until carmelized. *Add* orange juice and orange liqueur; *cook* 5 minutes. Then *add* grated and julienned orange peel, salt, pepper and pan juices with fat removed. *Stir* and *cook* over low heat for 5 minutes longer. *Pour* sauce over roasted ducks.

Serves 4

Photo at right by David Robbins: Diane and Mike McBride guiding kayakers through China Poot Bay.

Loonsong Mountain Zucchini

The McBrides offer an outstanding get-away cabin high on a remote mountain lake, where the rainbow trout fishing and scenery is unsurpassed. Loonsong Mountain offers scented cottonwood groves, cascading waterfalls and the laughter of loons in late evening. You may forget the need to eat; the wondrous beauty of this environment is food enough for the soul. But eat for the body you must, and you will enjoy this light, tasty dish while taking in one of the grandest settings available—your own private restaurant and cuisine with the best view in southcentral Alaska.

2	pounds zucchini, unpeeled and thinly sliced
1	cup chopped celery
1	red pepper, chopped
1	medium yellow onion, chopped
1	garlic clove, minced
⅓	cup olive oil
	salt, pepper and basil
3	tablespoons butter
3	slices bread, trimmed
¼	cup Parmesan cheese
¼	cup Romano cheese

Preheat oven to 375 degrees.

In a saucepan, *saute* zucchini, celery, red pepper, onion and garlic clove in olive oil. *Add* salt, pepper and basil to taste. *Cover* skillet and *cook* on low heat 5 minutes. *Transfer* to casserole dish. *Butter* bread and *dice*. *Place* diced bread on top of dish and *sprinkle* with Parmesan and Romano cheeses. *Bake* uncovered at 375 degrees for 20 minutes.

Serves 4—6

Broiled Tukcross Tomatoes

Tukcross is Alaska's own variety of a hearty, flavorful beefsteak tomato that has adapted well to the Alaska environment. They complement most halibut, cod or salmon dishes. Serve them right from the broiler and watch your dinner guests smile with delight.

3   **medium tomatoes**
½   **cup bread crumbs**
½   **teaspoon dried basil**
    salt and pepper
1   **tablespoon margarine, melted**
    Parmesan or Romano cheese, dried or fresh

Cut tomatoes in half. *Make* four deep slashes across tomato halves. *Mix* bread crumbs, basil, salt, pepper and margarine; *sprinkle* on cut side of each tomato half. *Sprinkle* tops with cheese. *Broil* six inches from heat until golden brown.

Serves 6

After a scrumptious evening meal, a wood-heated sauna, pictured here, is one of the many comforts that guests enjoy at Kachemak Bay Wilderness Lodge. Several pairs of boots on the porch await the more adventurous, for a quick cool-down in the bay.

Kachemak Bay Crab Chowder

At Kachemak Bay Wilderness Lodge, guests revel in the many natural wonders of the area. After lunch, Mike McBride delights in taking clients to check the crab pots (see photo page 222), where he describes the conservation and biology of the crab, and the role the crab plays in the Kachemak Bay marine environment. At dinnertime, one truly appreciates not only the taste of the fresh-caught delicacy, but the "walk-softly" approach to the wise use of natural resources.

1   10-ounce package frozen cauliflower
2   cups milk
2   tablespoons sliced green onion
2   tablespoons diced pimiento
½   teaspoon salt
1   cup light cream
3   tablespoons all-purpose flour
1   7½-ounce can crab meat and juice
1   3-ounce package cream cheese, cut in cubes
    salt and pepper

In a 3-quart saucepan, *cook* cauliflower according to package directions; *do not drain. Cut* up any large pieces. *Stir* in milk, green onion, pimiento and salt. *Heat* and *stir* just until boiling.

In a separate bowl, *combine* the light cream and flour, *add* to hot milk mixture. *Cook* and *stir* until thickened and bubbly. *Add* crab meat and juice and cubed cream cheese; *heat* and *stir* until cream cheese melts and chowder is heated through. *Season* to taste with salt and pepper.

Serves 4

China Poot Corn Soup

Kachemak Bay Wilderness Lodge nestles in ecologically rich China Poot Bay, an area that is the starting point for a variety of wilderness adventures. Some of the most spectacular adventures begin right at your feet in the simple things we often take for granted, such as a tidal pool or a group of intertidal wildflowers.

Diane and Mike McBride are active members of the China Poot Bay Society and Center for Alaskan Coastal Studies, whose primary goal is teaching others about Kachemak Bay and the areas related to it.

The smallest of God's treasures reveal surprising facts about the world around us. This simple-to-make recipe is a testimonial that a meal or adventure doesn't have to be elaborate to be memorable.

3	cups frozen corn
2	cups chicken stock
1	carrot, chopped
1	small onion, chopped
2	garlic cloves, minced
1	teaspoon chili powder
½	teaspoon ground cumin
¼	teaspoon red pepper
¼	teaspoon black pepper
1½	cups milk

Roast frozen corn under broiler until golden brown.

Combine chicken stock, carrot, onion and garlic in a large pot and *bring* to a boil, then *simmer* 5 minutes. *Add* corn, chili powder, cumin, red and black peppers; *simmer* 10 minutes longer.

Pour soup into a blender, *add* milk and *blend* until smooth. *Reheat* before serving. *Top* with a spoonful of plain yogurt or sour cream.

Serves 4

Growler Island Wilderness Camp

*A*laska's Growler Island is an ice-age remnant, a green emerald in the sapphire sea of Prince William Sound, one of the most scenic and biologically rich areas in the North Pacific. Your adventure departs from Valdez, which is road-accessible from Anchorage or Fairbanks. During the three-hour cruise to Growler Island aboard the *Glacier Spirit*, you'll see the Alyeska Pipeline Terminal, gold mines, cascading waterfalls, and possibly mountain goats, black bear, eagles, sea otters, whales and porpoises.

As you enter Columbia Bay, the ship is dwarfed against the massive, 20-story face of Columbia Glacier. Ten-story chunks of ice calve (break off the glacier), creating an explosive spray as they drop into the sound. As Captain Stan Stephens turns off the engines of the sleek ship, you'll quietly float among the turquoise-blue icebergs, listening to the snap and crackle of the ice. As you stare in awe at the ice-age spectacle, you may feel that you are being watched. Turn to meet the huge black eyes of spotted seals gazing at you as they bask in the sunshine on the chunks of ice.

Columbia is the largest tidewater glacier in Prince William Sound and is one of the largest in North America. The glacier covers over 424 square miles: the approximate size of Los Angeles County. Columbia Glacier was first reported by the Spanish explorer, Fidalgo, who thought the loud booming noises were from a volcano. In 1794, explorers identified the booming sounds as ice calving from the glacier. Columbia is in a state of change. It is one of the last remaining North American iceberg calving glaciers to undergo a drastic retreat from its neoglacial position.

*W*hen you arrive at Growler Island, you'll notice that boardwalks link the tent cabins with the dining hall. Because of the fragile nature of the flora environment, these boardwalks have been constructed for guests to explore the wonders of this special island without destroying the beauty of the delicate plants.

Seal on an iceberg.

Your wilderness headquarters will be Growler Island Wilderness Camp. You'll stay in heated tent cabins or Weatherport huts equipped with cots, bunks and linens. You'll have access to kayaks, skiffs or canoes to explore the coastal flora and fauna of scenic Elder Bay. Be sure to disembark occasionally and walk the beaches, or watch salmon migrate into freshwater streams. You can charter a larger boat and fish for halibut, salmon or rockfish. A full support staff and resident naturalist can customize a variety of activities to meet your family's desires. The camp offers special ramps suited for the handicapped.

The Glacier Spirit and Nautilus bring guests into the harbor at Growler Island Wilderness Camp.

Photo above: Growler Island offers one of the most spectacular scenic views available to diners: a backdrop of Columbia Glacier, the rugged Chugach Mountains and magnificent Prince William Sound.
Photo below: Growler Island guests spend their days fishing, kayaking or exploring remote beaches. Stroll along the gravel beach and touch huge icebergs washed ashore by the incoming tide.

*A*fter you've worked up an appetite, visit the dining hall for a gourmet's delight of chicken, salmon, halibut, fresh sourdough rolls and salads prepared by Chef Jim LaChance. The spectacular beauty of nearby Columbia Glacier complements the banquet. After dinner, explore the island and or photograph the little-noticed residents of tidal pools, such as tiny crabs and starfish. The next morning, stroll along the gravel beach and touch huge icebergs washed ashore by the incoming tide.

Mary Helen Stephens, wife of Stan, is a gracious hostess and will be happy to answer questions you have about the Prince William Sound ecosystem. The resident naturalist conducts tours of the island and is familiar with the location of eagles' nests and other natural treasures.

Access to Growler Island Wilderness Camp is through Stan Stephens Charters & Cruises. The Stephens family oversees the operation of the camp, and has offered tours and remote camps in the Prince William Sound region for over 20 years. Stan Stephens says it best: "We love Alaska and want to share its intricate beauties and natural treasures with all our guests."

For more information on Stan Stephens Cruises, see page 304.

James Lachance, Chef, Growler Island Wilderness Camp

Jim first became interested in cooking when he was eight years old. He remembers his mother telling him, "Try everything once, to see if you like it." Years later, those words spurred him to try a cooking career. After two years of study at the Culinary Institute of America in Hyde Park, New York, he landed his first cooking job at the local Ramada Inn. Jim advanced in his newly chosen profession, working as a sous chef at the Peabody Hotel in Memphis and at the Hilton in Greenville, South Carolina, and as a dining room chef at the Marriott Hotel in Marco Island, Florida.

Why does he love the food business? "I never wanted to do anything else with my life than to be a chef," he said with a smile. "Cooking is an art form, and the artistic expression comes from within. Presentation is very important. It's fun to watch people sit down and smile while they're eating. Anybody can cook, but not everybody can be artistic with food."

Jim had a couple of friends who told him that Alaska is a wonderful state and he should see it. Jim sent resumes to the Holland America Cruise Line, who employed him as kitchen manager at the Westmark Hotel in Valdez. While there, Jim met Stan Stephens. Stan hired Jim as the chef at Growler Island. Jim reminisces about his first day on the job.

"When my friends told me how wonderful Alaska is, I could not have imagined I would be working in a kitchen with the best view in the world," he said. "From my kitchen and dining room, I look out over Columbia Bay to Columbia Glacier, and the sight is breathtaking."

Jim enjoys the freedom of using his own recipes and menu planning. In 1991, he came out with a recipe book, *Yes! It's Applesauce*. The recipes in this chapter are from Jim's book, reprinted with permission.

What foods do Growler Island guests request most? "Vegetarian food," says Jim. "Except for chicken and beef, we don't use animal fat or products in anything we cook. Salmon and chowder are the most popular items we serve.

"The secret of cooking salmon is to cook it slow," Jim advises. "Don't overcook it. I also like to use a sauce or glaze on the fish."

Being a free spirit, Jim wants to explore new opportunities. He hopes to stay in Alaska and buy his own restaurant.

"It's a lot easier to be yourself here than in a big city," he said. "In Alaska you can still start small and afford it. There's a tremendous opportunity for growth for people who want to work hard."

See the Sound Ribs

*G*rowler Island is a mid-way point for those travelers who have just completed a tour of the majestic wonders of Columbia Glacier. The spicy smell of these ribs greets guests on their way up the boardwalk to the dining hall. Once there, they are treated to one of the most spectacular views in Prince William Sound and an all-you-can eat wilderness feast featuring these delicious ribs.

1½ cups teriyaki sauce
2   cups brown sugar
2   tablespoons garlic powder
2   tablespoons ground cayenne pepper
1   10-ounce jar hoisin sauce*
2   tablespoons powdered ginger
6   pounds beef ribs

In a large bowl or baking pan, *combine* teriyaki sauce, brown sugar, garlic powder, cayenne pepper, hoisin sauce and ginger to make a marinade.

Place ribs in the marinade, *spooning* it over the ribs. *Marinate* for at least 24 hours, *turning* the ribs every 6 hours.

Cook over grill, *basting* ribs with marinade while cooking.

Serves 12

*Hoisin sauce can be found in the oriental section of most food markets.

Photo at right: *Few areas can match a close-up tour of Prince William Sound's Columbia Glacier, with its ice-capped mountains, huge icebergs, and resident marine and wildlife. Here two rafters explore icebergs in the bay off Growler Island, while Columbia Glacier looms in the distance.*

Sockeye Salmon Chowder

*T*he Pacific Northwest Indians considered the sockeye salmon of enough food and bartering importance to name it "sau-kie" meaning "chief of fishes." While the spelling has changed, the sockeye salmon has not. Experienced anglers and cooks know that the sockeye is the tastiest salmon found in Alaska waters and the prime ingredient in this delicious chowder.

4	slices bacon, diced
1	carrot, diced fine
1	onion, diced fine
1	stalk celery, diced fine
1	15-ounce can of clams, chopped
4	potatoes, diced
1	cup water
2½	tablespoons fresh dill
2	tablespoons chopped garlic
1	tablespoon chopped fresh basil
1½	teaspoons thyme
½	teaspoon oregano
4	cups heavy cream
¾	pound sockeye salmon fillet, coarsely chopped (can be raw, cooked fresh or leftover)
4	cups milk
½	cup cornstarch
	salt and pepper

In a 4-quart stockpot, *saute* the bacon until it starts to get clear. *Add* carrot, onion and celery. *Saute* until onion is clear. *Add* clams with their juice, potatoes and water. *Cook* at a slow boil until the potatoes are tender. *Add* dill, garlic, basil, thyme, oregano, heavy cream and salmon. *Cook* for 15 minutes, *stirring* constantly.

Mix milk with the cornstarch; *add* mixture to the soup, *stirring* constantly. *Cook* until soup thickens. Salt and pepper to taste. *Serve* immediately.

Serves 8—10

Chugach Cheese Soup

The Chugach Mountains, which tower over Prince William Sound, contain some of Alaska's most beautiful and rugged peaks, glaciers and wilderness valleys. Take a cup of this soup, relax and drink in the scenery slowly, so you can appreciate the goodness of both.

This soup is a good base for many additions, including broccoli, cauliflower, asparagus and seafood.

½ **cup butter**
1 **onion, diced fine**
1 **clove garlic, chopped**
1 **stalk celery, diced fine**
1 **large carrot, diced fine**
3 **tablespoons flour**
1 **quart chicken stock**
2 **cups heavy cream**
2 **cups milk**
¼ **pound American cheese, coarsely grated**
¼ **pound Cheddar cheese, coarsely grated**
¼ **pound Swiss cheese, coarsely grated**
1½ **teaspoons thyme**
1 **teaspoon white pepper**
1 **teaspoon basil**

Melt butter in heavy sauce pan. *Add* onion, garlic, celery and carrot; *saute* until carrots are soft.

Add flour and *cook* for five minutes, *stirring* constantly, to make a roux. *Add* chicken stock and *cook* for 15 minutes at a slow boil until slightly thick.

In a bowl, *mix* cream and milk; *add* very slowly to soup, *stirring* constantly. *Cook* on low for 10 minutes.

Add cheeses, *stirring* constantly; *cook* until melted and well blended. *Stir* in thyme, pepper and basil. *Serve* immediately.

Serves 6

Chicken Island Soup

An abundance of mini-islands are scattered throughout Prince William Sound. One of these is Chicken Island, only three-tenths of a mile long. While many islands are larger, few share its simple yet robust character, which best describes this chicken soup with its homemade Bridal Veil Noodles, page 239.

Stan Stephens, captain of the *Glacier Spirit*, is a full-time Alaska resident who has cruised the waters of Prince William Sound for over 20 years. He shares his intimate knowledge of wildlife concentrations and natural wonders of the sound as you cruise among the islands on your way to Growler Island Wilderness Camp.

1   **medium onion**
1   **stalk celery**
1   **large carrot**
2   **tablespoons olive oil**
2   **quarts water (or homemade chicken stock)**
1½ **tablespoons chicken base**
2   **teaspoons fennel seed**
1   **tablespoon anise**
¾   **pound leftover cooked chicken meat**
1   **batch uncooked Bridal Veil Noodles, page 239**

Chop the vegetables coarsely. In a large pot, *saute* the chopped onion, celery and carrot in olive oil until the onions are clear. *Add* water and chicken base or stock; *simmer* slowly for at least 30 minutes. *Add* fennel seed, anise and chicken chunks. *Simmer* for another 30 minutes.

Add the fresh noodles and *cook* just until noodles are tender.

Serves 6

Bridal Veil Noodles

On your drive down the Richardson Highway through Thompson Pass to Valdez, be sure to stop and admire Bridal Veil Falls. Like the falls, these noodles are wispy, yet delight the senses enough to make a long-lasting impression. Serve these noodles in Chicken Island Soup, page 238.

2   small eggs
1   cup flour
1½ tablespoons curry powder

Combine egg, flour and curry powder in a food processor. Mix with plastic dough blade just until ingredients stick together. *Remove* dough from the food processor and *place* in a bowl. *Cover* tightly and *let rest* for one hour.

Place dough on a lightly floured board; with a rolling pin, *roll* out the dough to 1/8-inch thickness. With a sharp knife, *cut* the noodles into ½-inch wide strips.

Add noodles to boiling water or Chicken Island Soup, page 238, and *cook* just until tender.

Serves 6

Thompson Pass is one of Alaska's most scenic, with snowcapped mountains and cascading waterfalls visible from the highway.

Northern Lights Coleslaw

*T*his coleslaw, with its reds, greens and yellows, reminds me of the wavering strands of northern lights that emblazon the horizon from early September through March. Serve this salad when you want to brighten up any meal in summer or winter.

½   **head purple cabbage, shredded**
½   **head green cabbage, shredded**
1   **yellow bell pepper, julienned**
1   **green bell pepper, julienned**
1   **red bell pepper, julienned**
1   **large carrot, grated**

In a large salad bowl, *mix* cabbage, peppers and carrot. *Pour* vinaigrette over vegetables and *toss. Chill.*

Vinaigrette

1   **cup cider vinegar**
¼   **cup granulated sugar**
1   **teaspoon curry powder**
2   **teaspoons ground cumin**
1   **teaspoon garlic powder**
1   **tablespoon celery seed**
¼   **cup plain yogurt**

Mix vinegar, sugar, curry powder, cumin, garlic powder, celery seed and yogurt together in a food processor or blender and *blend* until smooth. *Pour* over vegetables.

Serves 10

Photo on opposite page: Prince William Sound is a large area to fish and explore, and subsequently, guests work up a big appetite. Growler Island Chef Jim LaChance serves a hearty plate to satisfy the hungriest sportsmen, with plenty available for seconds. Shown is Fog Island French Toast. See the Sound Ribs, Sourdough Rolls, Northern Lights Coleslaw, halibut and three-bean salad.

Stephens' Sourdough Bread

$\mathcal{M}$ary Helen Stephens, wife of Captain Stan Stephens, is a very cordial and gracious hostess to guests aboard the *Glacier Spirit*. She ushers hungry travelers up the boardwalk and into the dining room on Growler Island. With the same softness as her sourdough bread, she sees to the needs and comforts of everyone while Jim LaChance serves the main course.

1   **cup milk**
⅓   **cup granulated sugar**
⅓   **cup shortening**
1   **teaspoon salt**
1   **package dry yeast**
2   **tablespoons warm water**
1½   **cups sourdough starter, room temperature**
5   **cups flour**
        melted butter for brushing tops of loaves

Grease a large bowl and two 9x5x3-inch loaf pans or two large baking sheets.

In a saucepan, *scald* the milk; *stir* in sugar, shortening and salt. *Let cool. Dissolve* yeast in warm water, *add* to milk mixture. *Stir* in sourdough starter and *beat. Stir* in flour and *mix* thoroughly. On a well-floured board, *knead* the dough for 10 to 15 minutes.

Place dough in a covered, greased bowl. *Let rise* in a warm place until double in bulk. *Punch* down and *let rise* again.

Divide dough into two balls. *Cover* with a towel and *let rest* for 10 minutes. *Shape* into loaves. *Place* loaves into greased pans. If making rolls, *shape* dough into rolls, and *place* ½-inch apart on baking sheet. *Let rise* again. *Bake* loaves at 400 degrees for 40 minutes and rolls for 20 minutes or until golden brown. *Brush* with melted butter.

Makes 2 loaves or 3 dozen large rolls

Photo at right: Jim LaChance puts the final touches on these Stephens' Sourdough Rolls before he serves them to hungry Growler Island guests.

Prince's Pumpkin Cheesecake

$\mathcal{S}$tory has it that when the clock struck 12, Prince William heard the Sound. He rushed out of the castle to find that Cinderella's coach had turned into a pumpkin. Being a sentimental nobleman, the Prince grabbed the pumpkin and made this spicy cheesecake in honor of his lost love.

½	**cup butter**
⅓	**box graham crackers**
2	**8-ounce packages cream cheese, softened**
¾	**cup granulated sugar**
1 ½	**cups pumpkin**
5	**eggs**
1	**tablespoon vanilla**
1	**teaspoon cinnamon**
½	**teaspoon ground ginger**
½	**teaspoon nutmeg or cloves**

Preheat oven to 325 degrees.

Melt butter in a small saucepan. *Crush* graham crackers. With a pastry brush, *brush* a small amount of butter on the sides and bottom of a springform pan. *Dust* the pan with a small amount of cracker crumbs. *Mix* the remaining butter and crumbs. *Press* into the bottom of pan to form crust.

In a mixing bowl, *cream* the cheese, sugar and pumpkin until smooth. *Add* eggs and *mix* until well-blended. *Add* vanilla, cinnamon, ginger and nutmeg or cloves; *mix* gently.

Pour mixture into graham cracker crust. *Place* springform pan in a larger pan of water and *bake* at 325 degrees for 45 to 50 minutes, or until a knife inserted in center comes out clean.

Makes one 9-inch cheesecake

Fog Island French Toast

*R*ight before sunrise, thin wisps of fog shroud many islands in Prince William Sound. Take Nature's advice and sprinkle a layer of powdered sugar over these slices of French Toast, photo page 240, for a breakfast dish as perfect as a Prince William Sound morning.

½   **large orange**
4   **large eggs**
1   **cup heavy cream**
1   **teaspoon cinnamon**
   dash of nutmeg
1   **tablespoon orange liqueur**
1½ **teaspoons vanilla**
1   **tablespoon granulated sugar**
8   **slices bread**
   powdered sugar
   thin orange slices, cut and twisted for garnish

Preheat greased electric skillet or griddle to medium.

With a zester, *remove* zest from orange. *Squeeze* juice from the orange into a bowl. *Add* eggs, cream, cinnamon, nutmeg, liqueur, vanilla, granulated sugar and zest from orange to juice and *blend* together. *Dip* slices of bread into the mixture one piece at a time and *place* on skillet or griddle. *Cook* until golden brown on both sides, turning the bread after approximately 3 to 4 minutes.

Cut bread in half, from corner to corner, *forming* a triangle. *Arrange* on serving plate and *sprinkle* with powdered sugar. *Garnish* with orange slices.

Serves 4

Gates of the Arctic Lodge

*A*t the turn of the century, prospectors traveled to arctic Alaska to find their fortune in the gold fields. Nowadays, travelers are still looking for gold, but of another kind. Anglers probe the clear depths of Walker Lake in the Brooks Range for golden lake trout and arctic char.

Alaskans Nick and Sue Jennings knew that Walker Lake offered a treasure chest of natural resources. Being environmentally centered, they made plans to renovate a lodge they had leased on Walker Lake. Rather than build several guest cabins, they housed their guests in neatly decorated rooms on the second floor. They flew in rough-cut birch for paneling, which gave the lodge a rustic, yet refined look. They added to the lodge: a water system one year, a bed of wildflowers the next, all with minimal impact on the surrounding land. Because Gates of the Arctic Lodge was the only commercial sportfishing lodge on Walker Lake, it became an angling oasis for those seeking lake trout, sheefish, grayling, pike, arctic char and chum salmon.

A very religious man, Nick Jennings never bragged about his accomplishments. Instead, he delighted in hearing anglers tell about their experiences. He had many talents and skills, as do most Alaskans who run a fishing lodge with the help of a spouse. He excelled as a fur buyer, trapper, bush pilot extraordinaire, professional photographer and fishing guide. Nick and Sue named their lodge Gates of the Arctic because they were on the boundary of Gates of the Arctic National Park, a popular wilderness Mecca for tourists wanting to experience the "real" Alaska. Nick was one of the few fishing guides who helped pioneer the spectacular sheefish fishing on the Kobuk River, which begins at the Walker Lake outlet. Nick flew anglers to the middle sections of the Kobuk for one-day or overnight trips for sheefish.

In Walker Lake, anglers could catch 20 to 50 fish a day in the 12- to 20-pound range. When I'd be visiting the lodge in mid-June, the midnight sun would blaze as the old day passed and the new day began, with no curtain of darkness between performances. Of course, Chris used the continuous daylight to fish himself into oblivion, returning to the lodge only to sleep or eat.

Gates of the Arctic Lodge was a haven for those who wanted to commune with the wilderness. Besides the angling guests, the lodge occasionally housed park and government employees working in the area. Even with six guests, the lake was never crowded.

While flying Chris and I from Bettles to Walker Lake, Nick said he wanted to share something very special. Instead of the usual approach from the southeast, Nick flew in from the west.

Walker Lake is above the Arctic Circle and receives nearly 24 hours of daylight in the summer. Here, Nick Jennings pours iced tea, as Chris Batin tells about the big sheefish that got away.

"This is one of my favorite thrills," Nick told us. We climbed toward the peaks of the mountains and broke over the top. The ground disappeared beneath the plane. We gasped in delight as the breathtaking scene unfolded before us.

The sheer wall of the mountain dropped rapidly to the royal blue waters of Walker Lake, edged golden orange by the midnight sun. "I enjoy flying for moments like these," he said. "Even if I die tomorrow, to have experienced this would have made life worthwhile."

Nick's genuine sincerity and Susan's hospitality and warm, caring spirit made us appreciate the special nature of a Gates of the Arctic Lodge moment in history.

But the owners of the private land the lodge was built on sold the land to the National Park Service, which converted the land back to public ownership and removed the lodge. The Jennings watched their hard work disappear overnight.

Just as Nick and Susan were beginning to build a new tourism business out of their home in Delta Junction, Nick died in an auto accident. Susan is now raising their three children and writing a book about her life with Nick.

*I*t is good that so many anglers enjoyed a part of Alaska that would not have been possible had it not been for the Jennings. It is unfortunate, and sad, that with the lodge's demise and Nick's death, fishing opportunities and wilderness adventures for thousands of anglers will never become reality.

While Gates of the Arctic Lodge is no more, the memories created at the hands of Nick and Susan Jennings—from the home-cooked meals to the sharing of the land they loved—will live on through their guests, and in a very small way, in a chapter of this book. The lodge and its lifestyle was a dream-come-true for a couple who made a go of it in the Alaska wilderness. When I think of Nick and Susan and our times together on Walker Lake, I remember a paraphrase of Don Juan's words in *Journey to Ixtlan*: Live every day to its fullest. Live it with all the vigor and intensity as if it were your last day on earth. As a couple, Nick and Susan Jennings did just that.

Susan Jennings, *Cook, Gates of the Arctic Lodge*

Seventeen-year-old Susan rode up the Alaska Highway with her family in 1974. They came from California in search of a simpler lifestyle. For four years they lived in a Christian Cooperative in the Glennallen area of interior Alaska. Susan was a baker at the Cooperative, baking 30 to 50 loaves of bread, doughnuts, pastries, muffins and other goodies every day on a wood cookstove.

Susan met Nick at the Cooperative, and they were married a year and a half later. In 1977, Susan helped Nick guide hunters in the Wrangell Mountains and cooked in base camps and spike camps. As a new wife, she was excited with the challenge of being in the bush. The next year they guided backpacking and river float trips in the Brooks Range.

Susan cooked one season at Iniakuk Lodge, where she was asked to use her own recipes when put in charge of menu planning and cooking.

In 1978, Susan and Nick moved to Delta Junction to build a log home, which became their home base.

An offer to lease Gates of the Arctic Lodge gave them the opportunity to get back into doing what they enjoyed, while working together as a family. Their first year managing the lodge was 1983.

Most of Susan's lodge-cooking experience came from on-the-job-training. However, she had taken cooking courses in international foods and enjoyed preparing Italian and Chinese dishes. Unlike most lodges, which have the same menu week after week, Susan created a different menu weekly.

She made everything from scratch, including salad dressings. Cucumbers, tomatoes, peppers, celery, lettuce, green beans, carrots, broccoli, cauliflower and green onions were grown in her 14x24-foot greenhouse. With only sand and gravel around the lodge, dirt was at a premium. All the potting soil for the garden had to be flown in from Fairbanks. Susan served these "Alaska-fresh" vegetables with pride. Fresh eggs, fruit and milk were flown in every other week from Fairbanks.

The most challenging aspect of cooking at the lodge was when unexpected guests dropped in. It was not unusual to have kayakers paddle up to her doorstep, or float planes land on the lake, bringing people in for dinner. Groups of backpackers would drop in unexpectedly to buy a meal. Susan always made extra food and kept it in the freezer for unannounced guests.

Susan described her style of cooking as homestyle and gourmet. Her favorites were marinated meat dishes, stir-fry and barbecue salmon. She catered to special diet requirements, but always had a homemade pie on the counter to tempt those less conscious of their waistline.

Kobuk River Sheefish

*K*obuk River sheefish are some of the largest in the world, reaching weights of up to 60 pounds. This delicately flavored, white, flaky fish is some of the best you'll find anywhere. However, you won't find this fish in the grocery store. Anglers may be tempted to take home a cooler full, however, most anglers and guides practice catch and release. Sheefish from the Selawik-Kobuk watershed grow much slower than in other parts of Alaska.

Harvesting only a few sheefish for lodge guests, Susan Jennings served this as the lodge specialty. You may substitute any white flaky fish such as catfish, whitefish, cod or mahi mahi.

1	**10 to 15 pound sheefish**
	lemon pepper
	seafood seasoning
	paprika
	salt
	fresh dill or rosemary
	butter
	lemon juice
	mushroom slices
	lemon slices

Preheat oven to 375 degrees.

Clean and *scale* sheefish, *cut* into fillets or *use* as whole fish. *Lay* fish skin side down in shallow baking dish. *Sprinkle* fish with lemon pepper, seafood seasoning, paprika, salt and fresh dill or rosemary. *Dab* with butter and *sprinkle* with lemon juice. *Top* with mushroom or lemon slices.

Bake at 375 degrees for 15 to 25 minutes depending on thickness of fillets. The rule of thumb is to bake 10 minutes per inch of thickness of fish.

Photo opposite page: Chris Batin serves Kobuk River Sheefish, the lodge specialty at Gates of the Arctic.

Dijon Walker Lake Trout

*W*alker Lake offers excellent fishing for lake trout in a true wilderness environment. There were days when we caught and released up to 40 fish per person. The water was so clear we could see the fish take the lure in 50 feet of water. Because these fish come from such a pristine environment, they are some of the best eating you'll find anywhere. But limit your take, as these fish grow extremely slowly.

1	**3-pound fillet of lake trout or halibut**
1	**clove fresh garlic, minced**
½	**teaspoon ground black pepper**
	soy sauce
5	**tablespoons mayonnaise**
2 ½	**tablespoons Dijon mustard**

Preheat oven to 350 degrees.

Place fish fillet in a lightly greased shallow baking dish or on foil-covered cookie sheet, with skin side down. *Sprinkle* minced fresh garlic and ground black pepper over fillet. *Add* several dashes of soy sauce.

Mix mayonnaise with mustard and *spread* a thin layer over fillet. *Broil* until brown; continue *cooking* in oven at 350 degrees, until done, approximately 15 to 25 minutes, depending on thickness of fillet.

Serves 4—6

Alaska-Mex Casserole

For many, the only thing better than a Mexican meal is Alaska's wilderness scenery. When you combine the two, as Susan does here, you have a meal that brings the best of both ends of the North American continent together, much to the delight of hungry anglers.

2	pounds ground beef, caribou or moose
1	medium onion, diced
1	8-ounce can tomato sauce
1	8-ounce jar salsa
½	teaspoon garlic powder
	salt and pepper to taste
1	pint cottage cheese
1	pint sour cream
1	4-ounce can green chillies, diced
1	15-ounce bag tortilla chips (plain)
1	pound Monterray Jack or mozarella cheese, grated

Brown ground meat, add diced onions and saute. Add tomato sauce, salsa, garlic powder, salt and pepper. Simmer 15 minutes. Remove from heat and cool. Mix cottage cheese, sour cream and chillies together in a separate dish.

In a 9x13x2-inch deep casserole dish, arrange half of the tortilla chips on the bottom of the dish. Pour half of meat mixture over chips, spread with half of cottage cheese mixture, and sprinkle with half of grated cheese. Repeat layers. Use chips around the perimeter of the dish to hold in ingredients.

At this point, you can freeze this dish or bake it. Heat oven to 350 degrees. Bake for 45 to 60 minutes; longer if dish has been frozen.

Serves 8

Swan Island Dressing

$\mathcal{T}$he last thing you might expect to see on a wilderness lake in the Brooks Range is a 30-foot sailboat. I was surprised when I heard stories of this fine ship, which had been built in California, trailored up the Alaska Highway to Fairbanks, and flown in on a C-82 "Flying Boxcar" in the winter, landing on a runway made of ice. Swan Island, on Walker Lake, is home to the sailboat, the "Martha M." Bud and Martha Helmericks homesteaded the island in the 1950s.

The island is a safe harbor for airplanes and boats; however one bright, full-moon night Martha was awakened by the howling wind. She arose and looked out the window just in time to see the sailboat tear loose from its mooring and drift toward their float plane. Martha rushed outside in her nightgown and lay down on her back on the floats of the plane, bracing her feet up against the sailboat to keep It from tearIng up the nose of the plane. While laying on her back, soaking wet, all she could think of was the beautiful full moon overhead. With memories like these, I'm sure that of all the thousands of islands in this world, Martha's favorite is Swan Island.

¼ **cup pimientos**
1 **teaspoon Worcestershire sauce**
¼ **cup chopped sweet pickles**
⅓ **cup chopped green onion**
½ **cup mayonnaise**
½ **cup sour cream**
　 dash vinegar or lemon juice
2 **hard cooked eggs, chopped**
2 **teaspoons granulated sugar**
1 **tablespoon ketchup**

In a bowl, *mix* pimientos, Worcestershire sauce, pickles, green onion, mayonnaise, sour cream, vinegar or lemon juice, eggs, sugar and ketchup. **Blend** well, *chill* before serving.

Makes 2 cups

Brooks Range Bleu Cheese

*I*n mid-June just before midnight, the sun drops behind the peaks of the Brooks Range and drapes the mountains in a pale shroud of blue. Minutes later, the sun rises as a Phoenix from behind the peaks and illuminates the mountains in orange light, just as this dressing sheds a flavorful light on salads.

4	ounces bleu cheese
2	ounces buttermilk
2	pinches garlic powder
3	drops hot sauce
4	drops Worcestershire sauce
2	cups mayonnaise
1	pint sour cream

In a blender, *blend* half of the cheese with the buttermilk, garlic powder, hot sauce and Worcestershire sauce. A*dd* mayonnaise and sour cream and *blend* well. *Stir* in remaining bleu cheese and *chill*.

Makes 3 cups

Exploring 17-mile Walker Lake is an all-day adventure. Anglers can expect to catch pike, grayling, lake trout and arctic char. The high-mountain scenery surrounding the lake is some of the best you'll find in the Brooks Range.

Anaktuvuk Raisin Pie

*D*uring the long winter months, when fresh fruit is unavailable in high-arctic villages, raisins are the fruit of choice when a fresh pie is desired.

1   **cup raisins**
2   **cups warm water**
1   **cup granulated sugar**
¼   **cup margarine, softened**
3   **eggs, beaten**
1   **cup nuts**
1   **teaspoon vanilla**
1   **unbaked pie shell**

Soak raisins in water until plump. *Cream* together sugar and margarine. *Stir* in beaten eggs. *Add* drained raisins, nuts and vanilla. *Pour* into unbaked pie shell. *Bake* at 350 degrees for 40 minutes.

Serves 6—8

Remote, family-run fishing lodges offer plenty of opportunity for families to explore the wilderness environment. Managers often understand the needs of families with young children, and offer programs that fulfill those needs, from overnight camping, berry picking and hiking to shallow-water fishing.

Arctic Cheesecake

1   **cup flour**
¼   **cup granulated sugar**
1   **teaspoon grated lemon rind**
1   **egg yolk**
¼   **teaspoon vanilla**
½   **cup soft butter or margarine**

Combine ingredients in a large mixing bowl and *blend* to form a soft dough. *Chill* for one hour. *Press* dough on bottom and sides of 9- or 10-inch springform pan. *Preheat* oven to 500 degrees.

Filling

5   **8-ounce packages cream cheese, softened**
2¼ **cups granulated sugar**
3   **tablespoons flour**
¼   **teaspoon salt**
¼   **teaspoon lemon rind**
6   **eggs**
1   **teaspoon vanilla**
1   **cup sour cream**

In a large bowl, *combine* cream cheese, sugar, flour, salt and lemon rind. *Add* eggs, one at a time, *blending* with an electric mixer until smooth. *Blend* in vanilla and sour cream. *Pour* into crust. *Bake* at 500 degrees for 10 minutes. *Turn* oven down to 200 degrees and *bake* for 1¼ hours. *Do not open* the oven. *Cool* away from drafts. *Chill*. *Do not remove* sides of pan until completely cool. *Top* with Blueberry Filling and Topping, page 187.

Serves 16

Coconut Custard Pie

3   cups granulated sugar
6   eggs
¾   cup buttermilk
6   tablespoons flour
1½ tablespoons vanilla
⅓   teaspoon salt
1½ sticks butter, melted
3   heaping cups flaked coconut (14-ounce bag)
2   unbaked 9-inch pie shells

Preheat oven to 350 degrees. *Beat* together sugar, eggs and buttermilk. *Stir* in flour, vanilla, salt, butter and coconut. *Pour* into unbaked pie shells. *Bake* 45 to 60 minutes at 350 degrees. *Serve* topped with whipped cream.

Makes two 9-inch pies

Sports Afield fishing editor Tony Accerano battles an arctic grayling in front of Gates of the Arctic Lodge, color photo on back cover. Walker Lake grayling average from 16 to 18 inches, with several in the 20-inch class. Lake trout and arctic char could also be caught within easy casting distance of the lodge.

Midnight Sun Coffee Pastry

*D*uring the month of June in the Brooks Range, the sun shines at midnight. Enthusiastic anglers, including my husband, Chris, will spend all night and into the wee hours of the morning fishing for lake trout. Susan made this coffee pastry for those early morning anglers who tried not to wake anyone while sneaking into the lodge looking for a snack. For those of us who slept in, she served this pastry for breakfast with baked eggs, cheese, onions and bacon.

1   **cup flour**
1   **stick margarine**
3   **tablespoons water**
1   **cup water**
1   **stick margarine**
1   **cup flour**
3   **eggs**
2   **teaspoons almond flavor**

Work one cup flour and one stick margarine together with pastry blender or two knives. *Mix* 3 tablespoons water in with fork and *form* two balls. *Place* on cookie sheet and *pat* into two oval-shaped pastries ¼-inch thick.

Preheat oven to 350 degrees. In a large saucepan, *bring* one cup water and one stick margarine to a boil. *Remove* from heat and *add* one cup flour all at once. *Beat* vigorously. *Add* eggs one at a time, *beating* vigorously after each egg. *Add* almond flavoring and *beat* well. *Spread* this mixture over oval pastries and *bake* at 350 degrees for one hour. *Drizzle* with icing.

Icing

5   **tablespoons milk**
½   **teaspoon vanilla**
2   **cups powdered sugar**

Mix milk and vanilla with powdered sugar to get a thin consistency, *drizzle* over top of baked pastry.

Makes two 8x6-inch oval pastries

Lodge manager David Coray, center, toasts with guests after a successful day of fishing.

Silver Salmon Creek Lodge

*J*n 1983, David Coray left his job as a social services counselor to pursue a lifelong dream...to start his own fishing lodge business. Thirty miles across Cook Inlet from his home town of Soldotna, a small house and a few outbuildings were for sale.

Coray bought the homesite and slowly turned it into a sportfishing lodge. "The first four years were the most difficult," he said. "But once our guests discovered the great silver salmon fishing we had to offer, they re-booked, and brought friends and business associates."

Coray hosts more than 200 anglers a year. Minutes before the bush plane lands on the sandy ocean beach in front of the lodge, he rides a three-wheeler to the strip to meet the plane. His gray-flecked black beard parts in a quick smile as he welcomes each guest to the Silver Salmon Creek Lodge family. And family best describes the group, as over 40 percent of his guests each year are return clientele.

The lodge complex contains the main lodge structure, a series of outpost cabins, volleyball net, basketball hoop, and a hand-carved fish rack for hanging daily trophies. The main lodge offers three nicely decorated bedrooms, each sleeping two anglers. The lounge and living areas exude a homey atmosphere for hundreds of anglers indulging in some of the best halibut and silver and king salmon fishing in this region.

The lodge is a cornucopia of adventure. Silver salmon begin entering the creek around August 5. Anglers typically catch from 5 to 10 silvers per day, usually lots more. Halibut fishing is good year-round, with 50 to 100-pounders common. Guests come to watch and photograph Alaska brown bear feeding on salmon. From May through September, look to the inlet for seals chasing salmon or Beluga whales breaching.

Pilot Will Satathite of Clearwater Air provides safe transportation to and from the lodge, as well as flightseeing trips over the rugged alpine glaciers, mountains and pristine lakes of the Lake Clark National Preserve. Chiswell Island Bird Sanctuary offers unparalleled bird watching, and Fossil Point is a must-stopover for the young fossil aficionado in the family.

Anglers wanting to fish in solitude for silver salmon and char against the magnificent backdrop of Mount Iliamna can stay at remote Shelter Creek Camp. Coray expects big appetites from exploring the many wonders of the area, and the evening table is loaded with huge

Shore lunches at Silver Salmon Creek Lodge feature fresh-caught silver salmon stuffed with onions, bacon, butter and herbs, wrapped in foil and cooked in the coals of a campfire.

serving plates of salmon, massive salads and
wonderfully decadent desserts. Food is on par with
the fishing...excellent!

If the tides are right, clam digging is the favorite
game. Neophytes often get so caught up in the chase
they lose all sense of self image, fall down in the mud,
laugh, have a grand time and collect a bucket of razor
clams for superb dining.

Explore the coastline in the lodge kayak, watch the
clouds of birds, or marvel at rafts of playful otters eating
crabs while floating on their backs.

Silver Salmon Creek Lodge offers outstanding
adventuring, near enough to Anchorage and the Kenai
Peninsula to be conveniently accessible, but distant
enough to be remote. And with an invitation like that, it's
easy to see why the Silver Salmon Creek Lodge family of
anglers keeps growing year after year.

For more information on Silver Salmon Creek Lodge,
see page 305.

Delores Waffen, Cook, Silver Salmon Creek Lodge

Delores and her husband, Tony, were avid anglers looking for a sportfishing lodge that was remote and catered to only a small number of anglers. Their travel agent in California recommended Silver Salmon Creek Lodge. They booked the trip and discovered it was exactly what they wanted.

The next year, the Waffens returned and stayed in the housekeeping cabin, which is less expensive and allowed them to stay longer. They returned again the third summer. In mid-August, they noticed that manager David Coray needed additional help because several employees had to return to jobs or school. Delores mentioned to Coray that she would consider taking an early-retirement from her job as a school teacher in California if he would consider hiring her as the lodge cook. She would work for him the next summer during the interim period of August through mid-September, when lodge personnel would be making the transition. Tony returned to California at the end of his vacation, and Delores stayed behind to smooth the transition of lodge personnel. She has been the lodge cook ever since.

The following year Delores was in charge of the kitchen. She planned menus and ordered and prepared food. A bush plane flies in food on a weekly basis from Soldotna. Rhubarb, blueberries and horseradish are grown in the lodge garden. Delores said that guests frequently request halibut and salmon for dinner. Clam chowder is a popular lunch item. Goosetongue surprises most people. Guests love it, but are amazed at first to find it on the dinner table after seeing it growing wild in the lodge's front yard, a tidal flat.

Delores classifies the food at the lodge as hearty homestyle. The lodge has a collection of recipes that former cooks have left behind. Delores strives to maintain a consistency in food preparation, while at the same time adding her own special flair.

Delores has a special interest in dogsledding. During the winter she comes back to Alaska to be part of the Iditarod Trail Sled Dog Race and indulge in some private dogsledding.

"Employee turnover at fishing lodges is a major problem," says Delores, "because lodge employees often think they are going to enjoy an extended vacation. Just the opposite is true. The hours are long and the work intense." She also observes that many young people have a sense of adventure, but no long-term commitment to their employer. Once the "newness" of working at a fishing lodge wears off, they drift on to the next adventure.

Delores has found many adventures in Alaska, but happily calls Silver Salmon Creek Lodge her "summer home."

All-for-the-Halibut Surprise

The halibut fishing out of Silver Salmon Lodge offers many surprises. Until the fish is brought to boat, anglers generally don't know what they have on. Some of the interesting catches include skates, cod, rockfish, Irish lords and sharks. Return these species to the water. After all, most anglers go "all for the halibut," or not at all.

1	**cup sour cream**
⅓	**cup mayonnaise**
2	**pounds halibut fillets**
	salt
1	**small jar artichoke hearts, drained and chopped**
1	**4-ounce can mushrooms, drained and chopped**
½	**cup grated Cheddar cheese**
½	**cup chopped green onions**

Preheat oven to 400 degrees. Lightly *grease* baking dish. In a small bowl, *blend* sour cream and mayonnaise, *set* aside.

Place layer of halibut in dish. *Sprinkle* lightly with salt. *Layer* artichoke hearts and mushrooms on top of halibut. *Place* another layer of halibut on top of artichoke hearts and mushrooms. *Bake* for 15 minutes in 400-degree oven.

Remove from oven. *Top* with sour cream and mayonnaise mixture. *Sprinkle* with cheese and green onions.

Return to oven and *bake* just until cheese melts.

Serves 4—6

Cook Inlet Salmon

*C*ook Inlet was named by the Earl of Sandwich for Captain James Cook, who explored and mapped this region in 1778. Cook Inlet extends southwest 220 miles from Anchorage to its junction with Shelikof Strait at Barren Islands.

Silver Salmon Creek Lodge is 30 miles west of Soldotna, across Cook Inlet. Guests fish for silver salmon in August when they begin to enter Silver Salmon Creek from Cook Inlet.

That's when I pull out this favorite recipe. It's very quick and easy. The sauce imparts a sweet, delicate flavor that doesn't overpower the salmon.

2	**silver salmon fillets**
1	**cup butter or margarine**
1	**cup brown sugar**
1	**cup soy sauce**

Preheat oven to 400 degrees. **Lay** the two salmon fillets, side by side, skin side down, in 13x9x2-inch baking dish.

In a small bowl, **melt** butter or margarine in the microwave or in a saucepan on top of the stove. **Add** sugar and *stir* to dissolve. **Blend** in soy sauce. **Pour** sauce over salmon and *baste* while baking.

Bake uncovered at 400 degrees for 20 to 30 minutes until salmon flakes, but is still moist. **Do *not* overcook.**

Serves 8

Springer Salmon Marinade

*S*pringer refers to the first run of king salmon that migrates past the doorsteps of Silver Salmon Creek Lodge in late May. David Coray, lodge manager, likes to grill fillets from these fish on the outside barbeque with the scent of sweet, spring wildflowers in the air.

This marinade gives king salmon the same color as "blackened fish." It's also excellent with chicken.

½	**cup olive oil**
¼	**cup soy sauce**
3	**tablespoons ketchup**
2	**tablespoons vinegar**
5	**cloves garlic**
	white pepper to taste
2 - 3	**pounds salmon fillets or steaks**

In a large, shallow pan, *mix* together olive oil, soy sauce, ketchup, vinegar, garlic and pepper. **Marinate** salmon in mixture for at least one hour before **grilling** on barbecue grill.

Serves 6

Photo at right: These tasty salmon fillets grilled on the outside barbeque are the perfect food to brighten any angler's day.

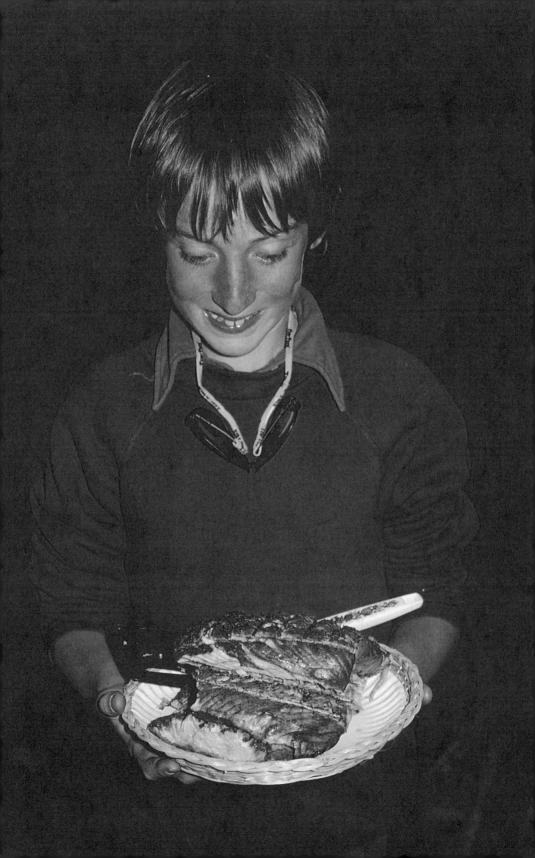

Sour Cream Chicken Breasts

A great dish to serve for a dinner party. It is very attractive and requires little prep time. Serve with rice and steamed broccoli.

1	tablespoon butter for pan
6	medium-sized whole chicken breasts, deboned and cut in half
	salt and pepper
	garlic powder
6	strips bacon, cut in half
1	can cream of mushroom soup
½	cup sour cream
½	cup slivered or sliced almonds

Preheat oven to 300 degrees. Lightly *butter* large, shallow baking dish or pan.

Season chicken lightly with salt, pepper and garlic powder. *Wrap* each piece of chicken with strip of bacon and *secure* with toothpick if necessary.

In a small bowl, *blend* soup and sour cream. *Arrange* chicken in baking dish or pan. *Pour* soup mixture over the chicken and *top* with almonds.

Bake uncovered in 300-degree oven for 2 to 2½ hours.

Serves 12

Goosetongue

*G*oosetongue, sometimes called wild spinach, is common to tidal areas in southcentral Alaska. It grows about 6 inches high in clusters, has a natural salt flavor and is an excellent fresh green vegetable.

"Guests are always surprised when I gather the goosetongue from the front yard of the lodge and serve it for dinner," says Delores Waffen, cook at Silver Salmon Creek Lodge. Guests' comments include, "Is this really the stuff that grows out in the tidal flats?"

It also tastes great with bacon and onions.

goosetongue
water
granulated sugar
Parmesan cheese
butter

Gather fresh goosetongue, *picking* the small tender shoots with no brown spots. **Wash** carefully, *changing* water a couple of times to rinse out the sand.

Cook as you would fresh spinach. **Boil** a small amount of water, add goosetongue and a pinch of sugar. *Cover* when goosetongue begins to change color. **Drain** all water.

Toss with Parmesan cheese and butter to taste.

Garnish with sliced, hardcooked egg.

Glacier Creek Clam Chowder

Silver Salmon Creek Lodge harvests clams and serves chowder as a popular lunch item.

4	slices bacon, chopped
1	medium onion, chopped
1	cup chopped celery
2	large potatoes, peeled and diced
3	cups water
1½	teaspoons salt
¼	teaspoon red pepper
½	teaspoon garlic powder
½	teaspoon basil
1	pound fresh clam meat, chopped
¼	cup cornstarch
2	cups milk
	parsley for garnish

In a 4-quart stockpot, *cook* bacon until limp. **Add** onion and celery. *Saute* until bacon is crisp and onion and celery are tender. *Pour* off bacon grease.

Add potatoes, water, salt, red pepper, garlic powder and basil. **Bring** to boil; *reduce* heat and *simmer* covered for 15 to 20 minutes or until potatoes are tender.

Add clams and *cook* on medium heat about 10 minutes. **Dissolve** cornstarch in milk. Gradually **add** to mixture. **Simmer** on low heat, *stirring* constantly until chowder thickens.

Garnish individual bowls with parsley and *serve*.

Serves 4—6

Termination Dust Squares

*I*n September, the first dusting of snow hits the Chugach Mountains. This natural indicator means it's time to conclude summer and fall projects and gear up for winter. At Silver Salmon Creek Lodge, the powdered sugar on these lemon squares is a type of termination dust that says it's time to relax after a good day of fishing.

2	**cups all-purpose flour**
½	**cup powdered sugar**
1	**cup margarine or butter**
4	**eggs, beaten**
2	**cups granulated sugar**
½	**cup lemon juice**
¼	**cup all-purpose flour**
½	**teaspoon baking powder**
¼	**cup powdered sugar**

Preheat oven to 350 degrees.

In a bowl, *sift* together 2 cups flour and ½ cup powdered sugar. *Cut* in margarine or butter until mixture clings together. *Press* into 9x13x2-inch baking pan. *Bake* at 350 degrees for 20 to 25 minutes or until lightly browned.

In another bowl, *beat* together eggs, granulated sugar and lemon juice. *Sift* together ¼ cup flour and baking powder; *stir* into egg mixture. *Pour* over baked crust. *Bake* at 350 degrees for 25 minutes.

Remove from oven, *sprinkle* with powdered sugar. *Cool* completely. *Cut* into 2-inch squares.

Makes 24 squares

Blueberry Cobbler

2   tablespoons butter
4   cups Alaska blueberries
½   cup water
¼   cup granulated sugar (up to ½ cup depending
    on tartness of berries)
2   tablespoons cornstarch
¼   cup cold water
1   teaspoon lemon juice

Butter a 9x9-inch casserole dish. Set aside.

In a 2-quart saucepan, bring berries and water to a boil and add sugar to taste. Dissolve cornstarch in cold water. Reduce heat and stir in cornstarch mixture. Bring to second boil. Cook for 2 to 3 minutes to thicken, stirring constantly. Remove from heat, stir in lemon juice. Pour into casserole dish. Top with biscuit dough to make crust. Bake 18 to 20 minutes at 400 degrees until crust is light brown.

Simple Biscuit Crust

1   cup all-purpose flour
1   teaspoon baking powder
½   teaspoon salt
2   teaspoons sugar
¼   cup butter or margarine
¼   cup water

Sift together flour, baking powder, salt and sugar. Cut butter or margarine into dry ingredients with a pastry blender or electric mixer. Moisten mixture with water, one tablespoon at a time, until consistency of biscuit dough. Drop by spoonfuls onto berries.

Serves 6

Red Glacier Grits

Red Glacier is near Hyder, in southeast Alaska. In 1926, it was named so by A.F. Buddington, U.S. Geological Survey, because the "moraine of this glacier is almost wholly of red quartz monzonite boulders." The white grits and red salsa, and rugged frontier taste, is a fitting tribute to this remote geological attraction.

As an entree, make this dish with pork sausage. Without the sausage, this makes a great side dish for breakfast or to accompany fish.

1	cup dry grits
5	cups water
1	pound bulk pork sausage (optional)
1	medium onion, chopped
3	4-ounce cans mild green chilies, diced (not jalepeno)
2	large eggs
2¼	cups grated Cheddar cheese
½	cup margarine
1	8-ounce jar mild or medium salsa
5-10	dashes hot pepper sauce

In a 2-quart saucepan, *cook* grits in 5 cups water until thick. *Set* aside. *Preheat* oven to 325 degrees.

In a frying pan, *saute* sausage and onion, *drain* fat. *Add* sausage and onion mixture, chilies, eggs, 2 cups cheese, margarine, salsa and hot pepper sauce to cooked grits. *Pour* into 9x13x2-inch oven-proof casserole dish. *Sprinkle* with remaining ¼ cup cheese.

Bake at 325 degrees for one hour.

Serves 12

Blueberry Griddle Cakes

This sweet batter is just right for tart Alaska blueberries. By not mixing blueberries into batter before pouring pancakes on the griddle, you avoid blue batter, making the pancakes much more attractive.

1¼ **cups all-purpose flour**
2½ **teaspoons baking powder**
4 **tablespoons granulated sugar**
¾ **teaspoon salt**
1 **egg**
1 **cup milk**
3 **tablespoons butter, melted**
1 **cup Alaska blueberries**

Preheat griddle (350 degrees for electric frypan).

In a large bowl, *sift* flour, baking powder, sugar and salt together. *Beat* egg in a separate bowl and *add* milk. *Stir* egg mixture into dry ingredients and *mix*. *Add* melted butter and *mix* thoroughly until batter is smooth.

Pour batter (approximately ½ cup for each pancake) onto preheated griddle or frypan.

Drop several blueberries on each freshly poured pancake. Pancakes are ready to be flipped when bubbles appear over the top. *Turn* pancakes and *cook* until golden brown.

Makes 10—12 medium-sized (4-inch) griddle cakes

Photo on opposite page: Author Adela Batin prepares Alaska blueberry griddle cakes for a group of hungry anglers. The blueberries were just picked, outside the cabin door.

Iliamna Lake Resort

*I*liamna Lake Resort is noticeably different from other Alaska fishing lodges. You'll find it near the village of Iliamna, a small community on the Lake Iliamna shoreline. The lodge complex is a series of two-story duplex townhouses complete with all the amenities. The townhouses are mansions when compared to the cold and cramped cabins of many other lodges. Each unit offers a deluxe kitchen, stocked refrigerator, elegant bath and cozy living room with television. The main lodge building consists of a lounge and trophy area, central dining room and kitchen. This is the focal point of activity at the beginning and end of each day.

A gravel road—also used as the town's airstrip—separates the guest cabins from the main lodge building. Not only do you need to look both ways when crossing over to your cabin, but you also need to look up over both ends of the airstrip to avoid having a Super Cub or Cessna drop down on you unexpectedly.

Manager Jim Winchester says the Iliamna area is the sportfishing Mecca of Alaska. Covering more than 1,000 square miles, Iliamna Lake is Alaska's largest. It is fed by a multitude of streams and tributaries, and is drained by the Kvichak River. Close by are the Naknek, Egegik and Ugashik drainages, which also contain world-class fishing.

Numbers of fish are another plus. Iliamna's sockeye salmon runs are awe-inspiring, with as many as 62 million fish returning annually to its myriad lakes and rivers. The Kvichak River alone is the largest producer of sockeye salmon in the world. And in even-numbered years, pink salmon are abundant to the point that they are ''aquatic pests,'' striking flies meant for other species.

*P*erhaps the most exciting part of Iliamna is its trophy rainbow fishery. Iliamna is the heart of the Bristol Bay Wild Trout Zone. The native rainbows in this region are among the largest in North America. Iliamna rainbows reach 10 to 15 pounds. At times, the only way to distinguish them from the chunky shape of 10- to 12-pound salmon is by color: salmon are red, rainbows are silvery blue. The life history of these fast-growing fish is worth knowing. They live in rivers until age two or three. Then they migrate into lakes, such as Iliamna, to live. In the spring they embark on seasonal migrations to tributary streams to spawn. In September, they return to those streams to feed on salmon eggs.

What species you will pursue at Iliamna Lake Resort depends on your preference, what's available at the time, and weather. Lodge pilots can fly you anywhere within a 200-square-mile radius of Iliamna, which includes trophy fish areas as far south as Ugashik, as far west as Bristol Bay, and as far north as the Mulchatna system. Much of the best fishing is directly south of Iliamna, and on the Naknek, Kvichak and smaller streams and creeks, and in Katmai National Monument.

A popular fishing hotspot for Iliamna Lake Resort guests is the Newhalen River, where anglers catch rainbow, grayling, char and a few of the millions of sockeye salmon that migrate into this river every year.

Good fishing is easily accessible by road from the lodge. Of the Iliamna tributaries, the Newhalen River is popular for salmon, grayling, rainbow and char. When gusty winds keep anglers on the ground, as it did to us one day, the Newhalen beckons.

*A*nglers spend as much time viewing the many sights as they do fishing. Chris and I were no exception. Flying to Lake Clark was a memorable experience. Bull moose sparred in the forests below, and herds of caribou migrated on top of long, snake-like eskers left from the last Great Ice Age. Although many have diminished in size, alpine glaciers still hang from mountaintops in Lake Clark Pass. I've flown through it many times, and each time I do, I am spellbound by its beauty. The ice-gouged mountainsides, rocky spires, long, feathery waterfalls, and lush river bottomlands offer as much—if not more— excitement than a day of fishing.

Iliamna Lake Resort specializes in gourmet lunches. While we were fishing for lake trout and grayling at a feeder stream emptying into Lake Clark, our guide, Randy, prepared a four-course lunch for us on a smooth gravel bar. After we had caught and released a dozen fish each, Chris and I took a break. We sampled the various appetizers, as well as pastas, entrees and soup prepared ahead of time at the lodge.

Iliamna Lake Resort is not a rough-it type of lodge. It's for those who want to experience the best comforts of civilization, from fine dining to end-of-day solitude in a private townhouse. As for the fishing, Jim Winchester and his guides are doing their best to ensure the Iliamna Lake area remains a world-class fishery for years to come.

Our guide, Randy, preparing a four-course lunch for us on a smooth gravel bar within casting distance of excellent lake trout and grayling fishing.

Elaine Wurster, Cook, Iliamna Lake Resort

In 1978, Elaine came from New England to enjoy a three-week vacation in Alaska, and liked it so much, she decided to stay! She landed a job in Anchorage with Merrill Lynch, working in sales and public relations, but she yearned to cook at a fishing lodge. Soon thereafter, Iliamna Lake Resort hired her through a mutual friend. Elaine says that the job more than meets her expectations. "It's like having a private dinner party in my home every night," she said.

Elaine pampers the lodge guests. She tailors her menu to them, paying special attention to preferences or dietary restrictions.

Elaine's favorite pastimes are traveling and cooking; in fact, she travels to eat. Her journeys throughout Europe have given her many ideas that she brings to her food preparation at the lodge. "The food in France is the best," she said. "Spain has lots of little snacks to eat all day. I was impressed that I didn't see any fat people in Europe. One theory is that the red wine served with the meal breaks down the fat and harmful cholesterol."

When preparing food, Elaine uses olive oil, subtle sauces, and lemon juice instead of salt. She fries very few foods and doesn't use any instant foods (potatoes, cake mixes or frostings), fixing everything fresh. Elaine grows her own herbs and rhubarb in the lodge's garden. Every week, Anchorage food brokers ship fresh Alaska sausage, eggs and milk to the lodge.

Elaine describes her food as European and gourmet.

While most cooks might get upset when anglers arrive late for dinner, Elaine goes with the flow. "I've served Veal Marsala for dinner at 10 p.m.," she said. "Everyone at the lodge has a 'can do' attitude, which makes the environment more exciting and pleasant for guests!"

Elaine spoils anglers at lunch, also. We were surprised to see a feast spread on the stream bank when we took our noon break from fishing. She had prepared everything ahead of time, and instructed the guides well on the proper presentation of the picnic setting, complete with wine. Spread on a red and white checkered tablecloth were a variety of appetizers and salads, hot soup, main course and dessert cakes. This moveable feast was fit for royalty.

Elaine's Pecan Salmon

Pecan Sauce:

4	tablespoons unsalted butter, softened
½	cup coarsely chopped pecans
2	tablespoons finely chopped onion
1	teaspoon lemon juice
½	teaspoon Tabasco sauce
¼	teaspoon minced garlic

Place above ingredients in a blender or food processor. *Process* until creamy and smooth, about 2 to 3 minutes, *pushing* down sides of mixture a few times with a rubber spatula. *Set* aside.

Fish Seasoning Mix:

½	cup milk
1	egg, beaten
1	tablespoon salt
1	teaspoon onion powder
1	teaspoon paprika
¾	teaspoon ground cayenne pepper
½	teaspoon white pepper
½	teaspoon garlic powder
½	teaspoon black pepper
¼	teaspoon dry mustard
¼	teaspoon dried oregano leaves
¼	teaspoon dried thyme leaves
1	cup all-purpose flour
1	silver salmon, filleted and cut into serving-size pieces
	vegetable oil for frying fish
6	tablespoons coarsely chopped, dry roasted pecans

Beat milk and egg in a pan until well-blended. In a small bowl, thoroughly *combine* the seasonings. In a separate pan, *add* 1 tablespoon of the seasoning mix to 1 cup of flour; *mix* well. *Sprinkle* some of the remaining seasoning mix lightly and evenly on both sides of the fillets, *patting* it in by hand. *Warm* the serving plates in a 250-degree oven.

Heat about ¼ inch oil in a very large, heavy skillet to about 350 degrees. *Dredge* each fillet in the seasoned flour, *shake* off excess; *soak* in the egg mixture. Just before frying, *drain* off egg mixture. *Dredge* fillets once more through the flour, *shaking* off excess. *Fry* the fillets in the hot oil until golden brown, about 2 to 3 minutes per side. *Drain* on paper towels and, while still on the towels and very hot, *spread* 2 tablespoons of the Pecan Sauce, page 280, over the top of each fillet.

To serve fillets, *spoon* a scant ⅓ cup Elaine's Sauce (below) onto each heated serving plate and *place* a fillet on top. *Sprinkle* each fillet with 1 tablespoon pecans.

Serves 6

Elaine's Sauce

1	**cup seafood stock**
¾	**teaspoon minced garlic**
¾	**pound (3 sticks) unsalted butter**
2	**tablespoons all-purpose flour**
¼	**cup Worcestershire sauce**
¼	**teaspoon salt**

In a 2-quart saucepan, *combine* stock and garlic. *Bring* to a boil over high heat, *reduce* heat and *simmer* 2 minutes. *Remove* from heat. In a 1-quart saucepan, *melt* ½ stick butter over high heat, *add* the flour and *whisk* 10 seconds until smooth. *Remove* from heat. *Return* stock mixture to medium heat. Gradually *add* the butter mixture, *whisking* until smooth. *Reduce* heat to low, *add* remaining 2½ sticks of butter, a little at a time, *whisking* constantly when butter is melted. *Whisk* in Worcestershire sauce and salt. *Cook* 5 minutes until sauce thickens, *whisking* often.

Makes 2 cups

Igiugig Lox

Igiugig is a point of land that acts as a gateway to the millions of salmon that each year enter Lake Iliamna. Slices of this specially prepared lox are carefully packed in Iliamna Lake Resort's famous shore-lunch baskets. They make for a tasty snack in between catching fish.

1	**3½-4 pound fresh red or silver salmon, filleted and deboned, with skin left on**
¼	**cup kosher salt**
2	**teaspoons white pepper**
¼	**cup granulated sugar**
	fresh dill sprigs
1	**shot bourbon**

Spread aluminum foil on baking sheet. **Lay** salmon fillets on foil with skin side down. **Mix** together salt, pepper and sugar. **Sprinkle** on salmon, *dot* with fresh dill sprigs (not dried). **Sprinkle** with shot of bourbon. **Lay** one fish fillet on top of the other with meat sides together, skin side out. **Wrap** fish tightly in foil.

Lay fish in pan, *place* a plate or board on top of fish, *weighing down* with clean rocks or heavy cans. *Place* in refrigerator.

Turn fish over 2 or 3 times a day for 3 days. After 3 days, *open* foil and *rinse* fish thoroughly. **Slice** fish diagonally in thin slices. **Serve** on fine, crisp crackers or bread with unsalted butter and a sprig of fresh dill or mustard sauce.

Serves 16—20

Lake Clark Carrot Soup

Lake Clark is a wonderfully diverse area with wilderness rivers, lakes, glaciers and forests that would take years to explore. The trout and char fishing is equally impressive, drawing anglers from around the world. It is only natural that a soup with this name has the fresh, invigorating taste that parallels the essence of this area.

6   **tablespoons unsalted butter**
1   **large yellow onion, chopped**
¼   **cup finely chopped fresh ginger root**
3   **cloves garlic, minced**
7   **cups chicken stock**
1   **cup dry white wine**
1½   **pounds carrots, peeled and cut into**
      ½-inch pieces
2   **tablespoons fresh lemon juice**
      pinch curry powder
      salt and freshly ground black pepper to taste
      snipped fresh chives or chopped fresh parsley
      for garnish

Melt the butter in a large stock pot over medium heat. **Add** the onion, ginger and garlic and *saute* for 15 to 20 minutes.

Add the stock, wine and carrots. **Heat** to boiling. **Reduce** heat and *simmer* uncovered over medium heat until the carrots are very tender, about 45 minutes.

Puree the soup in a blender or food processor fitted with a steel blade. **Season** with lemon juice, curry powder, salt and pepper to taste. **Sprinkle** with chives or parsley. **Serve** the soup hot or chilled.

Serves 6

Koktuli Fruit Galette

*W*hile the Koktuli doesn't have any fruit trees, anglers do delight in the river's rainbow trout fishery. The light nature of this dessert suggests the best way to float this river: pack a minimal amount of gear, a lightweight flyrod and plenty of gossamer tippets for these tail-dancing rainbows.

1	**9-inch round of puff pastry, well-chilled**
2	**tablespoons all-purpose flour**
½	**cup granulated sugar**
4	**firm, ripe, unpeeled nectarines, halved, pitted and thinly sliced**
1	**egg yolk**
1	**tablespoon heavy cream**
1	**tablespoon cold, unsalted butter, cut into small pieces**

Preheat oven to 400 degrees.

Place the circle of puff pastry (available in frozen food section of grocery store) on a parchment-lined baking sheet. With the tines of a fork, *prick* the pastry surface except for a ½-inch rim. *Sprinkle* only the punctured area of the circle with flour and ¼ cup sugar.

Starting just inside the unpunctured edge, *arrange* the nectarine slices, cut edges toward the center, in concentric circles *covering* the pastry entirely.

Beat egg yolk with heavy cream to make a glaze. *Brush* the egg yolk glaze on just the exposed rim of puff pastry, *sprinkle* the remaining ¼ cup sugar on top of the fruit and dot with butter. *Bake* for 18 to 20 minutes at 400 degrees until the fruit is tender and the pastry has puffed and turned golden brown. *Serve* immediately.

Serves 6

Photo on opposite page: Elaine Wurster prepares to serve lodge guests Koktuli Fruit Galette.

Brooks Bread Pudding

3   eggs
1¼   cups granulated sugar
1½   teaspoons vanilla
1¼   teaspoons nutmeg
1¼   teaspoons cinnamon
¼   cup unsalted butter, melted
2   cups milk
½   cup raisins
½   cup coarsely chopped pecans
5   cups very stale French bread cubes, with
     crusts on

Preheat oven to 350 degrees. *Grease* a 9x5x3-inch loaf pan.

In a large bowl, *beat* eggs with an electic mixer on high speed about 3 minutes, until extremely frothy and bubbles are the size of pinheads (or with a metal whisk for about 6 minutes). *Add* sugar, vanilla, nutmeg, cinnamon and butter and *beat* on high until well-blended. *Beat* in milk, then *stir* in raisins and pecans.

Place bread cubes in greased loaf pan. *Pour* egg mixture over them and *toss* until the bread is soaked. *Let sit* about 45 minutes, until liquid is absorbed by bread, *patting* the bread down into the liquid occasionally. *Place* in oven and immediately *lower* the heat to 300 degrees and *bake* 40 minutes. *Increase* oven temperature to 425 degrees and *bake* until pudding is well-browned and puffy, about 15 to 20 minutes longer. While bread pudding is baking, *prepare* Levelock Lemon Sauce and Brooks Cream, page 287.

To serve, *pour* 1½ tablespoons warm Lemon Sauce into each dessert dish, *add* ½ cup hot bread pudding and *top* with ¼ cup Brooks Cream.

Serves 8

Levelock Lemon Sauce

1   **lemon, halved**
½   **cup water**
¼   **cup granulated sugar**
2   **teaspoons cornstarch**
¼   **cup water**
1   **teaspoon vanilla**

Squeeze 2 tablespoons juice from the lemon halves into a 1-quart saucepan; *add* the lemon halves, water and sugar; *bring* to a boil. *Dissolve* cornstarch in ¼ cup water. *Stir* into lemon mixture and *add* vanilla. *Cook* 1 minute over high heat, *stirring* constantly. *Strain, squeezing* the sauce from the lemon rinds. *Serve* warm.

Makes ¾ cup

Brooks Cream

⅔   **cup heavy cream**
1   **teaspoon vanilla**
1   **teaspoon brandy**
1   **teaspoon orange liqueur**
¼   **cup granulated sugar**
2   **tablespoons sour cream**

Chill a medium-sized mixing bowl and beaters until very cold. *Combine* cream, vanilla, brandy and orange liqueur in the bowl and *beat* with electric mixer for one minute on medium speed. *Add* the sugar and sour cream and *beat* 3 minutes on medium speed, just until soft peaks form. *Do not overbeat.*

Makes 2 cups

The Batins' home outside Fairbanks.

Adela Batin's Best Recipes

I enjoy traveling, seeing the sights of the world with a pack strapped on my back. The huge cathedrals of Germany and the skyscrapers of New York are enthralling. But no matter where in the world I go, my heart always yearns to be back home in Alaska, in my log home amid our white birch forest, with the gentle breezes carrying the spicy smell of highbush cranberries into my kitchen.

Chris and I share our home with our Amazon parrot, Juliet, who imitates everything from the ringing phone to the neighbor's cat. This is sometimes confusing to our dog, Tiger Lily, who upon hearing Juliet, roams our acreage looking for the cat. She settles for chasing squirrels up the spruce trees.

I've lived in this log home since graduating from Boise State University with a degree in Advertising Design and Photography. In 1979, I started a graphic design agency, Award Design. Since then I've designed books, brochures, corporate logos and exhibits. My photographs have appeared in many books and national publications, including *Sports Afield, Western Outdoors, North American Fisherman, In-Fisherman, Alaska Outdoors and Family Adventures,* to name a few. I've been on the cover of nine national magazines and was featured in *Trout* magazine as one of the top women anglers in the country. In 1986, the American Business Women's Association chose me as one of the Top Ten Business Women in the United States.

I visited my first fishing lodge, Freebird Charter & Fish Camp on the Kenai River, in 1981. There are few things more stimulating to the appetite than spending the day fishing, breathing the fresh air and challenging the strength and prowess of the giant Kenai king salmon. I caught my first king salmon on that trip, a 56-pound fish that was an International Gamefish Association world record for the 25-pound-test line class.

After an exhaustive day of fighting fish with Freebird, we came "home" to Sheary Suiter's deliciously prepared family-style meal. The exhilaration of the day's events and the comfort of a home-cooked meal brought back the warm, nostalgic feelings of my childhood. I was happy.

Since that first trip, Chris and I have spent every summer sampling the full spectrum of Alaska fishing, from tent camping to full-service lodges. As outdoor photo-journalists, we write about the Alaska fishing lodge experience for national magazines and our books. We meet people from a wide range of economic and professional levels from all over the world. The lodge setting gives us the unique opportunity to meet and mingle with people we'd never meet otherwise. All these people have one thing in common—the desire to experience wilderness Alaska and its fishing, or to retreat from the hustle and bustle of civilization to cleanse their souls. Fishing lodges have a way of breaking down the civil pretenses we often exhibit at home or work.

For instance, while having dinner one evening at Wood River Lodge in the heart of the Tikchik-Wood River area, one of the lodge guests, an attorney I'll call John, was late for the evening meal. Before he arrived, there were various comments made by his fishing partners that John had just taken a shower and was drying his hair.

Their comments didn't make much of an impression until John arrived and sat down across the table from me.

I saw that he was completely bald, except for a small group of long hairs, carefully combed and pasted across his forehead. The look of astonishment in my eyes quickly turned to embarrassment as his lawyer friends burst into laughter when John returned my stare.

This was the candid side of John I would never have seen had I met him in a courtroom.

This is what makes the lodge environment so intriguing. People from all walks of life meet and have the love of the outdoors in common. Even if you have never experienced this at an Alaska fishing lodge, you might have experienced it in other ways.

I first felt this camaraderie in my youth. In 1963, my adventurous mother and I moved from Texas to Alaska. We knew only two people when we arrived: my Aunt Esther and Uncle Curtis. They introduced us to several families in the neighborhood. Two days later, one of the families invited us on our first Alaska outing—raspberry picking.

As I climbed into the front seat of the neighbor's car I nervously glanced at the two young boys my age in the back seat. "Are they going berry picking too?" I asked.

"No," was the reply, "they are going fishing."

My, I thought, we are going someplace where we can go berry picking and fishing at the same time? I was impressed with Alaska.

As we drove along Turnagain Arm I was overwhelmed with the beauty of the water and the way the road curved and snaked around the cliffs. Alaska was definitely more intriguing than the flat plains of west Texas.

We arrived at Bird Creek, and the boys bounded out of the car, grabbed their fishing rods and scurried down to the water's edge. Pat, as Mrs. Ward insisted I call her, pointed the way up the trail on the side of the mountain, where we would search for the precious wild raspberries. As we climbed the trail, we came to a clearing where there was a large boulder about the size of a one-car garage. Being a tomboy, I insisted on climbing the rock so I could see the creek below and the boys fishing. It looked as if they were having a lot more fun than me, and I couldn't figure out why I hadn't been asked to go fishing instead of berry picking.

$\mathcal{T}$hat first trip was a very important link to future adventures in the Alaska wilderness. I was hooked on harvesting food from the land. Pat and I spent the summer days picking blueberries, raspberries and cranberries at all her secret berry spots. I was eventually invited on a few fishing trips. But most often I was invited to dinner.

It was at the Ward's dining table that I tasted my first emperor goose, moose steak, caribou summer sausage, buffalo roast, sheep steak, baked salmon and roasted wild duck. I remember how lucky I felt their family was, to be able to eat such an abundant harvest of wild game.

At dinner, the conversation would quickly turn to the fishing adventure that produced the feast we were eating. The fish was the big one that didn't get away. Those exciting stories made me appreciate the food even more.

$\mathcal{D}$uring the past 30 years in Alaska, I've felt fortunate to experience a wilderness lifestyle most people only dream about. And I'm thankful for the many people who have shared these experiences with me. Alaska is a special land; her people share an independent spirit. We thrive in living off the land, while at the same time respecting those resources that give us so much pleasure. But we must savor each moment and manage our resources wisely, so future generations can also enjoy this precious lifestyle.

Adela Batin with a king salmon she caught and released in a river of the Susitna watershed.

Garden Stuffed Salmon

*W*hen the sockeye salmon are running and we bring home our winter supply, I always set aside a fresh fish to use for this dish. Serve with Goldstream Cornbread, page 297, and Fruit & Yogurt Salad, page 295.

2	**cups fine dry bread crumbs**
1	**cup finely grated raw carrots**
1	**cup finely chopped onion, sauteed in butter**
1	**cup chopped fresh mushrooms**
½	**cup chopped fresh parsley**
1	**egg, beaten**
1½	**tablespoons lemon juice**
1	**clove garlic, minced**
2	**teaspoons salt**
¼	**teaspoon pepper**
1	**6- to 8-pound sockeye salmon, dressed**
2	**17-ounce cans stewed tomatoes**

In a large mixing bowl, *combine* bread crumbs, carrots, sauteed onion, mushrooms, parsley, egg, lemon juice, garlic, salt and pepper. **Mix** thoroughly. *Set* aside.

Lightly *grease* bottom of oblong baking pan. *Lay* salmon in baking pan and *open* to expose body cavity.

Spoon mixture into salmon until stuffed. *Close* sides of salmon together. *Spoon* rest of mixture around the edges of salmon to fill baking dish. *Pour* stewed tomatoes over salmon. *Bake* at 375 degrees for one hour.

Serves 6—8

Variation

Instead of using dressed fish, butterfly whole fish. This is a double fillet held together by the skin, and allows for easier serving of fish and stuffing without the bones.

Creekside Croquettes

*T*his is one of my all-time favorite recipes. The original recipe was handed down from my mother, who laboriously made her own white sauce. I'm always in a hurry and substitute a can of cream of mushroom soup for the white sauce. For a different flavor, use half cream cheese and half mayonnaise.

4   **cups flaked salmon (or leftover salmon from Garden Stuffed Salmon recipe, page 292)**
1   **can cream of mushroom soup (or white sauce)**
¼   **cup chopped onion**
¼   **cup chopped celery**
2   **teaspoons dried parsley**
1   **teaspoon lemon/herb seasoning**
½   **teaspoon pepper**
½   **teaspoon dried dillweed**
½   **teaspoon paprika**
1   **cup flour**
½   **sleeve Ritz crackers, finely crumbled**
1   **cup bread crumbs**
2   **eggs, beaten in separate bowl**
    vegetable oil

In a large bowl, *mix* salmon, mushroom soup, onion, celery, parsley, lemon/herb seasoning, pepper, dillweed and paprika. *Stir* until thoroughly mixed. Be sure to *remove* all fish bones.

Pour flour on a plate. *Shape* salmon mixture into 10 three-inch patties and *dredge* in flour. If time permits, *refrigerate* patties until chilled. *Mix* crackers and bread crumbs on a separate plate. *Dip* each patty in beaten egg, then *coat* with cracker/bread crumb mixture.

Heat vegetable oil on medium high in frying pan or electric skillet. *Be careful* not to get the oil too hot, otherwise the bread crumbs will burn. *Fry* the patties approximately 5 minutes per side or until golden brown. *Drain* on paper towels to absorb excess oil.

Serves 5

Stuffed Zucchini

*I*n Fairbanks, the power goes out quite often in the wintertime, usually during cold spells of 20 below zero or colder.

One evening I had just prepared this dish and was ready to put it in the oven when our power went out. Unfortunately, we were also expecting guests for dinner. I put the casserole on top of one of the wood stoves we heat our log home with and completely encased the top of the stove with aluminum foil, creating a "stove-top oven." This stuffed zucchini cooked beautifully, and was the hit of the evening.

1	**pound ground caribou, moose or beef**
½	**medium onion, chopped**
2	**cups cooked rice**
¼	**teaspoon pepper**
1	**teaspoon garlic salt**
1	**tablespoon dried parsley**
1	**4-ounce can mushrooms, chopped**
1½	**cups grated pepper jack cheese**
1	**large or two medium zucchini**

Preheat oven to 350 degrees. In a skillet, *brown* ground meat. *Add* onion and *cook* until onion is clear.

In a large bowl, *mix* rice, pepper, garlic salt, parsley and mushrooms. *Add* meat mixture and 1¼ cups cheese.

Cut zucchini in half and *scoop* out the inside. *Chop* up the insides of zucchini and *stir* into the rice/meat mixture.

Lightly *grease* baking pan and *lay* hollowed-out zucchini halves in the bottom with the scooped-out side facing up. *Stuff* zucchini with the mixture, but don't pack it down. *Sprinkle* ¼ cup cheese on the top.

Cover and *bake* at 350 degrees for 45 minutes. *Uncover* and *bake* 15 minutes longer to brown the top.

Serves 4—6

Fruit & Yogurt Salad

This fruit salad is a refreshing companion to a seafood entree.

2   **bananas, sliced**
1   **17-ounce can fruit cocktail, drained**
1   **7-ounce can mandarin oranges, drained**
1   **red delicious apple, cut in ½-inch pieces**
½   **cup sliced almonds**
1   **cup low fat strawberry banana yogurt, stirred**

In a salad bowl, *combine* bananas, fruit cocktail, mandarin oranges, apple and almonds. *Stir* in yogurt until well-mixed. *Cover* and *refrigerate* until ready to serve.

Serves 6

Author Adela Batin enjoys cooking over a campfire as much as preparing elaborate dinners in the kitchen. Here she is cooking a jack salmon next to the stream in which she caught the fish 20 minutes earlier. For fuel, she is burning driftwood in the stove which uses a convection fan, operated by a solar panel.

Good Neighbors Bread

*I*t's been said that you shouldn't plant zucchini unless you have a lot of friends. Zucchini grows almost too well in Fairbanks gardens—you need lots of friends to give the zucchini to and lots of recipes that allow you to enjoy its "fresh, juicy goodness."

Zucchini bread freezes well, so you can bake plenty of loaves to take to the neighbors or to that last-minute potluck. It slices well when frozen, and is great to serve when a neighbor knocks on your cabin door for a cup of tea.

3	eggs, beaten
1	cup vegetable oil
2	cups granulated sugar
2	cups grated zucchini
3	teaspoons vanilla
3	cups all-purpose flour (or half wheat, half white)
1	teaspoon salt
1	teaspoon baking soda
¼	teaspoon baking powder
3	teaspoons cinnamon
½	cup flaked coconut
½	cup chopped pecans

Preheat oven to 350 degrees. *Grease* and *flour* two 9x5x3-inch loaf pans.

In a large bowl, *mix* eggs, oil, sugar, zucchini and vanilla until well-blended.

In a separate bowl, *sift* flour, salt, baking soda, baking powder and cinnamon. *Stir* into egg/oil mixture. *Fold* in coconut and nuts.

Pour into two loaf pans. *Bake* at 350 degrees for one hour or until a toothpick inserted in the center comes out clean.

Makes 2 loaves

Goldstream Cornbread

¼ cup granulated sugar
1 cup yellow cornmeal
1 cup all-purpose flour
1 tablespoon baking powder
1 teaspoon onion salt
¼ teaspoon garlic powder
1 egg
1 cup milk
¼ cup vegetable oil
¼ cup chopped green pepper
1 teaspoon dried parsley

Preheat oven to 400 degrees. *Grease* an iron skillet or 9x9-inch baking dish.

In a bowl, *sift* together sugar, cornmeal, flour, baking powder, onion salt and garlic powder.

In a separate bowl, *beat* together egg, milk and oil. *Add* to dry ingredients, *stirring* until thoroughly mixed. *Stir* in green pepper and parsley. *Pour* into iron skillet or baking dish. *Bake* at 400 degrees for 35 to 40 minutes or until golden brown.

Serves 6—8

Variation

1 19-ounce can creamed corn
¼ cup chopped onion
2 tablespoons chopped pimiento
½ cup shredded Cheddar cheese
¼ cup chopped green pepper
1 teaspoon dried chives

Replace milk in above recipe with can of creamed corn. *Substitute* onion, pimiento, cheese, green pepper and chives for green pepper and parsley.

Chocolate Truffle Delight

2	cups heavy cream
3	egg yolks, slightly beaten
16	ounces semi-sweet chocolate
½	cup light or dark corn syrup
½	cup margarine or butter
¼	cup powdered sugar
1	teaspoon vanilla

Line 8½x4½x2½-inch loaf pan with plastic wrap. In a small bowl, *mix* ½ cup heavy cream with egg yolks.

In a 3-quart saucepan *stir* chocolate, corn syrup and margarine or butter over medium heat until melted. **Add** egg mixture and *cook* for three minutes, *stirring* constantly. **Cool** to room temperature.

In a mixing bowl, *beat* 1½ cups heavy cream, powdered sugar and vanilla until soft peaks form. **Fold** into chocolate and *stir* lightly until no streaks remain. **Pour** into loaf pan. **Refrigerate** overnight or *chill* in freezer three hours. **Slice** loaf into 12 slices and *serve* each slice with raspberry sauce.

Raspberry Sauce

2	10-ounce packages frozen raspberries, thawed
⅔	cup light corn syrup

Puree raspberries in a blender. **Strain** to remove seeds. **Stir** in corn syrup until well-blended. **Spoon** raspberry sauce onto individual plates and *top* with slice of chocolate truffle loaf.

Serves 12

Red Rhubarb Crunch

2	tablespoons butter
1	cup all-purpose flour
¾	cup oatmeal
¼	cup unprocessed bran
1	cup brown sugar
1	teaspoon cinnamon
½	cup butter, melted
1	cup granulated sugar
2	tablespoons cornstarch
1	cup cold water
1	teaspoon vanilla
4	cups rhubarb, cut into 1-inch pieces

Butter a 9-inch deep-dish pie plate or 9x9-inch baking pan.

Mix flour, oatmeal, bran, brown sugar and cinnamon together in a large bowl. *Add* melted butter and *stir* until all the butter is absorbed by the dry ingredients. *Press* half of the crunch mixture into pie plate or baking pan.

Combine granulated sugar, cornstarch and water in a 2-quart saucepan. *Stir* and *cook* over low heat until thick and clear. *Stir* in vanilla and rhubarb and continue *stirring* until rhubarb is well-coated with mixture. *Pour* rhubarb mixture into pie plate.

Sprinkle the rest of the crunch mixture evenly over the rhubarb. *Bake* at 350 degrees for one hour.

Serve warm with vanilla ice cream.

Serves 6—8

Epilogue

_T_hroughout this book, we've introduced you to notable individuals in Alaska's fishing lodge business—from lodge owners and fishing guides to cooks just beginning to realize their goals and dreams. Some chefs have excelled elsewhere and they are now searching for that elusive something not found in the elite restaurants of the world.

What are these people looking for? Or a better question for many is, what have they found? Why do culinary chefs, who would ordinarily be preparing one or two meals a day in a well-equipped kitchen maintain a grueling schedule of three to four meals a day at an Alaska wilderness fishing lodge with limited resources? And, why do they swear they wouldn't want to be anywhere else? The challenge? Perhaps. But let's dig deeper.

What lures a corporate president away from his business in New York city or a lawyer or doctor away from the intense challenges of her Boston practice?

We have seen them sit in a spike camp and, forsaking the fishing nearby, indulge in steaming hot char bits and fresh-baked blueberry muffins.

For these individuals and others, there is more to the allure of an Alaska fishing lodge than just the fishing. The lodge environment is perfect for developing a unique type of camaraderie, of becoming one with Nature. For many, this entire process of heading afield with friends, catching fish for dinner, pulling crab traps, digging for clams, picking huckleberries for the morning's pancakes, or gathering a few greens for the salad is a sacred bond, and not one to be taken lightly. It's the act of bringing the harvest back to the collective group at the lodge, and to the preparers, where in the heady spirit of success and friendship, the day's events are relived.

This, my friend, is what brings the veteran chefs, the business people and us to Alaska's fishing lodges...the sharing and reliving of our day's experiences at a table in the Alaska wilderness. Here we see people drop their professional facades. Business executives, used to formal behavior in corporate board meetings, now pull the chef aside after dinner to cast a few flies on the streamside and talk about food, fishing and fun. How often do any of us do this with the chef at our favorite restaurant?

At Alaska's fishing lodges, guests and lodge personnel share a common bond in an uncommon land.

The following pages detail how to contact some of these lodges. We invite you to enjoy these unique lodge experiences yourself. We would also like to hear from you, our friend in Alaska sportfishing. Send us your comments, suggestions and stories on Alaska cooking, sportfishing and the lodge experience. Chris and I look forward to hearing from you.

Adela and Christopher Batin
P.O. Box 83550, Fairbanks, Alaska 99708

Christopher and Adela Batin discuss slide selection for a magazine cover, while their pet Amazon parrot, Juliet, observes and comments.

Information Supplement

Contact the following businesses for more information on enjoying Alaska's fishing and fine dining.

Alaska Sausage and Seafood means more than just fine cuts of meat and sausage. It's Alaska's favorite place to purchase smoked red, king or silver salmon, lox/kippered products, smoked salmon strips and squaw candy.

They can prepare your fish to take home from your Alaska fishing trip or they will ship you an order to prepare the recipes in this book.

In 1963, owner and operator, Herbert Eckmann, a German chef, started Alaska Sausage, which is the largest processor of wild game in Alaska. Their gift packs of Alaskan Sausage with Reindeer meat and Alaskan salami make an ideal gift for a business associate who wants a "taste of Alaska."

Kachemak Bay
WILDERNESS LODGE

Gorgeous sea and mountain panoramas. Exquisite accommodations, private chalets, fine dining, professional naturalist and fishing guides. Fish for salmon, trout, char, halibut. Dig clams, incredible 25' tides for tide pool exploring in China Poot Bay.

Numerous national and international awards. Called **"America's Best Wilderness Lodge"** by publisher of The Guinness Book.

Abundant bald eagles, puffins, bird and seal rookeries, sea otters. Glacier and coastal hiking, sea kayaking. Great for families. 12 guests maximum. Remote brown bear photography camp near McNeil River Sanctuary, 6 guests maximum. Boat and floatplane access only.

Kachemak Bay Wilderness Lodge
Box 956-AB, Homer, AK 99603
(907) 235-8910 Fax (907) 235-8911

Chosen as the "Wilderness Lodge Hideaway of the Year 1996" by Andrew Harper's Hideaway Report.

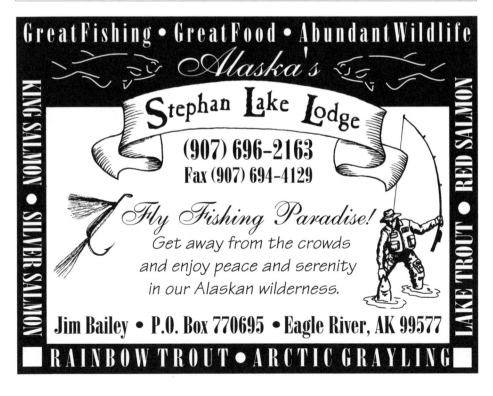

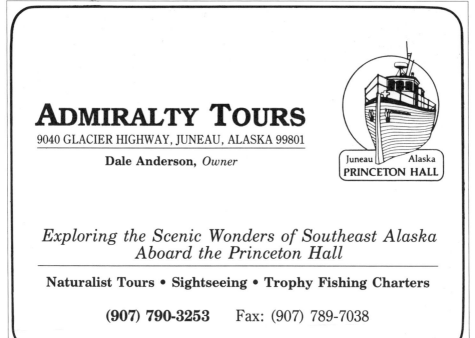
Best Recipes of Alaska's Fishing Lodges

"Best Recipes of Alaska's Fishing Lodges"
Author, Adela Batin, Will Teach
Your Cooking Club or Outdoor Group
the Secrets of Alaska Cooking and the Outdoors

Now your group can benefit from a wealth of Alaska outdoor cooking information by scheduling one of **Adela Batin's Alaska Cooking Seminars**, and make money for yourself, your club or organization at the same time.

This simple plan yields big results for everyone.

First, when your recommendation results in a seminar booking, you personally receive 10 percent of Adela's honorarium, which can mean as much as $500 for you.

Second, your organization can make money from this workshop.

Third, **Adela Batin's Alaska Cooking Seminars** are content-rich, stimulating events that are specially designed to meet the informational and entertainment needs of your group. Adela's outstanding photography and enthusiastic stage presence will entertain and educate your audience for an hour, a day or a weekend.

Her seminars are perfect for:
- Women's outdoor groups or cooking clubs
- Business or professional groups
- National and regional sport shows
- Instructional seminars at your lodge

Adela Batin brings over three decades of Alaska travel and cooking experience to these seminars. An accomplished outdoorswoman, she enjoys cooking over a campfire as much as preparing elaborate dinners. She became successful by helping others achieve their Alaska outdoor dreams. Call today and take advantage of this opportunity for you or your group to tap into the experience and knowledge of this Alaska outdoorswoman.

Here's what a satisfied participant said about Adela's seminar **"Cleaning and Cooking Your Catch"**:

"Adela is a wonderful teacher. Finally, I can fillet a fish. She had plenty of good information—all gathered from experience. And very good, simple recipes that can be made easily outdoors. I know I will use what I learned."

To savor the Alaska experience and enjoy a true taste of Alaska, write:

Adela Batin's Alaska Cooking Seminars
P.O. Box 82222-Q, Fairbanks, AK 99708

Or call (907) 455-8000 or fax (907) 455-6691

Index

How to catch Alaska's Trophy Sportfish

By Christopher Batin

"Alaska Fishing Book Unparalleled" *Rich Landers Field and Stream magazine*

Over 30,000 anglers around the world have benefited from this advanced guide.

Anyone can catch four-pound rainbows or 12-pound salmon. But if you want to catch 60 to 80-pound Alaska king salmon, 300-pound halibut, 20-pound silvers, 30-inch rainbow trout, trophy grayling and steelhead, **"How to catch Alaska's Trophy Sportfish"** is your must-have, on-stream guide.

How to catch
Alaska's Trophy Sportfish
by Christopher Batin
Foreword by Homer Circle
Angling Editor of
Sports Afield

ISBN 0-916771-03-2

This book is also a must-have volume to fully understand the author's fishing recommendations in "Fishing Alaska on $15 a Day."

"Batin's long time on Alaskan waters (over 30,000 hours) gives his new book singular value. What fisherman wouldn't pay for a decade of experience condensed into plain English? The author's experience shows. No matter what the species being sought, Batin's book is a great place to start." Joe Bridgman *The Anchorage Times.*

This book can make your Alaska fishing trip a success with its:

This Book Gives You A PH.D. Crash Course In Alaska Fish Habits and Biology Necessary for Success

"How to catch Alaska's Trophy Sportfish" translates volumes of biological data into terms every angler can understand and use to catch trophy sportfish.

You'll learn about:
- aggravation responses that catch 70-pound salmon,
- social hierarchies that tell you where to find fish before you reach the water,
- stream equations necessary for catching the largest trout and char.

We show you how each species of Alaska trophy sportfish respond to stimuli, and how you can duplicate those responses through our proven field tips and techniques. If you order NOW, you can have this knowledge today...at your fingertips.

Use this book when you go shopping for flies and tackle.

You receive sixteen full-color pages showing the different sportfish and the best flies and lures you need for success, all of which have earned the highest marks for catching trophy sportfish in 10 years of testing.

With this advice, you'll spend your time catching fish, rather than wondering what to catch them on.

- 368 pages and 120 action-filled photos showing you the fish-catching secrets that has enabled the author to catch and release thousands of sportfish.

- Fly fishing techniques for Alaska's lakes and streams.

- Detailed information, life histories, and feeding habits for all of Alaska's 17 major sportfish species.

- Over 500 specific areas in Alaska where you can catch your trophy sportfish.

- 16 full-color pages identifying Alaska's trophy sportfish plus color charts of the most effective lure and fly patterns.

- Detailed charts and illustrations showing you where to find trophy sportfish.

- Fish-catching secrets of over a dozen guides and biologists.

"If you plan to go to Alaska, or already live there, read this book thoroughly and you fish it better. Chris Batin IS Alaska fishing." Homer Circle *Angling Editor, Sports Afield magazine*

How to catch Alaska's Trophy Sportfish
Softcover........$25.95 (Canada $27.95)
Hardcover-Limited Edition............$45.

Chris Batin's 20 Great
Alaska Fishing Adventures

by Christopher Batin

The greatest adventures in Alaska sportfishing that you can experience today!

Frustrated by shoulder-to-shoulder crowds... mediocre Alaska fishing opportunities...and fish that are small and too few in number?

If so, get ready to fly into a glacial-rimmed volcanic crater and fish nearby streams where you will land 50 salmon a day... a wilderness mountain retreat where you catch 11 different species of sportfish in one week... or discover a remote river where anglers catch several, 10 to 17-pound rainbow trout each day!

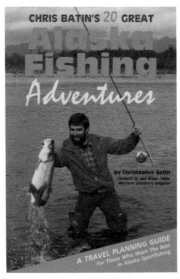

ISBN 0-916771-09-1

Free information on contacts, charter pilots, lodges, road-access routes, telephone numbers...everything you need to plan your Great Alaska Fishing Adventure THIS YEAR!

It's an adventure book you won't want to put down!

This book is also chock-full of Alaska wilderness fishing adventure stories and anecdotes that not only entertain, but inform. Only a handful of anglers experienced in the world's best fishing have known about many of these areas.

At your fingertips is everything you need to duplicate the author's successes...as well as specific travel details necessary for you to plan one of Alaska's 20 finest fishing adventures NOW.

Many fisheries are so remote, only a handful of anglers visit them each year!

This book has over 150 photos and maps...showing you what you can expect first-hand. See the rivers...country... fish...and the adventure you can expect on each trip!

This book offers you detailed information on where to find fish at each location...forage fish and hatch information...and personal observations on the habits of these sportfish so you can make outstanding catches...and releases... of trophy fish Alaska is famous for.

A comprehensive listing of the most productive flies for each area, based on actual field tests.

"In 20 Great Alaska Fishing Adventures, Chris Batin captures the spirit and excitement of Alaska sportfishing adventure!"

Jack Brown, Western Outdoors magazine

"In recent years, Chris and Adela Batin have become synonymous with and trusted sources for Alaska fishing information.

Twenty Great Alaska Fishing Adventures stresses the best in Alaska sportfishing and details trips that qualify in that 'adventure of a lifetime' category. The book also offers a commendable emphasis on catch-and-release fishing."

The International Angler

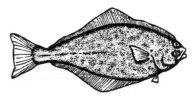

Chris Batin's 20 Great Alaska Fishing Adventures..............$24.95
(Canada $26.95)

Fishing Alaska on Dollars a Day

A Comprehensive Guide to Fishing & Hunting in Alaska's National Forests

by Christopher and Adela Batin

A seven-day stay at a premier Alaska fishing lodge will cost over $4,000, a price beyond the financial reach of many anglers.

However, if you can row a boat, cook your own meals and handle cast-after-cast excitement for feisty, fresh-from-the-sea salmon, you can enjoy comparable Alaska sport-fishing for only dollars a day.

Fishing Alaska on Dollars a Day reveals Alaska's best angling hideaways where you can catch trophy steelhead, salmon and trout. The book is the result of years of research and travel to some of Alaska's best fishing hotspots.

All the information you need for planning your trip is in this one book, saving you hundreds of dollars in research time and phone calls.

3rd Edition

Fishing Alaska On Dollar$ A Day

A Comprehensive Guide to Fishing, Hiking & Outdoor Recreation in Alaska's National Forests

By Christopher and Adela Batin

ISBN 0-916771-26-1

■ **Detailed USGS topographic maps and fishing charts** help you pinpoint the best fishing and hunting areas. If purchased separately, these maps alone would cost you over $150. These maps are **FREE** with the book, and are invaluable in helping plan your trip.

■ **Specific advice on flies and lures,** as well as 100 photos to prove these recommendations work!

■ **With this book you'll also learn where you can inex-** pensively hunt for moose, goat, brown and black bear, wolf and Sitka blacktail deer, as well as waterfowl. You'll have the comforts of a wilderness cabin to enjoy at the end of a successful day's hunt.

This 352-page book provides you with:

■ **Specific details on over 200 wilderness cabins,** exact locations, how to get there, free boats for your personal use, free cabins and shelters, and where you'll find the best wilderness sightseeing, wildlife photography and adventuring opportunities, as well as pages of alternate contact sources for more information.

■ **Available for the first time are the names and locations of over 375 Alaska steelhead streams.** Discover where you can average 8 to 12 steelhead per trip; choose from over 200 cutthroat waters, many located in Alaska's finest scenic mountain wilderness, or the best intertidal areas where fly fishermen catch over 20 silver salmon per day!

The book is profusely illustrated with over 150 maps, photographs and charts, When used in conjunction with our award-winning book, *"How to catch Alaska's Trophy Sportfish"*, you have all the information you need to plan a complete and successful Alaska fishing adventure.

"An excellent book that is essential for anyone considering making the trip."
San Francisco Examiner
"If you've dreamed about an Alaska adventure but can't afford the $2,000 to $4,000 price tag for most outfitted trips, this book is the answer."
Allentown Morning Call
"A comprehensive guide destined to become dog-eared by dedicated anglers. Written by Chris Batin, perhaps the best-known fishing authority in Alaska." **Akron Beacon**

Fishing Alaska on Dollars a Day....$24.95
Canada............$26.95

How to Catch Trophy Halibut:
Proven Tips, Techniques and Strategies of the Experts

by Chris Batin & Terry Rudnick

This 368-page book reveals the inside secrets of how to catch trophy halibut from 80 to 400 pounds.

Catching a slab-sided halibut is the dream of every angler...a fish so heavy it takes several people to hoist it onto the scale!

Catching these huge flatfish requires specialized skills and knowledge that takes a lifetime to acquire.

Now, you can obtain this information in hours rather than years.

ISBN 0-916-771-15-6

THIS BOOK REVEALS HUNDREDS OF TIPS FOR HALIBUT SUCCESS:

• A newly discovered, remote area where halibut average 80 to 100 pounds, and the world's best hotspot for 300 to 400-pound "barn-doors."

• How to make super-effective metal jigs in your own home for pennies, and specialized techniques that outfish bait.

• New type of leadhead jig that so closely imitates a crab that it drives big halibut into a feeding frenzy.

How to Catch Trophy Halibut reveals the success secrets of the experts with decades of on-the-water experience.

This book reveals time-proven bait rigs, specialized techniques, floating jig secrets, drifting methods, flyfishing tips, and world-record strategies that will help you catch trophy halibut **wherever you fish along the California, Washington, Oregon, British Columbia and Alaska coastlines.**

Whether you fish from your own boat or hire a charter, this book provides the inside information that will give you that added advantage over other anglers in catching trophy halibut.

• A new floating jig that enhances bait presentation by over 200 percent.
• In-depth research that shows how you can create a powerful scent field that attracts schools of halibut...as recorded on sonar units.
• Specific advice on the new technology lines, hooks, and equipment that will increase your catch size and amount.
• Exact guidelines for identifying 16 prime holding and migration areas favored by slab-sided halibut.
• Secret baits favored by huge halibut. Learn the Injection Effect to triple your catch. Illustrations showing best knots, leaders, rigs, double rigs, and more.

Information-packed Chapters Include.................................

SPECIAL TRAVEL SECTION:
Over 100 pages of secret hotspots, best charter operators, local secrets and best times to fish Alaska, British Columbia, Washington, Oregon, and California.

AND MUCH MORE:
Memorable Halibut Battles • Halibut Guides Reveal Secrets • For Flyfishers Only: Two Deadly Flies that Catch Halibut in Shallow Water • Photo Guide to Filleting Fish

• Money-Saving Tips on Freezing, Packing, Shipping Halibut • Scientific Studies Reveal Preferred Foods of Big Halibut • Making the Record Books with Your Fish • Halibut Recipes • New Seasickness Remedy that Works • And hundreds of additional tips with photos of record catches to prove this information can help you realize your dream of catching huge halibut.

How to Catch Trophy Halibut
..................$25.95 (Canada $27.95)

Alaska's Favorite Recipes Notecards

These beautiful, full-color, 5"x7" notecards look good enough to eat! Each card features a photograph by Adela Batin of a recipe prepared from her book, **Best Recipes of Alaska's Fishing Lodges.**

The notecards are blank on the inside. On the back of each card is the complete recipe and easy-to-follow directions. These are the most requested recipes by Alaska's visitors: Lowbush Cranberry Nut Bread, Alaska Wild Blueberry Cobbler, Alaska Sourdough Pizza and Cook Inlet Salmon.

Alaska's Favorite Recipes Notecards
8 notecards (2 of each design) and 8 envelopes...........................$15.95

Alaska Underwater Portfolio Sportfish Notecards

Actual scenes of sportfish in Alaska's wilderness rivers.

These one-of-a-kind, full-color 5"x7" notecards capture the essence of Alaska sportfish in a way drawings or illustrations cannot. Wild salmon on their spawning run. Sockeyes competing for territory. Char pursuing a fly...scenes often imagined by anglers, but never seen, until now.

Each underwater scene was photographed by veteran Alaska sportfish photojournalists, Chris and Adela Batin. The back of each notecard gives interesting and seldom-known facts on each Alaska sportfish species: Sockeye Salmon, King Salmon, Arctic Grayling, Rainbow Trout, Arctic Char and Northern Pike. These beautiful notecards are perfect for framing to add Alaska's colorful sportfish to your home or office.

Alaska Underwater Portfolio Sportfish Notecards
12 notecards (2 of each design) and 12 envelopes.......................$23.95

Alaska Angler® Information Service

Want to know the best rivers to catch all five species of Pacific salmon? Anxious to discover the Top 10 do-it-yourself trips for wild, 8 to 10-pound rainbow trout? Or a listing of Alaska's five-star lodges that serve you early-morning coffee in bed and at night, place European chocolates on your pillow?

The answers to these and other Alaska sportfishing questions can be answered by calling the **Alaska Angler Information Service**.

The Information Service provides "answers for anglers" who are planning a fishing trip to the 49th state.

"There's a common misconception that Alaska fishing is good year-round, no matter where or when you go," says Chris Batin, editor of **The Alaska Angler®** . "Alaska has over 3 million lakes and 3,000 rivers covering a land mass one-fifth the size of the continental United States. Planning is crucial for success. A miscalculation of several days can have anglers staring at fishless water rather than a stream filled with salmon."

He stressed the information service is not a booking agency.

"Objectivity is the key to the Alaska Angler Information Service," Batin said. "We do not receive any remuneration or benefit from recommending one stream or fishing service over another. This ensures that our customers receive objective information on fishing opportunities, guides and lodges that surpass industry standards for service, quality and professionalism. We can provide all the information anglers need, from the best flies for a particular watershed, water conditions to expect, type of hatches, and even the flora and fauna in the area."

Travel agents and booking agents are often unfamiliar with Alaska's myriad sportfishing options.

"Many travel agents sell a limited selection of trips that offer the best commissions for them," he said. "It's not cost effective for them to recommend quality, inexpensive trips, even though it may be perfect for the angler's needs. The Alaska Angler Information Service provides unbiased information so the angler can personally decide whether to spend $25 or $4,000 for a trip.

The crew of **The Alaska Angler** spends over 180 days a year fishing Alaska, searching out the best do-it-yourself and full-service adventures for the company's information service, periodicals and books.

The cost is **$30** for **15 minutes of consultation.** Before consultation begins, callers provide a Mastercard or Visa credit card number. To expedite matters, have ready your list of questions. To benefit from the Alaska Angler Information Service, call 1-907-455-8000 10 a.m. to 6 p.m. Alaska Standard Time, Monday—Friday.

Place your order through our website: http://www.alaskaangler.com

Interested in other books and Alaska cooking products?
Send us your name and address. We'll send you more information.

Ship to _____

Address _____

City _____

State _____ Zip _____

Daytime Phone (____) _____

Send order to:
Alaska Angler® Publications
P.O. Box 83550-Q
Fairbanks, Alaska 99708

Or call (907) 455-8000
24 hours a day, 7 days a week
Fax your order (907) 455-6691

Quantity	Item	Price	Total
_____	Alaska's Favorite Recipes Notecards	$15.95	_____
_____	Alaska Underwater Portfolio Sportfish Notecards	$23.95	_____
_____	Best Recipes of Alaska's Fishing Lodges, softcover	$24.95	_____
_____	Best Recipes of Alaska's Fishing Lodges, hardcover, spiral bind	$29.95	_____
_____	Bear Heads and Fish Tales	$9.95	_____
_____	Chris Batin's 20 Great Alaska Fishing Adventures	$24.95	_____
_____	Fishing Alaska on Dollars a Day	$24.95	_____
_____	How to Catch Alaska's Trophy Sportfish, softcover	$25.95	_____
_____	How to Catch Alaska's Trophy Sportfish, hardcover	$45	_____
_____	How to Catch Trophy Halibut	$25.95	_____
_____	Hunting in Alaska	$25.95	_____
_____	''Alaska Angler® '' poplin leisure cap, one size fits all	$14 ppd	_____
	Circle color: Teal Green Red		
_____	''Alaska Angler® '' leisure cap, one size fits all	$16 ppd	_____
	Circle color and fabric: Teal Green Red Corduroy Ripstop Nylon		
_____	''Alaska Angler® '' Polo shirt, Circle color and size	$38.50 ppd	_____
	Teal Green Red Men's sizes: S M L XL		

Gift Section

Book(s) personalized to: (please print)

Name _____

Title of book(s) _____

_____

Book(s) personalized to:

Name _____

Title of book(s) _____

_____

Book(s) personalized to:

Name _____

Title of book(s) _____

_____

Book Shipping Charges

Priority Mail delivery............................$6 _____
   Each additional book Priority Mail.........$3 _____
Apparel postage paid............................0
Express Mail delivery.......................$20 _____
   Each additional book Express Mail.........$7 _____
Foreign countries, Airmail, per book....$15 _____
   Each additional book Airmail................$7 _____

ORDER AND SHIPPING TOTAL _____

Payment Method

Enclose your personal check, money order or credit card information.
☐ Check   ☐ Money Order   ☐ VISA   ☐ Mastercard

Card Acct. Number _____

Exp. Date — Signature _____

☐ **Send me a FREE Alaska Angler Resource Guide**
☐ **Send me more information on Alaska Cooking Products**